To Took 6 yrs to write (slow writer)
Pake McEntire

HEROES & HIGH BOBBIN' GOOD TIMES

PAKE MCENTIRE

Pake McEntire
Rt 1, Box 675
Coalgate, OK 74538
phone# 918-720-7840
phone# 918-625-5281

Cover photo by
McCoy Studio
Ada, Oklahoma

Copyright © 2013 Pake McEntire
All rights reserved.

ISBN: 1491044942
ISBN 13: 9781491044940

This book is available for purchase through createspace.com, amazon.com and other retailers.

Table of Contents

Introduction vii

Chapter 1	Names	1
Chapter 2	Mama	7
Chapter 3	Little Ropentire	12
Chapter 4	The Till House	18
Chapter 5	John Wesley McEntire	25
Chapter 6	Old Pap McEntire	30
Chapter 7	Pap's Ladies	34
Chapter 8	Uncle Keno	36
Chapter 9	Uncle Peck	39
Chapter 10	Reba	42
Chapter 11	Limestone Gap School	46
Chapter 12	Louie Sandman	49
Chapter 13	Rattlesnakes	50
Chapter 14	Steer Roping	54
Chapter 15	Brownie	65
Chapter 16	New Steer Ropers	70
Chapter 17	June Ivory	74
Chapter 18	O Cross	78
Chapter 19	School of Hard Knocks	80
Chapter 20	Ranching	84
Chapter 21	John Sharp	95

Table of Contents

Chapter 22 Garner Boyd 100

Chapter 23 Kiowa 103

Chapter 24 Money 109

Chapter 25 Kiowa High School 112

Chapter 26 Mr. Harold Toaz 116

Chapter 27 Kiowa High School Band Class 120

Chapter 28 Ballad of John McEntire 123

Chapter 29 My Red Ford Pickup 127

Chapter 30 Hardcore Country 129

Chapter 31 Wardville Boys 132

Chapter 32 Mischief 137

Chapter 33 Matches 139

Chapter 34 WH Corral 142

Chapter 35 Wayne Sexton 147

Chapter 36 John McEntire Memorial Steer Roping 149

Chapter 37 Big Mule 159

Chapter 38 Wild Trips 162

Chapter 39 Cheyenne 166

Chapter 40 OS Ranch 172

Chapter 41 Summer of '74 177

Chapter 42 Pendleton Round-Up 181

Chapter 43 Let 'er Buck Room 190

Chapter 44 The Big Change 194

Chapter 45 Ray Bingham 199

Chapter 46 RCA 204

Chapter 47 On the Road	209
Chapter 48 Terry Inscho	227
Chapter 49 Gary Coffee	228
Chapter 50 Gene Stipe	231
Chapter 51 Little Kids	233
Chapter 52 Butt Hole Buttons	242
Chapter 53 The Bremmer	244
Chapter 54 CBS Special	246
Chapter 55 Cancun	255
Chapter 56 Basketball	258
Chapter 57 The Ghost	262
Chapter 58 Fiddle	265
Chapter 59 The Zone	270
Chapter 60 Ten by Twelve	275
Chapter 61 Sound Tracks	285
Chapter 62 Back Surgery	290
Chapter 63 Cairo	292
Chapter 64 Steph	295
Chapter 65 Songwriting	312
Chapter 66 Party of a Lifetime	315
Chapter 67 Ornery Friends	320
Chapter 68 Pocket Knife Blues	338
Chapter 69 Around the Kitchen Table	341
Our Birth Story	351
Chapter 70 The End Gate	361

INTRODUCTION

Today is July 31, 2008 (all day long).

A few days ago, Robin Lacy sent me a self-written family book entitled, *Kiowa in My Rearview Mirror*. I can't tell you how much I enjoyed reading what all he wrote. It was about him growing up in Kiowa, Oklahoma, where I also went to school for ten years.

Thank you, Robin, for sending me one of the limited copies of a very special memory effort. I have wanted to write a book for about thirteen years but didn't know where to begin. Your book did the trick and got me kick-started.

I recall most of the people and some of the events Robin wrote about. All my life, I've had upfront goals that I kept working diligently toward, but now I feel the need to reflect back on these endeavors, while having fun doing it. You may remember the stories or events I tell about; maybe you remember them differently, but these are my recollections, so I hope you have fun with them too.

This ain't to say I'm hangin' up my ropes, tie strings, my fiddle, singing, and quit runnin' Mexican steers to do this. Hell no! Ever heard the old saying, "Success is biting off more than you can chew, and then chewing it."?

Robin Lacy and Pake, 2012—Sherry Loudermilk Photo

INTRODUCTION

DISCLAIMER

You may get the wrong impression in this book that I make fun of women ruthlessly, with the intention of downgrading them. That is not my intention. In fact, I simply adore most women and love to talk to and about them. I marvel at just the sight of them. Their beautiful skin texture and softness therein. Long slender legs that begin at the ankle and go all the way up to their...midsection...connected to round, tight buttocks that demand male hands caressing them. So round, so firm, so fully packed, peach-color breasts, with nipples standing at attention, sensitive to the touch. Unbound shoulder-length hair, silky in nature, blowing in the breeze—when in public, catching everyone's attention. Rosy-red lips with a small crease in the middle of the upper, with the bottom full, eagerly longing to be kissed. Big, round, sparkling eyes with long eyelashes that stare deep into my soul. When leaning into her, closing my eyes, taking a long deep breath, she smells like I just walked into a flower shop. Now you tell me, how could anyone downgrade something like this? Makes one wonder why in the hell there are any queer men! I would rather visit with a woman over a man any day. A woman will usually open up and tell me what she thinks. I have a mother, three sisters, three daughters, an ex-wife, a few ex-girlfriends, and an all-but-perfect girlfriend living with me today. I have been around women all my life, and I truly do like them. But, I ain't gonna shit ya' and tell ya' that I have them figgered out, but I really do like them.

She said, "Oh God, oh God!" I said, "No, honey, it's just me—Rod!"
—ROCKIN' ROD HARTNESS

Here's my disclaimer: The stories within this project are true to the best of my memory. Up until now, nobody has indicated that my memory is slipping, so I figured I'd better start writing some stuff down before the Alzheimer's or Sometimer's sets in. It's kinda like you and I sat down together, and I just started telling you about things in my life I like to talk about.

There will be some off-colored words within this book, simply because I love to cuss. Not to the point of embarrassing myself or anyone around me, but at the right time and in the right company, I do like to cuss. I do respect the folks who resent hearing cuss words, so I refrain from using them around such folks.

This book is not for the faint of heart. In the event of shocking your modesty to the point of making your eyes bleed, discontinue. Side effects may include: lowering the value of your home, nausea, vomiting, migraine headaches, insomnia, ingrown toenails, bleeding ulcers, loss of appetite, drizzlin' dysentery, or loss of bladder control—Depends.

Discontinue if you start pulling your hair out with both hands, running the wrong way down Highway 69, screaming, "Willie! Willie!" Do not read if you are pregnant, for excessive reading may cause birth defects, such as your child being born naked! Do not read while operating heavy machinery or consuming alcohol. If an erection lasts for more than four hours, consult your psychiatrist to resolve your sexual issues! If you develop suicidal thoughts, just stop reading! Like the guy on *Hee Haw* that came into Archie Campbell's doctor's office, raised his arm, and said, "Doc, it hurts when I do that!" Archie said, "Then don't do that!" If this book doesn't meet your standards, then lower your standards!

The slang words and bad grammar that may drive you and my very best friend Clark Rhyne slap-ass nuts are there because I like to say them that way, so I write them that way. You may have trouble getting my drift, but sift through it the best you can.

The old blind sow finally found an akern!
—JAC MCENTIRE

I'm gonna try real hard not to tell anything that will hurt anyone's feelings. But, in order to tell it like it was I may get real close. To help keep the facts straight for these stories, I have sent a copy to some friends to look over before sending it to the press. Reba said she didn't do this with her

INTRODUCTION

book, but wishes she had, because she thinks she got a few things incorrect. I hope I tell more off-colored things about myself than others.

I hope to keep this upbeat and positive, like my grand pap John McEntire would want me to. You are reading this because you probably know me real well, maybe even better than I know myself, and you know that I don't do anything unless I enjoy it and call it fun.

> *A man was walking down the road with one shoe on. Another man met him in the road, stopped and said, "Excuse me, sir, but, you've lost a shoe!" The man looked at him and said, "No I didn't; I found one!"*
> —JUNIOR EDGE

CHAPTER 1

NAMES

I am proud to have been born at 9:40 a.m., June 23, 1953, on a hot summer morning, to Clark Vincent and Jacqueline McEntire (can't tell ya her middle name—she'll brain me) at St. Mary's Hospital, McAlester, Oklahoma. My second cousin, Ray, and his wife, Ruby Williams, were there at St. Mary's when I was born. Seems Ruby was having surgery, so Ray went upstairs to see Clark and Jac. After I was born, one of the nurses mistook Ray for Clark, walked up to him, and told him he had a new baby boy. Ray looked at her and simply said, "Thank you!"

Del Stanley "Pake" McEntire—Family Photo

I was born with a three-inch (catch your breath now) birthmark on the outside of my right knee (well, its three inches now); ironically it's the same spot where my grandma Alice Kate Hayhurst McEntire had one. Clark tells it that he went off rodeoing, which was their only means of income, soon after he brought Jac and I back home from the hospital. He came home months later and couldn't believe it was me in the baby bed 'cause I had grown so much. He turned me over to see the birthmark and knew it was me.

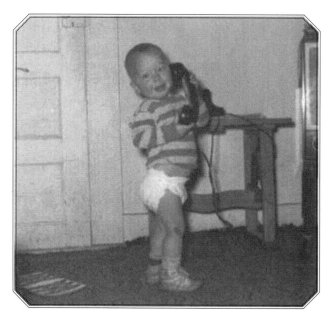

Pake gossiping with cousin Doris Jean. 1954—Family Photo

Our last name has been misspelled every way under the shinein' sun—McIntire, McIntyre, McEntyre, McEntier, and MacEntire, just to name a few. They even had my grand pap John's name spelled wrong in the past world champions steer roping book of the PRCA (Professional Rodeo Cowboys Association) up until a few years ago.

They named me Del Stanley McEntire. "Del," after a steer roper named Del Haverty, and "Stanley," after Stanley Gomez, a bull rider. You're thinking, "How in the hell did 'Pake' come into play?" When they were expecting my older sister Alice, instead of calling her "the baby" or "it" or whatever, they made up Mexican names. Hers was Pedro Joe, and mine was Pecos Pete. After I was born, instead of calling me "Del," they shortened "Pecos" to "Pake." Quite confusing actually—all my life. My driver's licenses would say "Del Stanley," my credit cards would say "Pake," the bank loan documents and the land ownership titles would read "Del Stanley," but my personal checking accounts would say "Pake." People who thought it would aggravate me called me "Del Stanley," those that liked the Western way of life to the fullest called me "Pecos Pete," and everybody else calls me "Pake." I didn't give a shit either way—as long as they called me to supper.

When I used to hang out with my cousin Gary Ray Thompson down at Stringtown, I pulled out my pocketknife (which got me into lots of trouble down through the years) and playfully threatened some older black friends of ours, Genie Boy, Johnny, and Teddy Joe Smith, who were pestering me, so they started calling me "Butcher Knife"! So my sisters Alice, Reba, and Susie, called me "Pecos Pete" Del Stanley "Doodle Bonk Butcher Knife" McEntire.

Cousins Sally and Molly Williams, Alice, and Pake.
Looks like I wuddin' too excited about taking a
picture with girls. 1954—Family Photo

"Pake" has been mispronounced by accident, with the likes of "Pate," "Peck," "Poke," "Pank," "Hank," "Pack," "Packe," "Take," "Paite," and "Pakay," which is what RCA records said some of the disc jockeys were calling me, so they made up some T-shirts with the name Pake and under it the right pronunciation like the dictionary would show.

As kids, Alice and I used to get into cuss fights, and I'd call her "bitch," and she'd call me "bastard." She was a standup broad-shouldered girl, with very little tolerance for a smart-mouthed kid brother. She was real good at keeping me in line until I was just about to catch up with her in size, then we had our more memorable moments. Like the time Delmer Woods came to visit, and I was going to show him how I could boss Alice around. I told her (I definitely did not ask her politely, like I should have) to cook me and Delmer something eat. She stood at the stove with a spatula in the hot frying-pan grease, looked at me, and slung that grease right in my face, and the fight was on. She stood flatfooted, punching me in the face, and I would run in and grab her and go to the floor with her, just a-gouging her with my spurs every chance I got! Delmer sat over in the corner about to cry—he had never seen anything like that before! This may make it seem like Alice and I were at odds most of the time, but quite the contrary. We played, laughed, cut up, acted up, and had more fun together than most kids.

Clark Rhyne, from Wardville, Oklahoma, was a teacher at Kiowa during my school years and taught music, art, and history. He was very good at teaching all of these. Not many students had a teacher as their best friend in school, but Mr. Rhyne was mine, and is to this day. There ain't much we haven't talked about. We know so much on each other, we have to be friends! Clark's dad, Tod, used to hang around my great-granddaddy Clark Steven McEntire, known locally as "Old Pap"—that's how far back the McEntires and Rhynes go.

Clark Rhyne told me that one day he was in class and was calling the roll from his grade book to ensure all students were attending. This particular day, he was feeling kinda chipper, so he started adding to their names, for example, Johnny "Appleseed" Smith, Mary "in the Morning"

Johnston, and so on. He came to a girl named Robin Vinski and said, "Robin 'Red Breast' Vinski!" The class began to laugh, and he looked over his grade book at this beautiful, young high school girl of eighteen years of age and about 110 pounds. She had on a tight bright red sweater, covering the finest set of breasts that the good lord ever made! He looked at her, and she had this stunned look like she didn't know what to think. He said he ducked down behind the grade book and went back to reading the row without all the added names.

I can't reveal the name of the cowboy who was talking to a lady in a bar after he performed at a rodeo. (This really did happen.)

He said, "What's your name?"

She said, "Carmen."

He said, "That's a nice name. How did you come by that name?"

She said, "It's because I like cars and men. What's your name?"

He said, "Beer Fuck!"

Within this book I will sometimes refer to my father and mother as "Clark" and "Jac." I began calling them by their first names when I lived with them a year to the day after my divorce from Katy in 2000. I call them by their first names instead of "Daddy" or "Mama" because it makes us closer. This way I not only have parents, but also best friends; and without a doubt, they are my very, very best friends. I can tell them anything without hesitation from stem to stern, and even though they may get mad at me on occasion, they still find eternal love for imperfect me. I have found that when we talk now, they don't talk to me as a kid anymore. But I know how parents are: even though I'm a grown man, I will always be their little boy.

When we were amateur rodeoing, we would all enter when we got there. So we would tell the secretary our name and the event we were competing in; then she would write down whatever she understood—"Pake" was not easily understood. One time I entered the team roping with Clyde Blair. When it came time for us to rope, the announcer called us, "Claude Blore" and "Poke McGuire"! (From that story, on occasion Clark Rhyne calls me "Poke McGuire.")

I told this story to Emer Beal, and he said, "Never in my life was I ever late to rope when called upon, but at one rodeo they called out, 'Armor Ball!' I was on my horse, sitting in the arena gate entrance, looking around behind me for Armor Ball. The announcer kept calling out, 'Armor Ball!' until someone hollered out, 'Could that be Emer Beal?' They looked at the sheet and yelled out over the microphone, 'Emer Beal!'"

An announcer called a calf-roping buddy of mine by the name of Butch Bode, (pronounced "Boadie") "Bitch Bode" (like "rode"). I once heard that a person's name is the most important word in the dictionary to them. Enough of the name calling.

So after about fifty years of this confusion, I went to the judge in Atoka County and told him I wanted to change my name. The judged asked, "Pake, what do you want to change your name to?" I said, 'Pake.' He said, "I thought it is 'Pake.'" I said, "No, sir, my legal name is Del Stanley, but most everyone knows me as 'Pake.'" He agreed.

> *This older man came home drunk one night and made it through the yard gate, walking up the sidewalk crossways, when his wife, who was standing inside the screen door, said, "Drunk again!" He said, "So am I!"*
>
> — GEORGE COOP

Chapter 2

MAMA

Jacqueline was the second child born to George Elvin and Reba Estelle Smith, and they lived near Capshaw corner. If you are not familiar with Capshaw corner, it is near Boggy Creek, Bethel, Wardville, and Kiowa, Oklahoma, halfway between Tulsa, Oklahoma, and Dallas, Texas, in the United States of America, planet Earth. Is that giving a thorough direction or what? If not, get out your Google Maps.

Imogene was the oldest; then came Jac, Dale, and Georgia. We call her "Georgie." Elvin was raised up an orphan, and he did what needed to be done to provide food and clothing for his family. He shot squirrels, milked a cow, had other cows that raised calves, and the whole family worked and raised a garden. I asked Jac, "Did you ever get tired of eatin' squirrels?" She said, "No, because if you get hungry, you'll eat about anything. We wouldn't eat rabbits even though they had twice the hind leg that a squirrel had, Because of the rabbit fever some of the neighbors had (and some even died from). Even through those hard times, we never ever went hungry. We raised everything we used and ate. A lot of other people didn't have what we had. Mama had a green thumb, and she could make just about anything grow. Lord a mercy, we had a "truck patch"—that's a bigger garden with the likes of tomato, beans, and watermelons.

MAMA

(Grandpa) Elvin, Imogene, Dale, Georgia, (Grandma)
Reba, and Jacqueline. 1959—Family Photo

Eggs and cream were all that was hauled to town for money. Jean and I would tote a number two washtub between us and a five-gallon bucket on each side. Then we had a smaller garden for the fine stuff, and then a flower garden in the yard. There was forty acres: the first track of land Mama and Daddy bought, and it had a big orchard on it of pears, apples, and peaches, and, boy, there wasn't any of it wasted.

There weren't any varmints that got into them because we and the nesters (other neighbors) ate the varmints like raccoons, possums, and so forth. Mama trapped skunks, and every morning before the school bus came, she would go down and check her traps. She wouldn't let us kids go with her, because the skunks would throw their musk scent, and she didn't want us to take the smell to school. She would shoot 'em, bring 'em to the house, and Daddy would skin 'em, turn 'em wrong side out, stretch the hide, and nail 'em to a board, and later sell the pelts. They would bring a quarter or fifty cents each, depending on the different pattern of the stripe down their backs. She saved that money and ordered Daddy a suit of clothes, a coat, shirt, and two pairs of pants, for fifteen dollars. Well, he wouldn't have it; he said, "No, no, I'm not gonna have a suit of clothes." So she sent it back, and we got two rocking chairs, the first rocking chairs we ever had. Daddy wore bib overalls except when he went to church, and then he wore a white shirt and slack britches with black shoes.

Sometimes Dale would ask Mama and Daddy for the truck, so he and I could go to the dance at Pittsburg. NY Thompson and Richard Johnson went with us and we stopped at Wheelers Café in Kiowa on the way. The two boys got themselves a beer; then we headed for the dance. We were having a great time when after about two hours, Dale told me that Richard had gotten real drunk and had puked on the stairs. We all decided it was time to go home. We loaded Richard in the back of the truck even though it was the dead of winter. While going through Kiowa, we stopped at Mr. Heath's gas station and thought it would be funny to hose Richard down with water. We pulled up to the faucet with a hose on it and let him have it from head to toe, and he barely even flinched. When we got back to his house to let him out, he was stiff as a board, and we thought we had sure enough killed him! We finally woke him up, and he stumbled into the house."

Grandma Reba Estelle Brassfield Smith was kin to the Grand Ole Opry star comedian Rod Brassfield. We all could have gotten some of our entertainment traits from as far back as Rod. Grandpa and Grandma Smith were real good about going to church. I remember when there was a church house at Chockie before some shit hook stole it and moved it to Kiowa. Have you ever heard of anyone stealing a church? Anybody who steals a church needs to go to church!

Chockie Church House when it was at Tipperary,
before moving it to Chockie—Family Photo

Anyway, we attended, and Grandpa and Grandma were always there. One Sunday morning, Herman Edge was preaching that we outta give 10 percent to the church, and then he moved on to another subject. Clark was raised up with Herman, so he spoke up, pointing to Mugs Self, and said, "Hold up a minute, Herman. You mean I'm supposed to give the church 10 percent, when I owe Mrs. Self over there a grocery bill?" I don't remember what Herman said, but his wife didn't like it very much because she spoke up, defending, "You are supposed to pay your bills *and* give 10 percent to the church."

We used to stay a few days with Grandpa and Grandma Smith, and they liked to go to church on Sunday morning and night at Chockie, and Wednesday night at Stringtown. I remember on the way home from Stringtown, every time he met a truck, Grandpa would stop and pull over on the side of the road in fear of getting hit. Every night before going to bed, they would kneel down at their recliners and pray to God. Grandma would pray out loud in a foreign language, and I never did know what that was all about and was too spooked to ask her. Rarely did I like going to church, except for the singing and the food, and I liked it when they fed outside. Except for when they would scream, holler, and slobber, wiping the spit running off their chin, the longwinded preachers were boring and hard to take. I liked to sit at the back and whittle things into the benches with my pocketknife.

Now you don't have to run and tell God that I don't like going to church; he already knows; we've talked about it. I don't want people, especially preachers, telling me what I need to do about my spiritual beliefs. I'll come closer to listening to a preacher that has a daytime job, over one that doesn't. I think preachers should quit giving advice and stick to the Bible and let people make their own choices. It's like doing right from wrong. It ain't that people don't know what the laws are—they just choose to break them. My relationship with my Lord is personal, not public. I don't have to answer to any preacher in the hereafter—only God—and that's between him and me. I don't ask God for help. God gave me two good hands and legs and a reasonably sound mind to work with and left the rest for me to figure out. How would you like to be God and everyday someone sits around on their dead ass and asks you for help? Let's help ourselves—he gave us that gift! I watch cowboys on TV at the NFR in Vegas, and they are thanking God for letting them win the go-round for $17,000. God didn't answer their prayers to win over someone else! I like to thank God for all the blessings of tools he has given to all of us on this earth, the ability to make a life as we choose of living right. Your faith is none of my business either, and I don't want to hear you brag about how you are going to heaven and I'm not. Last I heard, only God makes the decision of who makes the cut, and he's not telling until the time comes.

Chapter 3

LITTLE ROPENTIRE

Clark McEntire. About 1935—Family Photo

J.V. Newberry tells, "I went to school at Limestone Gap and had Mrs. McEntire for my teacher. One day she sent me down to the McEntire house to check on Clark, because he was at home by himself. I walked down there and found that Clark was OK and outside roping a dummy steer head." The cowboys nicknamed Clark "Little Ropentire." Clark's grandfather, Ib Hayhurst, was on his deathbed, and Clark, a little boy then, was roping the bedpost. It aggravated the women there at the time, and they told him to stop. Grandpa Ib said, "Let that boy rope!" He then laid over and died with that being the last thing he said.

A good friend of Grand Pap's, Happy Carden, came to the house one day looking for Pap, and no one was home except Clark, who was outside (you guessed it) roping the dummy. Happy said, "Clark, where's John?" Clark said, "He's gone to Fort Worth to the rodeo." Happy said, "When will he be back?" Clark said, "Day before yesterday."

Clark and John McEntire. 1929—Family Photo

The McEntire house was just under the hill about two hundred yards northeast from the Limestone Gap Schoolhouse. Clark had a dog named Fido that would follow Clark to school. Clark didn't want to go to school even though Grandma was a teacher; he thinks they let Fido go so he would go.

Clark said, "I expect Fido went a total of fifteen years to school. He started out with me in Mrs. Stiewig's room; she was a pretty lady, small in build, and Fido would be laying up near the blackboard, so sometimes she would have to straddle Fido while she wrote on the board, and Fido would snore and poot. Then me and Fido moved on up, and Mama was in the next room; we went in there, and after that, Old Lady Wilson, and then Van Kelly's room. All the teachers liked him, and when the young boys would play Wolf and Dog, we couldn't ever catch NY Thompson because he could outrun us all. They had a one o'clock bell that rang, and if we hadn't caught NY by the time the bell rang, I'd say, 'Git 'em, Fido,' and Fido would run in and grab NY by the lower britches leg, tripping him to be tagged out."

Clark said, "Sometimes the goat would come to school." I said, "What was his name?" Clark said, "Billy, and ole Billy was bad. They had stairs that ole Billy would get up at the top of, and he'd rear up on his hind legs and wouldn't let the girls come up! They would go and get some bigger high school boys like Emer and Jones Beal to grab him by the horns, kick his butt, and he'd go on about his way."

Clark said, "Jones, Emer, and Babe Beal were brothers, and all three started to school at the same time. When they came home from school, they would wave to their mama, and she would go behind the door for all of them to nurse. Peeler, the dad, said it was funny to see one grab the other by the hind foot and pull him off, so he could suck."

Clark said, "Emer told it that his grandad Old Man Beal, Peeler's dad, had a place east of Durant and was bad to drink. His wife, who was a Marcum, kin to Claude Marcum who married my aunt Bessie, came home one day and found his horse tied up at the lot next to the barn. She thought he was up in the hay loft passed out drunk, so she set the barn on fire and burned it to the ground. Her plan backfired (no pun intended). Seems old man Beal had gone off with someone in a wagon."

When Clark was a small boy, there was a store at Limestone Gap, across the highway and up the hill south. Late one evening after dark, Grandma sent Clark walking to the store to get some jar lids for canning. He really didn't want to go, because the rattlesnakes were out, but she insisted. He walked along, looking up at the spooky trees, and somewhere around the tunnel at the railroad track, he heard a panther squall. He stopped in his tracks, and the hair began to stand up on the back of his neck. He wanted to run as fast as he could back to the house, but instead he hotfooted it on to the store. He made it back from the store, more than glad to be back safe at home, when she said, "You'll have to go back; you got the wrong size!" As Clark told it, "I was afraid of that walk down through there, but I was more afraid of that ole woman!"

Clark, Reba, Susie, and Pake in front of Grand Pap's house at Limestone Gap—Family Photo

Clark was born November 30, 1927, and at an early age of four, he and an older man named Shorty Harbison, got typhoid fever drinking from a spring at Limestone Gap Creek. A man named Isabel had died a year earlier from the spring, but folks kept on drinking from it. This spring still runs today from the side of the hill on the south side of the road, east of the railroad track tunnel just as you begin to cross the creek. Jake Weaver from Kiowa came by and saw how sick Clark was and reached in his watch fob pocket in his Levi britches and handed a wadded up five dollar bill to Grandma; it looked like he had saved it for years. He told her to give it to the doctor, so he went back to town and sent Doc Harris down there. Clark barely lived, and Shorty died. Clark said, "I'd a shore died if Jake hadn't been there. I remember I had to learn to walk all over again after that."

Clark and Grandma Alice, suppertime. Ain't it just like a young boy to stand and watch? 1928—Family Photo

Then Clark had appendicitis, which kept him out of school to the point of getting behind. Instead of holding him back, they kept him in from recess and made him study, in hopes of catching him up with the rest of the class. Clark resented not getting to go play with the other kids, so he balked like a Missouri mule! He played dumb, but (dumb butt?) anyone who knows Clark, knows he is not dumb. He is however just short of a genius! Clark is illiterate when it comes to education. I've seen times when he would have over a million dollars borrowed for cattle and asked me how to spell *beef*! He is a good listener and really good at improvising. For example, I've been riding out in the pastures and found a tailgate sticking out of the ground where Clark had gotten stuck and taken the tailgate off of his truck, jacked it up, and stuck it under the back wheel to get out!

He learned to read by reading road signs, while rodeoing with his dad, John. And because of his hatred toward school, he finished the eighth grade and started the ninth, but John had him gathering steers up in the hills that fall, so he never went back. Pap didn't want him to go to school either. He wanted Clark to be a steer roper and a cattleman. Ironically, Clark's memory is sharp as a razor when it comes to things that matter to him. As pertaining to his genius side, I've known a lot of people in my time, but I have never met a man who was as brilliant at making right decisions as Clark. He has a real knack for it. He simply sees things different than other people.

A man's profession molds his personality.
— PAKE MCENTIRE

CHAPTER 4

THE TILL HOUSE

In his early twenties, Clark rode by the Smith house one day and saw Jac carrying two five-gallon buckets of water to some hogs. Clark thought, "A gal like that could fit purty good in my business!"

Clark and Jac have been married for fifty-nine years. Ironically, Alice, Reba, Susie, and I have all been divorced, and Alice twice. I think part of the reason is because we had it too good to stay married and had other options. Mama's sister, my aunt Jeannie, had a rule that when her kids got married, they could not come back home. I think this stopped the, "You son of a bitch, I don't have to take this; I'm going home to Mama; I hate this shiiiiiiiit!"

Clark and Jac first moved into the Till House just about a half a mile up the holler from Pap and Grandma Alice's house at Limestone Gap. They had to run the hogs out of it before moving in. Clark said, "Uncle Till Elmore and Aunt Liza lived there from 1932 to 1947. Aunt Liza was real poor and slim and never grinned a day in her life. One time Uncle Till was on a high-steppin' mare and got turned around and lost his bearings up near Rob Davis's and came by the house, and I was outside ropin' the dummy. He got halfway to the mailbox when he turned around and headed home. I saw him the next day, and he told me that he was so mixed up that when he got home, the old woman didn't even look right! We wuddin' kin to them; we just called them 'Aunt' and 'Uncle' 'cause all their nieces and nephews did."

Although they had a well for water, there was a creek real close for swimmin' and bathin'. Clark said, "When I'd come in of an evening, I'd stop by and see Mama, and she'd ask me to sit down and eat, so I would. Then I'd get home, and Jac would have supper fixed, so I'd eat again."

There's three things a man duddin' need. A roguish sow, a fence-jumpin' cow, and a red-headed wife. I'll be damned if I didn't wind up with all three!
— CLARK MCENTIRE

July 4, 1951, Clark and Jac went to Carrollton, Texas, to rope at a calf roping on a borrowed horse named Doug, owned by Doug Caesar from Canadian, Oklahoma. He noticed the horse was not feeling well when they left home, and by the time they got there, he was even sicker! Just so happened he drew a calf that was not feeling very good either. They were giving away a brand-spankin' new Ford car to whoever won the calf roping, and Clark won it!

Rodeo History: This is a photo of the richest calf ever tied in rodeo at the time. Clark McEntire was richer when the flag went down on his tie. Besides the first place money, he won a trophy buckle and a '52 Ford—Carrollton Texas Rodeo Photo

Carrollton Texas Rodeo Photo

Clark says that Jac drove it out of the arena and hung the gatepost with it. Mr. Caesar wanted two hundred dollars for the horse before Clark won the car, but when they got home, he wanted a thousand dollars, so Clark just took him back to Canadian. He traded the car and five hundred dollars to Uncle Dale for eighty acres between Boggy and Bethel Corner and moved into the house that sat up on a hill. When Boggy Creek would get up, the place was bad to get underwater, with only the house sticking up out of the water. They bought another eighty acres next to it across Boggy Creek, called "the Capshaw place," for twelve dollars an acre.

This is the only known photo of me with my rocky horse. I remember roping him and dragging my rope back to Mama, so she would coil my rope up and build a loop for me. August 1955 Family Photo

Pake, Alice, and Clark in the house at Bethel before
Oklahoma City bought them out. 1954—Family Photo

There's no limit to what a man can accomplish when he doesn't care who gets the credit.

— RONALD REAGAN

Oklahoma City bought their 160 acres for fifty dollars an acre because of flood control for Lake Atoka, when they damned it up southwest of Stringtown back in the late fifties. Recently, I read an article in the Atoka paper, where an inmate in prison told that a fellow inmate and former lawyer told him, "Those dumb farmers in southeastern Oklahoma believed everything I told them—that they had no rights but to sell at the price I offered them."

Alice, Reba, Clark, Pake, and Jac at the Chockie house. March 1958—Family Photo

Clark went to a public auction in Atoka and bought 4,779 acres on the east side of Chockie for $25,000 with about 2,400 acres of mineral included. Now some folks advised Clark—even warned him—not to buy the hill country, for everyone else that did went broke. Clark thought it was a bargain, but finding a banker to finance the place was next to impossible. They considered the place worthless. Clark later found Mid-Continent Life Insurance Company, who put up the money for it and some more land, making the note for $28,000.

Clark and Louie Sandman tore down some old houses and barns for the lumber and helped Leroy Newberry, who was a part-time carpenter, build the house we were all raised up in. The house has a sheet-iron roof, and it is good sleeping when it rains. Not well insulated like today's houses, but we were kept plenty cool in the summer and warm enough in the winter. Clark said it cost less than five thousand dollars. Susie's boys EP and Sam live there as a boar's den to this very day.

Mama, Susie, Pake, Daddy, Reba, and Alice. 1958—Family Photo

Alice, Reba, Susie, and Pake. 1959—Family Photo

Clark kept running steers there and adding to the place until he wound up with eight thousand acres. The sale of cattle, timber, rock, electrical highline, gas leases, gas pad locations, pipelines, and gas royalty has made the Chockie place a cash cow ever since.

Chockie used to be called "Burg," but Captain Charles Leflore, a prominent Choctaw Indian marshal, had two daughters, one named "Chickie" and the other named "Chockie." Burg was changed to "Chickiechockie." When Chickie died, they shortened it to "Chockie." The post office was closed in 1934. Someday I would like to do a book on just the history of Chockie and Limestone Gap.

Chapter 5

JOHN WESLEY MCENTIRE

John and Alice McEntire, younger and
older years—Family Photo

Grandma Alice died July 1950, in Poteau, Oklahoma, at the hands of a quack doctor. Alice Kate Hayhurst was raised just west of where I live now at Cairo, Oklahoma, on Mail Route Road, and taught school at

Limestone Gap until she died. Do the math, and see that I didn't get the pleasure of meeting her. Wish I had.

Keep in mind that back then, school discipline was much different than now. More than one student in her class told me that when the kids were getting too rowdy, Grandma went down the aisle grabbing them by the hair of the head, jerking them back and forth, and sure enough getting everyone's attention.

I could write an entire book about the man Alice Hayhurst married, John Wesley McEntire. I knew him well. Born February, 19, 1897, Pap (short for Grand Pap) was my granddaddy and my best friend. As a young man, Pap used to plow the fields for Old Pap (his father) near Cairo, about a mile northeast of where I live now. He would make the rounds with a team of mules. In this particular field, there was a low spot where Pap and the mules would get out of sight from Old Pap, who was shaded up under some shade trees. Old Pap noticed when they went down under the hill out of sight, it took Pap too long to get out in the open again. Every time he went under that hill, it seemed to take even longer. Finally Old Pap decided to go see what was taking Pap so long. He discovered Pap had his rope hid out over there and was roping a fence post!

This was back during the Great Depression, and like most folks around here, they didn't notice it nearly as bad as the folks in the major cities because they never had any money to lose in the stock market. So their lives didn't change much. People were so caught up in putting bread on the table they lost sight of making a future of getting ahead. Old Pap wanted Pap to farm, but Pap knew that where they lived was not farming country. He used to tell me, "Pake, if you wanna be a farmer, move from here; this just ain't farming country." Farming was the furthest thing from my mind, so Pap didn't have to worry about that. Ranchers around here that wear caps and love tractors and machinery are really farmers in a ranch country.

For some reason, Pap wanted better than southeastern Oklahoma farming. Don't get me wrong here: there is nothing wrong with being a farmer or, for example, working at the navy or army ammunition depot at Savanna. But Pap preached toward something that involved working for yourself. Having time and money freedom—meaning, letting money work for you instead of working for money—is what the free-enterprise system is all about. Working for someone else involves a limited income without the chance of getting ahead. Grand Pap and Clark would rather be broke working for themselves than have money in their pockets working for someone else. To me a *job* stands for just over broke!

In the free-enterprise system, the chances of going broke, busted, or belly up are at a greater risk. This scares the living daylights out of some folks, but that's OK if you just keep believing in what you are doing and continue on. Lace Bowen used to say, "Clark, you're gonna go broke buying those steers." Clark said, "Lace, I'm broke to start with!"

Show me a successful person, and I'll show you one that has probably been broke once or twice. To us, working for someone else would be like being in hell with your back broke!

Clark took care of his family and was close with his money. Clark, like Pap, was not big on machinery. They noticed that every time a rancher went broke, the first thing they did was pile up a bunch of rusted-down machinery and call the auctioneer. Clark never worked for anyone his entire life and was a free-enterprise man all the way. I think the fear of having to work at the army ammunition depot kept him working harder with more and more determination.

It's only work if you'd rather be doing something else.
— UNKNOWN

Pap quoted phrases like, "Hit 'em a lick!" "Go for it!" and "If they can, you can too!" Pap taught Clark and me those ideas and that way of thinking, and even though Reba and Susie were not around Pap very much, they too inherited the idea, maybe through genetics or listening to Jac and Clark. Even though Alice Lynn was a wage earner for years, I hear her saying she wants to buy more steers.

The womenfolk in our house didn't like Pap coming over to our house for obvious reasons. They don't take kindly to grown men spitting tobacco juice on the floor or tracking in with muddy boots on. He liked to sit at the table with his feet sticking out away from it, and when they passed the tea pitcher to fill everybody's glasses, no matter if Pap's was full within an inch to the top, he'd get his glass and hand it to them to fill to the top. He drank from glasses or cups with his little pinky finger sticking out.

Clark tells of how Pap was gone a lot, and I don't doubt it. If Pap had chosen to put in eight hours a day working on the railroad like other men his age, he would have fallen out of the free-enterprise system and into the job rut. Ya see, Pap didn't have it all figured out, but he was on the right track. Clark also learned what not to do from Pap. For example, a ten dollar bill would burn a hole in Pap's pocket, so he would give it to someone he thought needed it more than he did. Garner Boyd recalls, "A man told me that John won a saddle at a rodeo. A little girl of six or seven rode her pony up and got off of a more-than-shabby saddle, touching and rubbing the one John had just won, saying that someday she would own a saddle just like this one. John asked her, 'Hun, you really like this saddle, do you?' The little girl said, 'Oh yes, it's a beautiful saddle.' John walked over to the little girl's pony, took the shabby saddle off her pony, laid it on the ground, reached and got that new saddle, and put it on her pony and cinched him up. After she rode off, the man said, 'John, why did you do that? Saddles don't come cheap!' John said, 'Did you see the look on that little girl's face when she climbed up on that new saddle? That was reward enough.'"

If Pap was breathing, he was telling stories. Usually rodeo stories. One I remember he told a thousand times—at least twenty. Seems this cowboy got thrown in jail, and a black lady came in to clean the cell. This jailer who was up front could hear her hollerin', "Mista Jaila! Mista Jaila! Come heah quick! This white sumbitch got me bent over and a chokin' me till I cain't hodly swalla!"

I never tried, but I learned that it was hard to hem Pap up in an argument. Guess the years of rodeoing and marriage put experience under his belt. One time we were down at the lots at Chockie, and Pap was trying to quit chewing so much Beech Nut chewing tobacco, so he had the end of a split rein in his mouth, sitting on a horse. Clark looked up at him and said, "Pap, get that nasty rein out of your mouth. You may as well have a horse turd in your mouth!" Pap replied, "Well then, hand me one!"

Neighbors tell that after Grandma died, one of Pap's nephew's was going to school at Limestone Gap, and one morning he stopped by Pap's house to visit before the bell rang. The youngster, of about seventeen or eighteen, noticed there was someone sleeping in one of Pap's beds and kept glancing toward the bed during the visit. Pap told the nephew to come here a minute. They both walked over to the bed. Pap said, "Lookie here!" He reached and threw back the covers, and there, sound asleep, was a lady naked as the day the good doctor spanked her little bottom. The nephew looked at that and squalled like a panther, ran out the door, and up the hill to school he went!

I've seen folks come up and greet Pap, just carrying on with him like best of friends, and I could tell Pap couldn't place who they were. Instead of asking them their names, he'd ask them questions like, "Where do y'all live now?" They'd say, "Same ole place!"

I don't think that Alice Hayhurst's dad Ib felt the same way about Pap as I did, 'cause hear tell he didn't want her to marry Pap. After they were married, Pap used to come into the house, lay down on the bed putting his nasty muddy boots on the clean white bedspread, and Grandma would never say a word. Now to me, this is a little out of line, but I don't like to be judgmental about someone else's marriage. Anyway, her bunch was well-organized with a nice team of mules, nice barn, nice enough house—they all sat down and ate together like normal people.

Chapter 6

OLD PAP MCENTIRE

Robert Lee McEntire, "Old Pap" Clark Steven McEntire, Carl Rupert McEntire, and Kenneth McEntire. These boys are Tump's kids. 1925—Family Photo

On the other hand, the McEntires, who lived a few miles east of them, were more than a little bit strange. Six boys and three girls in the family rarely sat at the table and ate at the same time. Great-grandma Helen Brown McEntire kept food on the table, and they'd go by all day and get 'em a pinch of this and that and take with them, eating it elsewhere. Guess that was to save arguments—who knows?

Great-Grandma would see visitors coming up the road, run around the back of the house, and peek around the corner to see who it was before going to greet them. Hear tell, sometimes she wouldn't greet them at all—just hide! The ole man, Clark Steven McEntire (whom I'll refer to as Old Pap), was the mayor of the weirdville family. Tragedy came over Old Pap in his younger child-raising years. He first married a lady named Alice Buie, who was Clark Rhyne's grandpa Buie's older sister, and they had two children. All three came down with influenza and died at the same time. Old Pap buried them somewhere around Ardmore. Clark and wife, Sue, named their oldest son James Buie Rhyne. Later Old Pap married Helen Brown and had the nine kids that started our family.

In his older and more cantankerous years, Old Pap built a lean-to hut out away from the main house he called "The Dutch Oven." He would get pissed off at the clan for sleeping in, so he'd get up real early on some mornings and chunk rocks at the house, trying to get 'em all outta bed. He would let hogs, dogs, and chickens hang out in his place. Had a bed with a pipe for a headboard, where the chickens would roost at night. So before he turned in, he turned the chickens to face the bed, so they wouldn't shit on his head while he slept. He took fun in going to town, wearing a vest with chicken shit on the front that hung on a chair where other chickens would roost.

The third child of the McEntire family was William Tump McEntire. When Tump was a young boy, Old Pap came back from town with a dresser that had a mirror with it. Tump climbed up on the wagon and looked in the mirror and said, "Look here, boys. Pap done brought home a wolf!"

One of Old Pap's daughters was named Margaret. She had a son named Ray Williams who used to hang out at the McEntire house 'cause there was something always going on there. Ray told us a bunch of Old Pap stories in eight hours of interview, and we caught them on tape.

On several occasions, a younger Ray would go to Coalgate, Oklahoma, with Old Pap, and Ray noticed that Old Pap liked to wear a rope-neck tie and nonmatching boots. They traveled in a worn-out hoopie called

"Truckie," and a lot of people would be walking to town. Now if they didn't have a hat on, Old Pap thought they weren't smart enough to earn a ride, so he'd pass them up and yell as they passed, "Better get a hat on, boy!" He'd pass by young boys on their way to town and tell them to hop on, since he was going about eight miles an hour. When he got to town, he'd tell them about what time he'd be going back home, so he could give 'em a ride home. Later when they got close to their houses, they'd just step off Truckie. One time he picked up a nice-dressed lady who wore bright red lipstick, and he insisted she sit by him up front. He looked over at her lips and said, "Yore mouth looks like a possum's butt after eatin' polk berries!" Ray said that usually when they got to Coalgate, he would purposely park in the sun and tell Ray to stay in the Truckie and hold the dogs.

He even had two girlfriends, named Miss Effie and Miss Tweedle, that, obviously, Grandmother didn't give two hoots about. I assume since he kept her knocked up nine times, that a good lettin' alone was OK with her! Now he was real public with these standup ladies (yeah, right) and would parade through town with them like he was footloose and fancy free, white, and twenty-one. Ray said, "Miss Tweedle had big buck teeth that stuck out in front, and she looked like she might bite'cha." (That's McEntire slang for "bite you"!)

One time Ray went over to their house, and no one was home. He went out to the barn, and there was Grandmother (as Ray called her) feeding some horses. He asked, "Grandmother, where's Pap?" She said, "Oh Ray, he's gone to Fort Smith to the horse races; let's pray to God he never comes back!" He stayed drunk a lot from visiting the whiskey stills up in the hills of southeastern Oklahoma. Clark said, "Old Pap rode a Paint horse; he could turn his head loose, and the horse could smell his way to the stills—he liked drinking out of the vats." One day while Old Pap was visiting a still, the feds showed up and raided it. Everybody ran for the hills except Old Pap, whom they arrested. There was a court date for him to appear in federal court in Muskogee, Oklahoma, and all the kinfolks urged Old Pap to get himself a lawyer. He replied that he didn't need no lawyer. On the day to go, my uncle Peck (Kelly McEntire) took Old Pap up there and suggested over and over that he needed a lawyer, with Old Pap repeating he didn't need no lawyer. They were waiting for their turn, when someone said, "The United States of America versus Clark S. McEntire, of Coal County, for making and selling whiskey." Old Pap stood up, and the judge said, "Well, Clark McEntire, I haven't seen you in years. What have you been up to?" Seems the judge and Old Pap were old friends since childhood! They carried on for a while; then the judge said, "Clark, they've charged you with making and selling whiskey—is that true?" "No, sir," said Old Pap, "I just walked up on these boys and their still, and I was just vistin'." The old judge said, "My advice to you is to stop visiting those places." He slammed down his gavel and said, "Case dismissed!" On the way home, Uncle Peck said, "Why didn't you tell me you knew the judge?" Old Pap said, "Didn't figure it was any a yore business!"

Clark said he hated to see Old Pap coming over to see them because Old Pap and Grand Pap argued most of the time. Grand Pap said that when he started roping steers, Old Pap went with him to one of the earlier ropings. Steer roper Raleigh Rooker threw a big slosher (a huge loop hoping just to catch anything) and roped this steer around the belly. (Back then it was catch as catch can, not like today when around both horns is the only legal catch.) He went to the end of it, jerked the big steer down, jumped off, tied the steer, and won the day money. Grand Pap said he looked up, and here came Old Pap, hollerin', "Do it like Raleigh did it! Do it like Raleigh did it!" Grand Pap told me that after that, Old Pap wanted to go every time Grand Pap went to rope, and he was so aggravating that one time Grand Pap was getting ready to go to New York, but he didn't go because he couldn't slip off without him!

Clark was over at the Hayhurst house one day when Old Pap came riding up. Clark remembers, "We were all standing on the front porch. He pulled up his shirt and showed us all a hole in his belly with his intestines half showing. He had passed out too close to a fire at a whiskey still and burned a hole in his belly." Old Pap lived to be in his eighties. And they say drinking, chasing wild women, and nasty personal hygiene will kill ya! Clark said, "Old Pap built his own coffin out of some used lumber and fed his horses out of it for a couple of years before he died in 1936." Old Pap is buried at Wardville, Oklahoma.

Chapter 7

PAP'S LADIES

Grand Pap John had this chemistry with women. One time Clark had a place rented near Clarksville, Texas, to run steers on. On the way down there one day, Pap, Clark, and I stopped at this east Texas general store stuck out by itself, way out in the country. Pap liked to unbutton his britches for belly comfort while he rode in the truck, so when he got out, he would hold onto his britches while he walked. I went into the store and noticed a real clean, nice-looking, older lady behind the counter. I remember her makeup was put on like a lady that could still see. Pap came stumbling through, banging the screen door, holding onto his britches, tobacco juice dripping out of the corners of his mouth, and looking like he hadn't bathed in a day or two, after working cattle with us. She took one look at him and hollered, "Why, John McEntire!" She came out from behind the counter, ran up to him, and planted a big kiss right on the mouth! They dry hunched around on each other, laughing and giggling like two teenagers. I looked at them in total amazement. I thought then and there about all the guys who worry themselves sick about their appearance when approaching women. The thing they forget to do is bring their big smile and personality, the one thing Pap *never* forgot to bring.

One day I asked Clark, "Where's Pap?" He said, "Oh, he's off galin'." That means sparkin', courtin,' pitchin' woo, settin' the gals—you get the drift. About three weeks later Pap showed up and told me this story. "Pake, a real nice lady from Prineville, Oregon, sent me a postcard saying she was coming to visit me and wanted me to pick her up at the Tulsie airport, (that's what Pap called Tulsa), so I did. We came back, and instead of coming to my camp, we checked into the Hollywood Inn, (that's what Pap called the Holiday Inn), in McAlester. We had one of those rooms where there were mirrors on the walls and ceiling. We stayed around there for a couple of days when she said, 'Hey, let's go to Miami, Florida!' I told her that if she wanted to pay for the meals, the rooms, and the gas, that I would furnish the hoopie [that's his Rambler car] and three pieces a day. She agreed, and off we went. We had a blast, and in about two weeks, we got back to the Hollywood Inn in McAlester. We stayed there again for a couple of days when she said, 'John, instead of me flying, why don't you just take me home?' I told her that'd be OK if she would agree to pay for rooms, the meals, and the gas; I'd furnish the hoopie, but I'm cuttin' it back to two pieces a day!" Guess he was startin' to get caught up!

Chapter 8

UNCLE KENO

One of Grand Pap's brothers was named Keno. Born January 15, 1901, his real name was Keener Brown McEntire, but we all called him "Uncle Keno." One time Pap, Keno, and Clark were building a fence up in the hills near the communication tower. They were trimming out a fence line with a chopping ax when Pap said, "Wait, Keno, don't cut down that bush. One time me and sweet thang came up here and had the best time of our lives right here." Keno said, "Oh hell no, don't cut down the little sentimental bush!"

Now, Pap and Keno were real close; they lived near each other at Limestone Gap but were complete opposites. During their conversations they rarely agreed on anything. For reasons unknown to me, Keno was a pessimist. Clark said, "Keno used to say, 'The whole world's against me.'" Most always with a tabacker plug of Days Work, he seldom spit, but when he did, it was unattractive. You may be wondering here, "Now, how in the hell can you spit tabacker juice attractive?" Well, Pap had it down pat, but Keno seemed to explode a huge wad out by blowing, splashing it all down his front. He held it in his mouth just short of drowning, so when he talked, he mumbled, usually with his back turned to ya, so you got about every third word and guessed at the rest. Every story he told was on the hush-hush. He'd say, "Now don't tell that!" What good is a story if you cain't tell it? I kinda liked the guy, but he was most aggravating. Other than all of this, he was a rather pleasant guy to be around!

Keno called on Jr. Edge to haul a load of hogs to Okmulgee to the sale for him. When they got there, they were backing up to the unloading dock when this black man walked over to their truck and said, "Did you boys hear? They shot the gov'na of Texas and killed the president!" Keno said, "What did you say?" The man said, "They just killed the president and shot the gov'na down in Dallas, Texas!" Keno looked as pale as a ghost and said, "I just knew something bad was gonna happen before I got them hogs sold!" Pap said that when Keno wrote a check for hogs, he could just write it out, no problem. But when he wrote one out for cattle, his hand would shake and quiver.

In the late twenties, he went to a goat roping Uncle Peck put on at Orphans Home between Wardville and Coalgate. Keno liked to dude up, with parts of his hair sticking out from under his hat, with a large envelope of a few land deeds sticking out his front shirt pocket, pretending to look important. That day he met Pauline Haney, who was a cousin to steer roper, and later politician, H. D. Bens. Pauline was an eye-catcher. Riding a spotted horse, trick rider Pauline was tall, slender, pretty, and a lady most any man would want to be with. Previously married, Pauline had a son named Hugh. Keno was a big name-dropper and led her to believe he was wealthy, with land galore, and soon talked her into marrying him. After moving into a hut, Pauline began to question the picture Keno had painted her. She said, "Keener and I hardly ever quarreled but liked to have starved to death! He laid around, wouldn't work, drank too much. I just couldn't stay." One day Pauline told Keno she'd had enough, got on her spotted horse, and rode off down the road, never to be seen again. Keno ran off to McGee Valley, between Stringtown and Daisy, and stayed drunk for five years. (It would be a cold day in hell before a woman would make me go off the deep end. Or anything else.)

Forty some years later, Keno pulled up to our house at Chockie, driving a brand-new Chevrolet pickup. Come to find out, Clark had bought and gave it to him for 160 acres at Limestone Gap. The deal was that Keno could use it, live on it, or whatever, as long as he lived. But Clark didn't get a deed when he handed Keno the keys. Many years later he courted Mary Roberts from Stringtown for a couple of years, and one day Clark told Keno, "Why don't you and Mary get married?" Keno was then about seventy-five years old and said, "I don't wanna rush into anything." Wasn't long after that they did get married, and Clark tried to get Keno to sign the deed to the 160 acres over to him. Keno told Clark that Mary ran the deal now, so Clark was to go talk to her, which he never did. After Keno died February 15, 1988, of course, it went to Mary. Years passed and Mary went to the rest home, and her kids sold it to Clark for $250 an acre. As it turned out, Clark bought it twice. I remember once Clark told me, "Now let that be a lesson to ya!"

Mary and Keno McEntire—Family Photo

Chapter 9

UNCLE PECK

I didn't know another one of Grand Pap's brothers, Kelly Clark McEntire (Uncle Peck), very well but admired him tremendously. Born December 18, 1898, for over a year, Peck batched under a rock sticking out of a bank with some lean-to tops out in front of it. Later on he moved into a real house; one day a lady came to visit Peck, and he took her sightseeing over his eight-thousand-acre ranch. They wound up under some pecan trees, and Peck put the smooth move on her. (Nowadays they call it "hittin' on her.") Well, like the steer roper once said, "She hit turned over and got up." (This is a steer roping phrase talking about when you trip a steer.) You get the drift. She didn't go for the deal. So Peck said, "Oh, I thought you wanted to friiiiiiiig!" I think he soon took her back to her car.

> *I won't say I did, and I won't say I didn't, but I will say this: a man who wouldn't cheat for a poke duddin' want one bad enough! Come on, darlin'.*
> —AUGUSTUS MCCRAE, IN *LONESOME DOVE*

Ruby Williams said, "Kelly [Uncle Peck] was going through some real tough times financially, and the banks were just about to foreclose on him. He came over to our house one night and asked to borrow some money from Ray and me. We assumed it was to pay down on his note to keep his place, but do you know what he did? He took that money and paid down on some more land!"

Ruby recalls, "Ray and I rented a place of about three thousand acres, near Hugo, and later Kelly bought thirteen hundred acres of it. In the summertime, we all loaded up and stayed down there until we got all the hay baled up. They hauled some of the hay back up here to Wardville. I remember, we stayed at the rock house, and I cooked for all the hay hands. One day, Bill Basket, from Adel [near Daisey], showed up and said, 'Do you all know why Old Pap McEntire walked stooped over?' Everyone there looked at each other with no comment. He went on to say, 'One time I was over at Old Pap McEntire's house, and Old Pap's son Judson showed up with a bicycle. No one could ride it because no one had ever seen one before. After some of the young boys tried, Old Pap insisted on giving it a try. They all tried persuading him not to because, like always, he was drunk, and they didn't want him tearing it up. He finally talked them into letting him try to ride it, and shore enough, he wrecked it, either breaking his back or slipping it out of place, leaving him walking stooped over for the rest of his life.'"

Grand Pap saw someone coming up the road to the house at Limestone Gap. A man got out of his car and told Pap and Grandma Alice that Peck was in trouble and in the hospital at Coalgate. When Pap got to the hospital, he asked the lady at the front desk, "Is Peck here?"

She said, "Yeah, he's in the backroom." Pap went down the hall to the farthest room, and there was Peck, lying in bed with his head all bandaged up. He said, "Where are you hurt?"

Peck said, "Right here at the back of my head."

Pap helped Peck raise up the bandage, and there was a pretty bad place where he had been hit. They talked for a while, and Pap left. When he got back home, Grandma Alice asked, "Did you find him?"

Pap said, "Yep."

She said, "Well where was he?"

Pap said, "He was in the hospital at Coalgate, like the man said."

She said, "What was wrong with him?"

Pap said, "He had been hit with something at the back of his head."

She said, "What happened?"

Pap said, "I didn't ask him."

Well, this went all over Grandma, so she said, "You McEntires beat all I ever saw; if it had been my brother Alfred, I'd have asked him what happened!"

Pap said, pointing to his mouth, "Yeah, and he'd had a pack of lies in the back of his mouth, just ready to tell you!" I learned later that while Peck was eating dinner one day, he was hit behind the head with a pair of berdezos, also called emasculators, used for clamping the cords on the outside of the bag on bull yearlings or calves, making a bloodless castration.

> *There are two kinds of pussy that'll get you killed—young and married!*
> —JOHN WESLEY MCENTIRE

October 11, 1978, Uncle Peck had a lease place in Paris, Texas. Story goes that he and two other men were down there one day working cattle when this five-hundred-pound calf hit a gate Peck was standing behind. The gate hit Peck and killed him. When his estate was settled, he had eight thousand acres and five hundred mama cows and only owed $250,000. Guess Old Pap was right when he said, "Peck was cut from a different cloth."

Chapter 10

REBA

On occasion, people ask me, "How does it feel to be the brother of a famous country music superstar?" Here's one answer I've never given, but it's true. All our family has enjoyed every stepping stone of Reba's career from the get-go. It was exciting from the first Grand Ole Opry appearance and record contract to the first #1 record on Billboard, every Country Music Award, and everything in between. After this it's hard for the family to get very excited when Susie and I do something in music, so they look at us and say, "Oh, that's good." This is only natural and not intended to be a complaint, just a true statement.

Ain't it funny how miscommunication and gossip spreads when it comes to folks in the so-called limelight? I've had people come up to me and say, "Are you really Reba McEntire's brother?" I say, "Well, that's what Mama says." They say, "No, you're not!" I say, "You know something—I don't know?" Reba has told me, "I've had people come up to me and say, 'Are you Reba McEntire?' I say yes. They say, 'No, you're not!'"

When Clark and Jac bought the Ed George place near Stringtown, rumor had it that Reba bought it for them. Bullshit! They bought that place themselves with years of hard work and determination. Reba did buy them a new van for their forty-first wedding anniversary that the whole family uses on occasion and to this day sits under their carport.

When I got off the road with RCA records in 1987, the American packing house in Durant sold; word was that Reba bought the slaughterhouse, and I got off the road to run it for her. Bigger bullshit! I have a lot of fun with star-struck fans when on occasion they say, "When's the last time you saw Reba?" I say, "On TV last night." They say, "No, I mean really saw her in person." I say, "Oh, she was in about a month ago, and by the way, she asked about you." They look at me all swelled up with pride and say, "*Really?*" Then they come to their senses and say, "Oh, she doesn't even know me!"

I've found out that sometimes when they ask the "What's your sister been doing?" question, I get it wrong; for example, I'll say, "Reba?" And they'll sometimes say no, Alice or Susie. Then when I ask if it's Alice or Susie they are asking about, they look at me like I have two heads and say, "No, Reba!" (OK, you don't have to get all huffy!)

When these people mention that Reba keeps me in money, I take full advantage of this dumbass remark. I say, "Keeps *me* in money? I have to loan *her* money! She makes forty million dollars a year, and she needs *my* money!" They sometimes give it back to me, sayin', "Ya know, Pake, I have the same problem with my kinfolk; you'd have money if you didn't have to loan it out to Reba!" Without bullshit, the world would not be as much fun, and I like to keep it fun.

At one of the Country Music Awards shows, Reba decided to wear a red dress that exposed the upper part of her chest with a see-through kind of mesh with sequins. This dress got more publicity than the girl that won the female vocalist that night. The rag magazines called me on occasion for some trash, but what I told them they didn't want to print because there was no trash. They called Jac so much that she got so fed up, she told them, "My name ain't McEntire—it's Smith. And I don't even know those damn people!"

She needed those folks like a hog needs a sidesaddle!
— GARNER BOYD

Reba, Jac, and Clark went to Los Angeles to be on a TV show that featured and interviewed moms of famous people. Whitney Houston's mom and a few others were on the show, and when they got to Jac, they held up the tabloid picture of Reba in the talked-about low-cut red dress. The tabloid read something to the effect, "Reba's mama says, 'Oh my God, Reba!'" They asked Jac about the article, and she said, "I didn't say that; they didn't call me on this one." When they saw they needed more about the dress, they walked down to the front row of the audience and had Clark stand up, put a microphone to him, and said, "Mr. McEntire, what did you think when you saw Reba in that red dress?" He said, "I thought she had it on backward!"

Just out of high school, Reba went to college down at Durant (if you are a local you call it "Dewrant"), and to say the least, she followed in the footsteps of Alice and me when it comes to having a good time at college. They used to frequent a nightclub called Arnolds, on Red River, bordering Texas, and one night there was a band playing. Her friends went to the band and asked if Reba could sit in, and they agreed. When they gave her a big buildup introduction, they couldn't find Reba! She was hiding under the table, and they all got a big kick out of that fun. Reba was always fun to be with, especially when it came to partying.

Pake telling Reba something really important after a New Year's Eve gig. Yeah, right! 1984—Family Photo

When I was in high school, I dated Reba's best friend, Brenda Lee. Brenda was a country girl, raised just north of Kiowa on Highway 69. One of about six girls, with no boys in the family, Mr. and Mrs. Lee farmed and ranched for a living and were exceptionally good people. One New Year's Eve, Reba, Brenda, and I all went out on the Kiowa town to celebrate and invited old granddad whiskey to partake in our social endeavors. I wound up celebrating more than they did, so when I became unable to drive, Reba and Brenda put me in the camper and started finding church house parking lots to cut doughnuts in while I hung on to the bed in the back for dear life! As if the world wasn't spinning enough already. When they took Brenda home, I remember them dragging me out of the camper and holding me up while I demonstrated to Mr. Lee, who was standing on the front porch, how to throw up old granddad whiskey. The next time I went to pick up Brenda for a date, Mr. Lee asked what was wrong with me that night. I think I told him I had the colic.

CHAPTER 11

LIMESTONE GAP SCHOOL

Limestone Gap School

Limestone Gap School was established in 1907 by prominent Oklahomans Captain Charles Leflore and J. L. Ward. The two-story brick building was first named Pushmataha. By 1921, Chockie and Bethel schools had merged with Pushmataha and became the first consolidated school districts in Atoka County.

The next year the school became known as Limestone Gap. Years later, more rural schools joined up with Limestone Gap. In August, 1938, the Workers Progress Administration (WPA) began tearing down the original brick building to replace it with a sandstone building to accommodate a larger number of students. The county road from State Highway 75 (now 69) went east under the railroad, through a tunnel (dating from 1910), then crossed Limestone Creek Bridge, turned right, and up the hill to the south, to the school. I totally enjoyed my first two years of school with Mrs. Eula Kelly, who took the place of Grandma Alice when she died in 1950, teaching grades one and two in one room. The first day of school, she told Donald Fred Smith from Wesley to take us boys down and show us where the restroom was. Donald Fred began to demonstrate to Buddy Lewis, Willie Tucker, a few more of us, how to wet toilet paper, wad it up into a ball, and throw it up, sticking it on the ceiling. We already knew how to use the restroom. We took spring class trips swimming in Limestone Creek; then all-day fun times in the gymnasium. I always felt at home there at Limestone Gap School. Was it because my Grandma Alice taught there before or because Grand Pap lived down the hill only a hundred yards to the north or because Daddy owned land around it in the hills? I never felt at home in schools after that. We completed the second grade at Limestone Gap with Mrs. Kelly in the spring of 1961, and because of declining student enrollment, they put it to a vote whether to continue on at Limestone Gap or close down the school and go elsewhere. They put the votes on a blackboard in one of the classrooms, and it was voted to leave and go to Stringtown or Kiowa. After the adults left the room, us kids went to the board and put our vote on the stay column.

Toward the end of the summer, our family loaded up with Clark and went to Okeechobee, Florida, to go to school and buy cattle. On the way down there, we stopped to eat, and I found myself collecting seashells they used for gravel in the parking lot. I liked the school down there and remember walking home with the hot sand burning my feet. I also liked climbing up into grapefruit trees and eating grapefruits. I learned from the locals how to cut a hole in the end of an orange and then squeeze and suck the juice out before breaking it open and eating the pulp, all without getting the juice on my hands. I got to skip some school and help Clark with the cattle and got to see how they bought them at the sale. Always before, the order buyers would send them to us, so I never got to see the buying process.

Burl Little was helping buy them; his wife was Jenny, son Little Burl, and daughter Marian. Jenny made me some bright-colored shirts that I took back home and wore for a long time. Mark Thompson from Wardville,

Oklahoma, was down there buying some cows, and I rode back with him. This was the first time I ever saw water sprayed on the windshield to clean it. Mark said there was a little boy underneath the hood peeing on it. Burl had a mama dog that had a bunch of pups, so he gave me one of them. Mark and I hauled this pup back to Oklahoma, and we named him Burl. Burl had a personality of his own, meaning that when the other dogs were working, he wouldn't; but when they all ran off after a deer, he would stay with the herd until they came back; then he'd quit again. I suppose our stay in Florida lasted about two or three months, because we were back home while deer season was still going. I met up with my Limestone Gap School friends at Kiowa, and it was sure strange seeing them in with a class full of other kids.

When we left Okeechobee and went to school at Kiowa, I was in the third grade under the direction of Miss Audrey Cason. I always wondered why Miss Cason never married. She had some intestinal problems and chewed her food like we all should—even cut the beans in half. Now if anyone could teach multiplication tables, she could. For example, she would write the fours on the blackboard and then reach in her desk and pull out her paddle and pound the blackboard, with everyone saying the tables out loud with equal enthusiasm.

After she retired, she did volunteer work at the McAlester Hospital and substitute taught at Kiowa. One day Miss Cason came into Mama's office and asked for Mr. Toaz. Mama could tell she was madder than an ole wet hen! Mama asked, "What's the matter, Audrey?"

Miss Cason sternly said, "I want Mr. Toaz to whip that Cooksey kid! He stood up in class and hollered out, 'I've got a hard on! I've got a hard on!'"

Chapter 12

LOUIE SANDMAN

Louis John Sandman was raised up on Boggy about halfway between Cottonwood and Cairo, Oklahoma. He is a real—and I mean *real*—likable guy. If you can't get along with Louie, you can't get along with anybody. Louie worked for Clark as far back as I can remember. Tall, slender, and very strong, Louie and his light blue car were so dependable and on time that you could set your watch to them. When Clark and Jac moved from Boggy to Chockie, they brought the old house with them. We called it "the bunkhouse," and Louie camped in it, which sat just north of the Chockie house. Since he half raised me, I asked him to come over to our house on January 5, 2009, and eat supper with Steph and me and tape our conversation to put some things in this book. We got to talking, and some of it went like this.

I said, "Louie, you worked for Peck [Grand Pap's brother], looking after hogs at Limestone Gap one winter, didn't you?"

Louie said, "You wouldn't believe how good an acorn crop there was that year. Peck turned out twelve hundred sows, and he gave me one hundred dollars a month to look after them. I'd stay with Keno most of the time, and John when I'd come in from the south."

I asked, "Which house was warmer?"

He said, "John's because he had a woodstove. Keno had a little propane stove he'd turn off while we were gone, and the house was cold when we'd get back. One day there was a little bit of snow on the ground, and Keno said, 'Let's go up to the salt rocks and put out some corn.' We took off walking with each carrying about twenty pounds of corn on our shoulders and wound up almost to Alec Staples. By the time we got back, that fifty-five-year-old man had this nineteen-year-old boy walked down!"

CHAPTER 13

RATTLESNAKES

I would like to know when the first rattlesnakes showed up at Chockie and Limestone Gap. They have been there all my life. At an early age, we were warned to watch out for them, so I have a habit to this day of watching where I step, even though there are no rattlesnakes here at Cairo. Rattlesnakes come in about three kinds: coon tail, velvet tail, and diamondbacks. They are the most common, and all are timber rattlers. Their sizes range from one to seven feet long at maturity, but the young ones of only a foot long have enough venom to do you in. "Rattlers," as we like to call them, are a popular conversation piece. It seems everyone around here has a snake story. They dwell on the east side of Highway 69 and are rarely seen west of Boggy or Buck Creek, which is between Kiowa and Stringtown. They require dens to hibernate in during the wintertime, so this makes sense because there are plenty of rocks east of 69 for them to exist. I don't enjoy looking for snake dens and have never seen one, but deer hunters found more than two on the hill between GB Flat and Highway 69.

MK&T railroad laid the first tracks in 1872, and for some reason, rattlers like to hang out around the tracks. Junior Edge thinks it's because the railroad cars leak out grain that the rats feed on, and the rattlers feed on the rats. I hear tell that rattlers will travel great distances to hunt their prey but make it back to their den when winter comes. Rattlers catch their prey by injecting venom into the victim, letting the rat or rabbit, for example, take off and run. The rattler then uses his scent-seeking forked tongue to track the prey, swallowing it after the rodent is dead. The snake's jaws unhinge to allow him to swallow large objects.

Rattlers are a calm, common-sense kinda snake. I say that because unless someone or something has really pissed them off before you find them, they pretty much wanna just be left alone. Upon approaching them, they will usually lay there comfortable with your presence, checking you out by sticking out their forked tongue, smellin' of you, or crawling off in the opposite direction. If 'in you prick with 'em, they will coil up, defending their long beautiful body, and put their head in the middle, raise it up, and prepare to strike. Seems they like to be coiled up before they strike. Unlike the water moccasin, who is aggressive and will come at you on occasion for unknown reasons to me, the rattler will send you a courtesy warning, by rattling his magnificent tail, with up to fifteen rattlers and a button, marking his territory, and you are to step aside and go around him. Now if you are drunk, deaf, or just plain piss ignorant, and you walk up on him, step on him, play with him, or do something he duddin' much like; if he gets a chance, he will bite you! Inside his mouth are two, sometimes three, fangs filled with lethal venom that will swell you up like a poisoned pup within a few minutes. Unlike the clap, penicillin won't fix this problem. Instead, an antivenom is required to get you back to normal, which is not found on every corner convenience store here in Oklahoma. Sometimes it has to be shipped in from Arizona or New Mexico. Now, his bite ain't always lethal, because he doesn't always leave venom. I like to call this his love bite—simply a passing bite that merely suggests to you, even though you have come too close, he is not serious about sending you home to your maker.

One day Louie killed a longer-than-normal rattler coming back from the roping pen, just east of the railroad fence that ran north and south. This rattler had a half-eaten rabbit in his mouth. Jac took a picture of him holding it up, and it was as tall as Louie, who is six feet two.

Alice and Carla Ogden walked up on one in the front yard, and they just picked up a big rock and threw it on him, holding him until Clark came and killed it.

Louie Sandman, rattlesnake, Reba, and Susie. July 1964—Family Photo

Jac said, "I was raised up near Bethel and Boggy, and we didn't have rattlesnakes; now, we had water moccasins and copperheads, but I hadn't ever seen a rattler until we moved to Chockie in the fall of '57. I was going down to the pond for something, where we got our water for the house. Clark was gone to Pendleton; I walked up on a rattler layin' in the road. I hollered for Louie, who was working for us at the time, and from the sound of my voice, he knew it was a rattler, so he came and killed it.

"Another time I went with Gary Ray [Mama's nephew] to run a trot line at Atoka Lake, and I saw something floating on top of the water. When our boat got closer, I saw it was a rattler all coiled up floating with his head and rattlers out of the water."

The first year I moved up the holler at Limestone Gap in 2000, I saw or killed twenty-one rattlers, and from then on about ten a year. The closest call happened near the house. The cattle lots were next to the house, and the horses were in a trap (a very small pasture of about three acres) just south of the lots.

I walked out this gate with a bucket of feed, went down past the wing, got them to follow me to the lots, went back through this same gate, put the feed in the trough, and the horses started eating. I went back to shut the gate, and there was the biggest rattler I'd ever seen. He wasn't as long as I'd ever seen but bigger around, and his head was huge.

Some folks go ape shit when they see a snake and think like the cowboys used to think about Indians: "The only good Injun is a dead Injun!" Well, they think the only good snake is a dead snake whether it's a rattler, copperhead, water moccasin, chicken snake, or even a little ole green snake. Most of the time, they don't know one snake from the other. Now usually when I see rattlers up in the hills, I just ride on off, because I remember what Pap used to say about coyotes: "Pake, don't kill 'em; their just like everybody else, lookin' for somethin' to eat or somethin' to fuck!"

But this one was just too close to the house, and I come in on occasion and walk from the car or truck to the house in the dark, and I could just imagine him layin' on the front porch. I began to throw rocks at him, and he tried to get away; but I stunned him, so he coiled up and put his enormous head under his body. I admired him and kinda felt sorry for him, but I was scared of him all at the same time. He never did strike or rattle. I wish he would have: I would have felt better about killing him. He only had eight rattlers and a button, but when I held him up, he measured from my nose to the ground.

Chapter 14

STEER ROPING

Long about 1920, Pap and his friend Wolf Marcum went to Pittsburg, Oklahoma, to see a steer roping contest. While they were there, they saw their first airplane. Jake Weaver put on the contest, hemmed up some big steers in the corner, cut one out, and headed him south, and the roper would take to him. They kept time with an alarm clock. Rope, trip, and tie—fastest time wins! At first glance, Pap and Wolf knew they just had to take a whack at that! They went home, made them up some tie strings, tied their ropes onto their saddles, and away they went. Just a-raring to go and couldn't hardly go for raring! Back then everything was outside. This means it was open range, so there were no barbed-wire fences to separate ranchers and farmers cattle from each other. One day Pap and Wolf rode out onto a prairie, and there was a herd grazing, just waiting for the young ambitious rookie steer ropers. They took after the herd, roping anything in sight.

John McEntire. 1920s—Griggs Photo

Now, if you have ever seen steer roping, you know that it is safer on the animal if the conditions are right. For example, today we make sure the ground is disked just right—not too deep, not too hard. Horns are tipped, fiberglass casted, rebarred, and wrapped to protect the steer. But in Pap and Wolf's day, none of that preparation was involved. Well, it didn't turn out to the best interest of the neighbor's cattle, and on some occasions, the rookie steer ropers would break a few horns, to say the least. When the neighbors got wind of this, the sheriffs came callin' at the McEntire house. Pap and Wolf saw them coming and snuck out the backdoor to hide the evidence—their ropes and tie strings. Pap told me this story and said, "We wuddin' bad boys; we just wanted to rope!"

John McEntire and Streak. The horse was killed in a trailer accident a few hours after this photo was taken—Family Photo

Steer Roping

Pap and Wolf continued to rope steers but built themselves a roping pen to get better practice.

Pap was up north rodeoing when he came back through Ada, Oklahoma, on his way home and saw a poster advertising the Ada Rodeo. The poster read, "Come see John McEntire bulldog a steer off the running board of a car!"

Pap said he didn't know anything about it. When they found Pap and asked him if he'd do it, he asked, "Has anybody ever done it before?"

They said, "Yeah."

He said, "Then I'll do it."

The stunt was scheduled to happen on the racetrack during the rodeo, and Pap was on the running board of a 1921 Buick Roadster. The steer was big with real wide horns, and the plan was for Pap to jump at the steer in front of the grandstand. When the steer was released at one end of the track, the hazer kept the steer close to the Roadster, and Pap jumped at him in a reckless hoolihan—that means the weight of Pap on the steer's head caused the steer to stick his head in the ground and flip over, making a qualified time. This is illegal today because they have to let the steer up and throw him by hand. Pap said it accidentally broke both horns on that big steer.

Pap's older sister Margaret had two very young boys, Wilburn and Ray, up in the grandstand that day. When Pap was getting ready to do this, she jumped up from her seat to leave and hollered out, "Come on, boys. John's gonna kill us all!"

Pap said the two youngsters started crying and pulling back, saying, "I wanna see Uncle John bulldog a steer!"

Pap did other events, like saddle bronc riding, bull riding, and calf roping. In 1934, he won the steer roping at the "Daddy of 'em All," the Cheyenne Frontier Days Rodeo, to earn the title of world champion steer roper. They gave him a gold watch, which he later gave to Babe Wallace, the wife of Claud Wallace from Atoka. The Wallace's claim they gave the watch back to Pap later, but Pap had no recollection of it.

John McEntire riding Plow Boy. 1934—Out West Photo

At rodeos, the cowboys loved to play tricks on Pap, like one time when Pap only had one silver dollar and told his cowboy buddies he was gonna head for the café to get something to eat. The buddies waited for him in a back alley where they knew Pap had to pass through to get to the vittles. They dressed up with handkerchiefs around their faces, so Pap couldn't recognize them. When they saw Pap coming, they came up from behind and put a make-believe gun in his back and said, "Stick 'em up!"

They robbed him of his dollar but gave it back to him later that night—again, all in fun.

It was at Butte, Montana, when Pap entered the bulldogging, or now called steer wrestling, that he drew this steer that was real hard to throw. Pap was on his back and had the steer by the head, with his nose turned back, but the steer's back end stood upright, spraddle-legged, and was determined not to go down. This went on for several seconds. Clark, who was a small boy, was sitting next to the fence with some cowboys. One of the cowboys said, "Clark, run out there and get 'im by the tail."

Clark ran out and grabbed the big steer by the tail and pulled him over, and the crowd whooped and hollered!

Pap quit rodeoing in the late forties, when Clark started going strong. Pap was more than supportive toward Clark's roping. He made sure that Clark had the best horses available. One horse in particular was Joe. Back in the late forties, Pap borrowed most of the money from Uncle Peck, his younger brother. Twenty-three hundred dollars, for a four-year-old horse and saddle, to boot, was quite a sum of money back then. Turned out to be the best investment and the best horse Clark ever had. When listing all-time great horses, more than a few cowboys listed Joe as being one of the best horses in their times.

At one roping they had some long-legged Bremmers that ran like hell. Dee Burk said, "Clark, do you know why you and Posey are beating us today?"

Clark said, "Why's that?"

Dee said, "You boys are tying on your calves while the rest of us are still trying to get a throw."

When other ropers rode him, Joe's lightning fast speed from the back of the box put some cowboys back behind the saddle almost falling off. Then, he stopped so hard he would sometimes throw the cowboy down on the ground.

Tragedy soon came when they were at Strong City, Kansas, at the rodeo in the spring of 1952, when someone tied Joe to a piece of iron on a camper. Joe was bad to pull back in a panic, and when he did, he jerked this piece of iron off and went running away with the iron dragging underneath him. In the ordeal, this piece of metal punctured into his belly, letting his guts stick out through the small hole. Cowboys gathered around, offering to help throw him down, stick his guts back in, and sew up the small hole, but Clark decided to take him to a veterinarian in Manhattan, Kansas, a short distance away.

The vet told his assistant to give Joe a sedative, "just a little," which put him on his side, and the doc began to sew up the hole. Clark looked at the horse and knew then and there Joe had been given too much sedative, and it killed him. This was a huge free fall for Clark in the rodeo world.

John, horse Joe, Clark, and horse Jiggs, Encampment, Wyoming. 1948—Mixer Photo

In the late forties, Pap, Clark, and Max Kinyon went to Ozona, Texas, to Joe Davis's big calf and steer roping. Clark was the only one of the three roping that day because of the limited supply of money.

This was a huge event held annually. The locals barbequed fifteen steers and over twenty-five goats to feed the large five-day crowd. Shoat Webster match calf roped a local boy Sonny Edwards, and the three Okies bet most all the little money they had on Shoat and lost. Clark wanted to draw out of the steer roping the next day, but Pap told him to give a hot check. If Clark didn't win anything, they would beat it home and go to the banker and sign a note until Clark won something at the next rodeo. Max said that Clark roped the best roping he ever saw him rope, won the average and $2800! Now back in '48 that was a bunch of lettuce! (Another word for money.)

Clark McEntire on Ole Joe in late 1940s—Mixer Photo

They slept in the horse stall that night, in the same barn where the thugs and gamblers were up all night gambling. Clark had the cash in his wallet, and they all slept with their clothes on. The next morning, Clark woke up, and his wallet was gone!

They looked and looked and found the wallet on the other side of the stall from where Clark slept, and all the money was there.

Drag 'em sixteen feet, boys—that's far enough!
— JOHN MCENTIRE

In steer roping, you get some breaks and some things taken away. For example, one year at Laramie, Wyoming, in about 1948 or '49, Clark was at the King Merritt Memorial Steer Roping. Normally they have a six-second time limit for the steer to remain tied after given slack. At this particular roping, the six seconds the steer had to remain tied started when the untie boys took the rope off the steer's head. The first place average prize money was more than four grand, and to win the roping, all Clark had to do was get a reasonable time on his last one. He tied this big red steer, but the untie boys were down at the backend of the arena, about half-drunk, getting the rope off a previously roped fighting steer. Clark looked at the judge and said, "What are we gonna do?" The judge said, "I can't start the watch until they get here to take the rope off." They waited for over a minute, when the steer finally kicked loose, and the judge waved Clark out for a no time! Back then four grand would buy over six hundred acres of land.

Winnin' ain't everything, but loosin' is nuthin'.
— GEORGE CARTER

Clark, Pake, horse Buddy, Shoat Webster, Troy Fort, Everett Shaw. 1957—Family Photo

Pap was so dedicated on making Clark a world champion that he often said, "Clark, if you're in the practice pen roping, and you turn around and see the house is on fire, you just keep right on a-roping. Me and your ma will put it out!" Clark went on to win three World Championships in Steer Roping: 1957, 1958, and 1961. I remember the '61 title real well. Clark took me, my first cousin Gary Ray Thompson, and Mike Miller, on a long rodeo trip. I was eight, Gary and Mike about fifteen, so Clark had to do all the driving. We stayed gone for about three months, but my best memory is of Cheyenne. We broke two or three bales of straw in a stall of an old wooden horse barn, put blankets on top of the straw, and slept in the stall for the whole week.

Clark and Pake and Buddy, Laramie.
1957—Family Photo

Clark 1961 RCA World Champion
Steer Roper—Devere Photo

Whether you win something or not, one of the great attributes of rodeo is getting to see all your old friends. The ropers had to feed their horses twice a day and came by and visited with us, shore 'nuff gettin' our visitin' in. Clark tied old Red Wood (his steer horse) up to the fence outside the stall, and we got used to the other horses kicking their stalls about the time to leave.

Reba, Alice, and Pake: Clark said this gray horse worked great at home, but when he got to a roping or rodeo, he worked like he'd never had a steer tied on him. 1955—Family Photo

Reba gave Alice, Susie, and me each a bronze sculpture of Clark for Christmas 2001, labeled, "Paying the grocery bill," Legends of Rodeo Collections, made by Edd Hayes. The table it is sitting on was made and given to me by my good friend Burt Quimby. 2011—Family Photo

STEER ROPING

Clark roping on Dough Belly at Ben Johnson Memorial Steer Roping.
This is the last steer Clark roped in competition. 1976—Family Photo

Chapter 15

BROWNIE

At nine years old, I began roping off a horse called "Brownie" that Clark gave $150 for. I wound up doing just about everything a kid could do horseback—things like barrel racing, pole bending, tire racing, flag racing, reining, western pleasure, trail rides, shipping cattle, or just plain riding him for fun. He was full grown, and soon after Clark bought him, I laid claim. Sort of a "first come, first served" kinda thing, meaning the one who rode a horse the most got to claim him. Still in my little kid saddle, I went to the roping pen with Louie to help him rope the steers. I sat on the front of the chute, opening the gate and turning out the cattle when he called for them. Clark had some real Corriente steers with wide horns that were good practice for young or green horses because they high loped, looking back at you left and right all the way down the roping pen. They had been roped so much that when you roped them and dallied up, they would stop and turn around, so you could ride up to them and take the rope off their horns. Then they would turn and high lope to the other end, and you could build your loop and rope them again before they got to the pond. Compared to today's arena, that one was huge. You could trail them past the plowed-up part and tie one down on the grass like at Pendleton if you wanted, but you had to watch out for the holes. Since it had a pond and a hay barn at the far end, you didn't have to move the steers after you roped them.

Before I started roping, there were some pecan trees in the middle of the arena you had to watch out for. One day, longtime friend Hugh Posey roped this steer and was gonna tie him down, but when he went to the end of it, the steer went on one side of the tree and Posey went on the other and they met on the other side! Shore do wish I could'a seen that!

Only Louie and I were down there the first day I roped off a horse. It felt like that horse's neck was twenty feet long and the steer was thirty feet in front of me. I remember I tracked the steer until we got to the pond before I'd throw, and my arm didn't give out. Hell, I was used to roping everything in sight on the ground, so my arm was in good condition. Not long after that, Clark had a new trophy saddle he'd won at the Ada Rodeo, and it was in the living room, stacked on top of the other saddles he'd won at other rodeos. I made up my mind I had outgrown my little kid saddle since I was now a steer roper, and it was time for a man's saddle. Now think about it: there was no need in riding a kid saddle when I was at the ripe old age of nine!

I caught everyone gone one day and led ole Brownie up to the front porch and dragged that new saddle out of the living room onto the front porch. Every time I'd start to put it on his back, he'd move over to where I couldn't get it on him. Although I was now a man, my short legs kept me from throwing this tree with leather on it from the ground up. I kept at it for more than thirty minutes (seemed like an hour), hell-bent on getting this shiny, great smell of new leather on my horse. Finally got it on him a little bit crossways, but managed to get it on him close enough to girt him up. Didn't know the consequences of this adventure, but I was willing to risk it. To my surprise, it turned out Clark didn't mind! Clark took off the stirrup fenders and put my little kid saddle fenders on so I could reach the stirrups. When I got legs long enough to reach the original stirrup fenders that came with the new saddle, Clark took the kid fenders off. Years later I realized that Ole Brownie and I wore that saddle flat out. Eventually Old Brownie wore out, and eventually decades later, ole Pake wore out, needing back, neck, and knee surgeries. Horses and saddles are useless if you don't use them. They are like violins—the more you use them the better they get.

When I turned fourteen, I added team roping, calf roping, breakaway calf roping, and ribbon roping to Brownie's agenda. When I turned fifteen, Clark bought old Jed from Jed Rowe in Ada, Oklahoma. Jed (the man) entered Everett Shaw's team roping like we did every other Sunday during the winter months, and we would stop back through Coalgate for supper and enter up in a "pitch till you win" smorgasbord for $1.25. The real nice folks who owned the Chuck Wagon then were from Boston and had the real Massachusetts accent. When Clark, Bill Hensley, SR Phipps, Bill Hamilton, and I—all huge eaters—got through after not eating very much dinner that day at Shaw's, it looked like two steers and ten chickens had crawled up on the table and died! The man who owned the place walked by one evening, looked at our table, and said with a Boston accent, "My, you fellas certainly do eat a lot!"

Pake roping calf on Slim at Vinita. I walked by a postcard stand in a restaurant somewhere, and saw this post card and recognized ole Slim and me. This post card was promoting rodeo through tourism. 1978 Color by Storer—

It costs very little more to go first class; you just cain't stay as long!
— BILL HENSLEY

I thought I was way past due to start tying down steers, and old Jed and I was a perfect match. Jac's brother Dale and his wife, Virginia, had three children: Don Wayne, who is Alice's age; Patricia Ann, who is my age (only four days apart); and Dianna Kay, Reba's age, made up the brother-sister, cousin families. Now Don Wayne didn't have any brothers, nor did I, so we were the closest thing to a brother each of us could get. He roped a lot of calves over at his house, but had no steers. I had steers but no calves. I rode over to his house, about three miles at Whiskey Corner, and we'd rope calves. Then he rode over to my house at Chockie, and we'd team rope.

Patricia Ann and Pake sharing a birthday party. June 1955—Family Photo

Don Wayne, Alice, Patricia Ann, Pake, Diana, Susie, and Reba. 1960—Family Photo

Don Wayne and Pake at Don's first wedding, to Kerri Grimes. We looked like two redheaded mafia gangsters. October 1971—Family Photo

Chapter 16

NEW STEER ROPERS

Don Wayne and I decided to enter a novice steer roping at Nowata, Oklahoma, at Sonny Waltman's place. We needed practice before this event, so Clark was down at the pen one day making sure we were all cinched up and didn't get hurt. I was so anxious to tie down that steer I missed the first two. Clark said, "Quit thinking about tying him down—just rope him!"

Then it all came together, and I felt like I'd just entered into the gates of heaven. All the years of listening to Pap and Clark talk about steer roping and watching my heroes—Clark, Everett Shaw, Sonny Davis, Shoat Webster, and Ike Rude—rope steers: now it was my turn. A new steer roper had arrived.

Pake and Jed at Post, Texas. 1972—Ferrell Photo

I'd always been left handed at about everything, and roping was no different. All arenas, with the exception of Pendleton, Oregon, are set up for right-handed ropers. They set the chutes up in the right-hand corner, so the steers will run down a fence on the right, and the ropers can go left after the catch and the trip. Left-handed ropers have nowhere to go because of the fence, except to outrun the steer, which takes a lot more time to get him on the ground. At the Waltman arena it was no different. I roped both steers, and they ran down the right fence and beat me to the back end. I had a "no time" on both steers. Don Wayne didn't win anything either, and he didn't enter much after that.

If I had known then what I know now, I would have gone home, put the rope in my right hand, and been a right-handed roper for the rest of my life, but it ain't that easy. It takes years of hard work, dedication, drive, grit, determination, and a lot of "want to," and at the time, I didn't think it was possible. Instead, I went home and kept practicing left handed, and the worst thing possible happened. I started winning. I know what you're thinking: what in the hell is wrong with that? If I had never won anything left handed, I would have switched to right handed sooner. I turned sixteen on June 23, 1969, and the next month, Cheyenne was coming up. Clark needed the car and trailer to go there, so he rigged me up with the feed truck. It was a one-ton International flatbed with square tubing sideboards.

There was an amateur steer roping at Tulia, Texas, and this was the weekend they landed on the moon, but that was the farthest thing from my mind. Clark got an Oklahoma and a Texas road map, and with an ink pen, he drew the trail I was supposed to take. I remember him saying, "Now the only way you can get into trouble is to drive too fast. There will be a guy by the name of Spicer Grip out there that will make sure you get your saddle cinched up tight enough." So we loaded up Ole Jed, cinched down my saddle on the cattle racks, picked up Philip Miller, and headed for Tulia.

The feed truck was too tall to jump Ole Jed up into, so Clark and I built a ramp of two-by-sixes and two-by-fours to load and unload Jed. We chained it across the back for traveling. The feed truck didn't drive well because of all the rough use around the ranch, mainly up in the hills, but I took it slow. After about a hundred miles, I got to thinking: this is a hell of a deal: just turned sixteen a month ago, going to a roping in a feed truck, and some guy by the name of Spicer Grip (whom I'd never even heard of) is gonna help me. I felt all grown up and excited to go.

Sure enough, when I was four ropers away from my time to compete, up walked Spicer. He was a real nice guy with a huge smile, and he had known Clark and roped calves and steers for years. Spicer is dead now, and they have an annual Spicer Grip Memorial Calf, Team, and Steer Roping at Hereford, Texas, every August in his name.

I placed a couple of times that day and won four hundred dollars. On the way home, I felt like a king. I wondered what in the hell the rest of the world was gonna do for money since I had just won it all. I went back out there the next year with Flip (a.k.a. Philip Miller), and the year after with Bill Hamilton in a newer and bigger feed truck, always having more fun.

Flip, Pake, and Jed going to Tulia, Texas. 1969—Flip Photo

Guy Allen, Marcia, and Philip Miller and Pake and Woodrow at Pendleton. 1996—Flip Photo

Chapter 17

JUNE IVORY

Gotta tell ya about my friend June Ivory. Before I tell these stories, let me tell ya that I really liked June. She was a great secretary for some PRCA rodeos we used to rope calves at, and she rarely made a mistake because she knew the business. She was very different, in a rough sort of way. If she liked you, she would kid you in a rough way, and if she didn't like you, then you knew it in a rough way. You may think this is downgrading her, or running her down, but if you knew her, you would understand this is the way she really was.

We were at Casper, Wyoming, and about twenty contestants were in the rodeo office paying their entry fees to June. The mustache thing was coming back in style with cowboys, when June looked up at Joe Dorencamp from Lamar, Colorado, and noticed he was growing one. Joe was a big guy, stood about six foot four and about 275 pounds. He roped calves and bulldogged—real nice and quiet kind of a guy.

Loud as always, June said, "Hey, Joe, what's that on your lip?"

Joe said, in his low, soft voice, hoping to seem invisible, "It's a mustache."

June said louder, "It's a what?"

Joe said, "A mustache."

June said even louder, "Oh I wondered what that was! I've had one between my legs for forty years!"

June Ivory—Ferrell Photo

Bo Ashhorn was a bull rider and borrowed money from other cowboys to keep rodeoing, but when he won something, he would pay them off immediately, down to his last dollar. Sometimes he would turn right around and borrow some of it back. At one rodeo, Bo and June got crossways in a name-calling incident, and Bo wound up calling June a "cunt." June reported Bo to the PRCA, and they fined him ten dollars.

Bo had to go before the PRCA board to get reinstated to ride bulls again. At an open meeting, with the room full of cowboys, Bo got the chance to defend himself in a statement to the board. Bo said, "Right's right, and wrong's wrong. June Ivory's still a cunt, and I want my ten dollars back!"

Bo and two other cowboys got thrown in jail after the last night of a rodeo. The next day, they went before the local judge. The judge gave them a choice of five days in jail or a five-hundred-dollar fine. The two other cowboys paid their fine, but Bo did the math.

Bo told the judge, "Sir, I'm not up at my next rodeo until Saturday, so if I pay the fine, I'll have to rent a motel and pay my meals; but if I stay in jail, look at all the money I'll save. I'm just gonna stay here with ya!"

Makes sense to me!

Now, I don't have to tell ya that cowboys like to talk nasty, especially around other cowboys, and sometimes it gets to be a habit to the point where one can say something unintentionally. Bo Ashhorn had been out on the rodeo trail for about five years steady and thought it was about time to go home and find a local girl, marry, and settle down. He called up a girl he knew from school and told her he was gonna be home for a while and wanted to take her out for dinner and a movie. She still lived with her mother, so when he came to pick her up, her mother met him at the door. Bo was all dressed up in his Sunday go-to-meetin' clothes and wanted to make a good impression.

Her mom said, "Why, hello, Bo. How are you doing?"

Bo said, "Oh, very fine, ma'am."

She said "Bo, come on in, and I'll fix you a glass of lemonade."

Bo said, "Oh, that's all right, ma'am. I'll just fuck around out here on the front porch."

Bo Ashhorn—Ferrell Photo

Kenny Call is a famous actor in movies like *Lonesome Dove*, *Silverado*, and *Cowboys and Aliens*. Kenny is a past world champion steer roper, and we used to rodeo together. A few years back, he asked me to sing at his dad, Jim Call's, funeral in Norman, Oklahoma. Clem McSpadden gave the eulogy, when Clem said, "About a week ago, one of our good friends, June Ivory, passed away. I know Jim is in heaven, and I think June is!"

Just as Clem said that, there was a loud *crack* from the back of the chapel. A bench that six people were sittin' on broke in two! Clem had a grin on his face, knowing that, as always, June had gotten the last word.

Chapter 18

O CROSS

Claud Wallace. About 1975—Family Photo

Claud Wallace from Atoka was around for as long as I can remember. He used to come to the house early in the mornings and bring a sack full of doughnuts from the Atoka doughnut shop. I liked him because he was a steer man plumb to the core. He talked the business with Clark and Pap, and I wanted to be like them someday.

When I was thirteen, I caught the itchin', scratchin', dreaded measles and had to stay in the house for four or five days, which I absolutely hated. One evening I saw a bobtail truck pull around on the east side of the house, and somebody jumped out three cows, three calves, and eleven heifers. When we ate supper that night, Jac asked Clark who brought the cattle. Clark pointed to me and said, "Oh, Claud bought 'em for Pake."

He had already branded them an *O* cross on the right shoulder 'cause that is what Claud branded, and he said that when he died, he wanted me to keep that brand. Clark branded a *Y O* with the *Y* on top, on the left shoulder; so later, with other cattle, we moved my brand from the right shoulder to the left to avoid confusion.

One of those cows got through the fence onto the railroad and got hit by a train, and the eleven heifers were slow to breed, so I sold the heifers and bought steers, selling them and buying back until I had 124 calves saved up and didn't owe a penny on them except what I owed Claud.

The two cows bred back year after year. Clark paid for the feed I fed them (guess I worked it off), and I was married and had kids when Claud finally let me pay for the first cattle with no interest. What a guy.

I was just out of high school and put those 124 head at the roping pen pasture across the tracks. I was gonna follow my big sister Alice and go to Eastern State College at Wilburton Oklahoma and get me a bona fide education! Clark was too busy to get over there and doctor my sick calves, so when I'd come home on weekends and rope them, I ended up losing 24 out of 124 head from sickness. After one semester, I hollered "calf rope" and announced that I got the hint: stay home and tend to business.

I think college is fine for the kids who don't know what they want to do or want to help build someone's estate and not their own. I don't understand why the younger generations don't want to continue the ranching that will make four generations of a great life. I think they think it will be easier in the outside world, but they'll find out they will have to work at that too.

Chapter 19

SCHOOL OF HARD KNOCKS

While at college, one day we were in this big auditorium of about five hundred students, when these state highway patrolmen gave a talk on highway safety. Me being "all cowboy," I raised my hand and asked if it was legal to drive with your spurs on. The crowd got a kick out of that, especially the kids from down around Broken Bow and Wright City, like Roger Ensley. The officer said, "Yes, it is legal."

He went on later to tell how it was illegal to carry a gun in the car. I raised my hand again and asked, "What if I'm changing a flat on the side of the road, and up drives these big guys threatening to rob me?"

He replied, "Use your spurs on them!"

The class really got a kick out of that.

Back home, I often heard Claud asking Clark, "When are you gonna let Pake learn about the steer business?" What in the hell had I been doing the past twenty years of my life if not helping Clark with his steer business? What else was there to learn? Here's where the school of hard knocks kicked in.

One day Clark and I were in Atoka, and he pulls up in front of the Kiamichi Production Credit Association. The first time Clark went into that building was several years before, and that day he walked in alone, and only the loan officer, Bill Sample, was there. They got acquainted, and Clark presented his loan inquiry to Bill, who looked at it and turned Clark down. Clark said since he didn't have anything else to do now that he had no money to buy cattle or operating expenses, he just kept hanging around for over four hours until Bill turned around and started typing with one finger at a time on an old manual typewriter. Clark thought he was going about his business and was ignoring him. Soon Bill started asking Clark questions, and it was then he realized Bill was typing up the loan application. Bill sent it into the home office, and it went through, and Bill and Clark did business for a long time.

Clark told Peck and Paul Hooe to go see Bill, and they did, but when Bill told them no, Uncle Peck jumped up and went home without the loan.

The day I was there, Clark started writing down some figures on paper in the truck seat between us, kinda talking out loud as if wanting me to hear. He reached for the door and said, "Come on."

We walked inside, and Clark told Bill he wanted to sign a note for me for some cattle and expenses. His plan included me stocking the thirteen-hundred-acre George Coop place at Scipio, about forty-seven miles northwest of Chockie. Clark told me that Pap was gonna go with me and help straighten the cattle up and go with me every day to feed—the whole nine yards, which suited me just fine. I would go by Limestone Gap and pick up Pap.

He lived in a one-room sheet-iron house. The west end was dirt, and down through the years we'd store cake (cattle cubes) in fifty-pound sacks and block salt; the east end was on a concrete slab where his two beds—one for him, one for company—table, ice box, and stove were. I asked him one time if he minded the mice running across the floor. He said, "Naw, when I see them, I know there ain't no rattlesnakes around!" He did actually find rattlers in the house on numerous occasions.

Before I came along, he tore the wooden floor out to recover his false teeth, which the rats had carried off. You could almost throw a cat through the walls of the house, so in the winter when it got real cold, Clark took Pap up to the Aldridge Hotel (Pap called it a "Whoretell"), and he would stay until it thawed out. Pap always looked forward to coming home to Limestone Gap because his friends knew where to find him.

On my way to Scipio, I'd stop by the Aldridge and get him; then we would go by the Oil Mill feed store, and they would load us up with a ton of cake, just enough to feed the five hundred steers. We did this process seven days a week for 195 straight days. He stayed up on the fifth floor, and one day we came out of his room, and there was a black lady housemaid sitting by the elevator, reading a newspaper. Pap, as always, spoke and said, "How'd do?"

She said, "Oh, not very good."

He said, "Well, you oughtta go to bed earlier." (I knew where this was going.)

She said, "Oh, I do's. I goes to bed with the chickens."

He said, "You ought to go to bed by yourself."

She said, "Oh, I do's. I do's go to bed by myself."

He said, "Well, it ain't very far to my room; it's just right around this corner."

She looked at him and raised the paper up in front of her face and pretended to read.

Now, this cattle deal at Scipio was gonna be like a profitable vacation. This was in October 1973: four hundred head of cattle cost $0.53 a pound and $214 a head delivered, and with the $32 per head for grass lease, plus feed, medicine, and interest, I had $100 of expenses, adding to the first cost a total of $314 per head. I threw in my all-paid-for one hundred head. (I know what you're thinking: he couldn't remember all of this if something bad hadn't happened.) This was supposed to be a paid-for vacation, getting away from having to do everything Clark said to do, but paid for it was not!

One year later, in October 1974, Pap and I had put three hundred pounds each on those five hundred head, but the market broke and kept breaking until we had to take $0.28 a pound. I went from one hundred head paid for to no head and owed $50,000! Oh shit. There were five or six cuts (cattle that didn't fit the herd, which the country buyer would not take) that we needed to send to the sale just to get rid of them, so I called Max Kinyon at the McAlester stockyards. He said three words, "Don't send them!" I did anyway, and they brought $0.08 a pound!

Just after I had the Coop place stocked, the price started falling. Clark bought three hundred head at the McAlester stockyards in one day for

$0.42 a pound. We all thought that was a bargain, but even they lost money. I remember the buyer, Dale Wright. He worked for Buster Wheat. Wright said, "Pake, it won't always be this bad."

I really didn't know how bad it was until I began working to pay off that debt. Clark had some equity built up from years before, and since he had signed my first note, the bank let him continue to sign. Four years later, running over eighteen hundred head a year of my own cattle in three states, we finally got back even. You really haven't been in the cattle business until you have paid off a dead note. The interest just keeps piling up, like the meter on a taxi cab that just keeps on running. The cattle are gone that created this loss and cain't gain to pay for it, which is why it's called a "dead note." The new cattle have their own interest and costs and have to do enough to help pay the dead note also.

Then I remembered what Claud had said, "Clark, when are you gonna let Pake learn about the steer business?"

They say you learn more from your mistakes than from the successes. I wasn't sure I had learned all there was to know about the cattle business but felt I had learned a lot. It wasn't anything Pap, Clark, or I did to make those cattle lose money because we got them over their sickness, kept the death loss at a minimum, and put the weight on them. It was just a market situation that made the event unsuccessful. Every so often this kinda thing happens. It wasn't the first time and certainly won't be the last.

The thing I did learn was to save up on the good years, so when this happens again, I'll be able to stay in the business. It also makes me appreciate the good years. Remember, this is a survival business.

Chapter 20

RANCHING

There are about two hundred miles of barbed-wire fence that has to be maintained on our outfit. To some ranches in west Texas or New Mexico, this would only be a small part of theirs. From 2000 to 2004, the hired hands and I put up over five hundred spools of barbed wire, with each spool being a quarter-mile long, and countless steel posts to replace the fences that have been there since the early or mid sixties, mainly on the outside fences between us and the neighbors. We unroll the wire from a plow disc turned over face-down with a welded stem rod sticking up; we place the spool of wire over the stem and then tie a rope to the end of the spool, and we take off horseback, dragging it on the ground while the spool stays spinning stationary. On flat straight ground, you can unroll a complete spool before stopping. We put up five strands of barbed wire, with steel posts about fifteen feet apart.

One day we had eight hands working in the hills east of Limestone Gap, and it took forty-five minutes just to get over there from the front entrance. We hadn't been over there but about two hours when this one kid of about twenty-two came up to me and said, "Pake, I've got to be back in Coalgate by noon."

I pointed and said, "OK, if you just cut right through that brush about four miles, you'll hit Highway 69. Go south about five miles, and you'll hit Highway 43; go about fifteen miles, and you'll run right into Coalgate."

He said, "You mean, you ain't gonna take me back to Coalgate?"

I said, "Hell, man, I've got seven other guys that wanna work. I cain't leave them here to sit on their asses while I take you back to Coalgate!"

He said, "Oh never mind, I'll just stay."

I'm an equal-opportunity employer; I hire Indians, blacks, girls, Mexicans, and whites. One day we were fixing a water gap down in this steep canyon, and I told this girl Kim to bring some wire, and she grabbed the end of the spool and took off running toward us, hanging the wire over her shoulder. The coils of the spool started turning and wound up in the back of her head, all tangled up in her long hair! I looked around, and she had her pocket knife out, cutting her hair, untangling it.

Billy West of Coalgate is the best hand I've had. Billy really likes it, puts his heart and soul into it, and can do it all: feeding, doctoring, cowboying, fencing, plumbing, carpentering—you name it. If he doesn't know how to do it, he'll figure it out. He is very dependable, rarely late, and most of the time early.

It is customary for the neighbors to split the cost of material and the labor, but some neighbors think that because our steers get on them, it's our obligation to keep up the fence. Some realize it is half their fence, too, and help with it.

The best way to have good neighbors is to be a good neighbor!
— CLARK MCENTIRE

After this major effort, we have to go horseback around these fences annually to repair when trees fall on them, deer run through them, or night hunters cut them from going through on four wheelers. Even though they are popular among other ranches, I refuse to have four wheelers on the place. I prefer the Western way of life.

Four wheelers have ruined many a good horse.
— PAKE MCENTIRE

Then there is the weather. Too hot, too cold, too wet, too dry, too windy, and lightning—all factors affecting the proper weight gain needed to overcome the expenses to make a profit. You may ask: what has lightning got to do with weight gains? Cattle like to bunch up in a lightning storm, usually under trees, and when the lightning hits the trees, it can and does sometimes kill all the cattle underneath it. Just recently, a friend had twenty-four head killed from lightning. If you know the weather in Oklahoma, you know it is usually changing and not all bad.

If you don't like the weather in Oklahoma, just wait a little bit.
—WILL ROGERS

Will **Rogers**—Jack Hull Photo

Seldom do people that make money at other things and then want to ranch make it work. Clark tells, "Lace Bowen and his brother made $150,000 in the oil business and came back to Bethel [near Wardville] and started ranching. I said 'Lace, why didn't y'all just stay in the oil business?' Lace said, ''Cause we wanted to be cowboys!'"

Guess there's a little bit of cowboy in all of us.
— Clark McEntire

It's really not a good idea to even pay monthly bills out of the cattle, so if you have a side income that can pay the monthly bills, this will let the cattle business grow. Back when you could win a bunch at steer roping, Clark lived on and invested his roping earnings.

I have supplemented my income by selling insurance or playing music jobs, usually called "moonlighting." For example, in 2008 we did fifty shows in a ten-state area to keep from spending out of the cattle. Now you are thinking: Who in the hell would want to work at a business when you can't even pay your monthly bills out of it? And what do you do with the yearly profits made off of the cattle? Think of it as a savings account. There will come a day when the cattle will lose money, and you can stay in business because of the equity built up in the paid-for cattle. (Seems the federal government should operate like this—don't you think?)

Be good to the cattle business, and it will be good to you!
— George Coop

My oldest daughter, Autumn, was in FFA in high school, and I attended an annual meeting at Kiowa, where she sang that night. They had a guest speaker from out of town come in, and he said, "I'd like to see a show of hands of the people here tonight that your grandparents farmed or ranched exclusively with no other income." A few raised their hands.

Then he said, "Now I'd like to see how many of your parents farmed or ranched exclusively." A few less raised their hands.

Finally he said, "Now I'd like to see how many of you here tonight are making your living exclusively from farming or ranching." No one raised their hands.

Clark had a nice immaculate place rented over near Bromide, Oklahoma. One day we were over there feeding when he mentioned to me and Pap that we needed to go to a funeral at Stonewall that afternoon. Pap asked who it was. Clark told him, but Pap didn't know the man. Clark got a little peeved and said, "Oh, Pap, you know. He lived over at [so-and-so], did [such and such]," and kept on until he had Pap noddin' and bobbin'. I think he did that just to get Clark to hush.

When we got to the church that day, several old codgers came up, speaking and shaking hands with Pap. When they all walked away, Pap whispered, "Pake, see that guy right there?" I nodded. He said, "I thought he was the guy that died!" He and I never did figure out whose funeral we were at.

After Clark quit steer roping in about 1976, he jumped into the steer business hook, line, and sinker. I remember him stacking up cattle like cordwood around the house at Chockie. Once there were over twelve hundred steers just in the traps around the house—more like a preconditioning feed yard. We couldn't get to the car to go to school because of steers getting up on the porch, so we had to build a yard fence.

I remember him talking to the order buyers on the phone like this: "I need steers to weigh [so-and-so] and cost [so-and-so]." The order buyers would tell him they couldn't send them for that price, and Clark would say, "See if you can!" Then he'd just hang up on them without even sayin' good-bye, kiss my ass, or nothin'. In a couple of days, I'd get up outta bed and look down the hill at the lots, and there would be five trucks, all lined up waiting for someone to come down there and help unload.

That gal's prettier than a mud hole in August!
—ANY RANCHER

He leased any pasture good enough to put on the pounds needed to make a profit: places like George Coop's at Scipio, Oklahoma, Cordis Martin's place at Limestone Gap, Pink William's place at Caddo, Kelly Spring's place at Redden, and Bus Ladd's place at Eureka, Kansas. These guys were retired from ranching but still had their places, so they would lease it out annually. Clark would then stock Chockie and Limestone Gap, running over four thousand head a year for several years and operating on a shoestring: no four-wheel-drive pickups, no round bales, no cake feeders mounted on the back of feed trucks to feed in bulk, all sack cake, with not nearly enough help. One winter we had a big snow, and Clark and Jac got up (early, of course), fed around the house, fed at Limestone Gap, headed for Caddo, fed there, came back through Stringtown and fed at Redden, headed east and hit the turnpike north to Scipio, and fed there just at dark. They stayed all night with George and Rose Coop and got up early and fed there and backtracked until they wound up at Chockie at dark, only to get up the next morning and start all over again! Now that makes for a long winter!

Bob Christopherson and Clark shipping cattle in east Texas. Late 1970s—Family Photo

Clark, you've got a goddamned sickness for them steers!
— CORDIS MARTIN

One spring, he leased a grazing association in east Texas, near Clarksville, that ran six hundred head. He found some steers from a pasture in Florida, just enough to fill the place. Pap, Clark, and I went down there one day, checked into a motel, and waited for the trucks to arrive from Florida that night. They didn't come all together, so Pap and I spent all night unloading. Pap dozed off in the pickup while I helped unload them. The last one came just before daylight and had three black drivers that I found out had left from Florida first. They had five dead ones on the truck, and we had to drag them off through all the piss and shit. When daylight came, I went to bed back at the motel, and Pap helped brand. This means we put a hot iron of Clark's brand (the *Y* with *O* just under it, not connecting) on their left shoulder for identification, injected a worm shot, a blackleg shot, and sometimes tipped their horns. Here's the part I wish I hadn't missed. Jim Clark was helping process the steers, and this is his story.

Pap couldn't walk or stand for very long in the late seventies, but he could ride a horse all day long. He was in the pen loading the steers in the chute horseback when they all looked up, and no cattle were in the chute. Now this was in the spring of the year, starting to get a little hot. They all looked to the back of the chute, and there was Pap, off his horse, sittin' on the ground with his boot off. Seems he had a rock in his boot. Clark lit into him, saying, "Every time I turn around, you're either in the way or tearin' somethin' up. All you have to do is keep your britches zipped up, and you cain't even do that!"

Pap didn't say a word—just put his boot back on, slowly stood up, put his foot in the stirrup, and was just about to pull himself up into the saddle, when he said, "Clark, you act like a feller that's used to handlin' forty head of cattle and has sixty!" Jim said that even Clark got a mild chuckle outta that one. I took it as to mean Clark was mentally stressed out, and the pressure was gettin' to him.

Jim Clark and Clark McEntire, east Texas. 1983—Family Photo

When I was at Chockie growing up, sometimes we would unintentionally not cut enough bag off of a bull yearling's nut sack after castration. It would fill up with blood and cream, like gravy, so we would have to go up in there and open it up to drain. The more effective way was without a knife, just open up the scabs with your fingers and run your hand up into the sack and let the corruption run down your hand and arm! (Grossing you out yet?) After very many of these, the next bull yearling got plenty of bag cut off to keep this from happening again.

Castration: gets their mind off the ass and puts it on the grass!
— CLARK MCENTIRE

Another surgery procedure I was not fond of was when some steers would come off the truck with an eye swelled up from a case of pink eye and sticking out past their eyelid, unable to close the eye completely, because the eye was swelled up with fluid inside. These steers were bargains at the sale barn, at about two to five cents a pound or about eight to twenty dollars a head, for only having one good eye. We liked to take advantage of this. We had to put them in the chute, pull their head around, and take a knife and slit the eyeball, draining the fluid from the eye. The eye was already damaged beyond repair, but it took the pressure off and made it feel better for the steer. Better stand aside and not bend over with your head down around it, or you'll get a face full of fluid that shoots out sometimes five or six feet!

Cordis Martin lived across Highway 69, just west of Limestone Gap, and had about three thousand acres of good ranchland. One day he came over to Pap's house, when Clark was younger, and wanted to borrow a chicken from Pap and Grandma. Later on, Clark went over to Martin's place and asked if he could borrow a wrench, but Martin said, "No, because you won't bring it back!" Clark said, "You didn't bring our chicken back." Martin looked at Clark and handed him the wrench.

When Jac quit being the school secretary in about 1974, she stayed home and helped Clark feed. Back then before the 2,500-pound automatic cake feeders, we had to load the cake in fifty-pound paper sacks on the back of a pickup truck and pour it out to the herd while someone drove. Jac could match Clark sack for sack and load the hay bale for bale. The bales of hay were about fifty to seventy-five pounds in weight, but this would tire a body out more than the cake. Jac said, "I was slim and trim back then. I think Clark and I became closer because I was home all the time." I don't think Clark liked her working at the school because it was a wage job, and he needed help at home.

Mama's part in the shipping process after the cattle gained as much as we thought they could for the summer was weighing the cattle either on the ground scales at the lot or corals or weighing them on the trucks.

Jac weighing cattle 1970's.—Family Photo

Mama said, "I first learned how to weigh cattle at Cordis Martin's place we had rented. Kelly McEntire was weighing them, and I was keeping books. Kelly was so precise, taking time to be correct, teaching me as he weighed."

Making sure the trucks are weighed normally at Cat Scales, ensuring correct weights, is obviously real important. She kept the books for me, Clark, Charlie Battles, Bob Christopherson, Jim Clark, Paul, E. P. and Sam

Luchsinger. Buyers have been Bill Jackson, David and Tommy Winters, Jim, Larry Runion, Bob Jones, Jim Gilbreath, Buster Wheat, Quinton Nolen, Joe White, C. A. Lauer, Dan Adcock, Max Kinyon, Ray Tucker, and Buel and Stanley Hoar.

To our knowledge Clark has never been hurt working cattle although he was in the thick of things all the time. Jac got hurt sometimes, like when she slipped on some cake in the back of the truck and came down on her knee and eventually had to have a knee replacement. Another time, a steer kept getting by her in the lots when she was loading the branding chute, and she was determined to outlast him; then he hooked her in the ribs, breaking two of them.

Pake brandin' and wormin' yearlings. 2006—Family Photo

Reba tells in her book, about a board that braced the back of the chute at the lots that we all had to stoop or duck our heads to walk under when we loaded them. Mama would forget to duck and often bumped her head. One day, she got mad and took off toward the house. Clark asked her, "Where are you going?"

She said, "I'm going to the house to get the chainsaw and cut off that goddamn board!"

We'd have fun hollering, "Duck! Duck!"—meaning to lower your head; and someone would say, "Where's a duck?" We had all got so used to ducking that after she cut that board off, we still ducked our heads there for nearly a whole winter.

One time we were just east of the house, trying to get about fifty wild Florida bremmers through a gate that stood between two trees out toward the house. This was a Mexican standoff. We were holding them and holding our breaths at the same time. These cattle were so wild that even scratching your head could make them swarm and run back through the cowboys. I heard someone coming up the hill in what sounded like a truck of some kind, from the lots on the other side of the house. When he rounded the corner at the house, I saw it was a septic-tank cleaning service. At the time, I really didn't know what a septic tank was because Clark just ran a six-inch pipe about one hundred fifty feet east of the house, and it came up on top of the ground and stunk a little. Well, it wuddin' too bad if in you were upwind from it. Sometimes it would stop up, so Clark would knock a hole in the top of the pipe about halfway and run a cable down toward the end, and that would loosen it up. He never did tell me to do it, and that was one job I was glad not to have to do.

Anyway, this ole boy got out of his truck and saw us out there, all horseback, holding this herd of idiot bremmers, and he got about halfway to us and hollered out, "Sir, I'm with Acme Septic Tank Cleaning Service. Could I interest you in letting me clean out your septic tank?" This ole boy couldn't have picked a worse time to ask Clark anything. His patience was past the boiling point with the aggravating steers, so Clark bellered out, "Hell no, feller. I ain't got no goddamned septic tank!" At this point, because of the loud hollering, the bremmers scattered, running back over us, and the septic tank man hotfooted it back to his truck as fast as he could, and away he went!

Elmer Earl Bowen, better known as "Hot Shot" Bowen, was a big man, to say the least. When he went to Doc Byrd at Coalgate, Doc had to send him to the feed store to weigh him. One day Hot Shot was helping his dad, Lace, work some calves at Bethel, and Junior Edge was there. They were dehorning, castrating, branding, and giving a worm and a black leg shot. Hot Shot was in the back, putting them in the chute, and they could hear him talking to the calves. He said, "Go on, little doggies; life is but a bitter pill; you are now entering therapy."

Chapter 21

JOHN SHARP

John Sharp. About 1975—Reba Photo

I just gotta tell ya about John Sharp! Some say John's elevator didn't go all the way to the top. Well, hell, that's probably been said about me and may be so. John's specialty was building barbed-wire fence. Like all of us, he'd rather build a new fence than patch an old one, but sometimes you just have to patch it because the wire and posts are still good: the fence just needs tightening or extra posts. Seems like patching fence is all we do. John liked anything pertaining to cowboying.

John used to call me "Pate." I'd say, "Damn it, John, my name ain't Pate; it's Pake!"

He'd say, "OK, Pate!"

John was born a hundred years too late. He stood about five foot six or seven, weighed about 165 pounds, was bowlegged, walked with his arms and elbows stuck out to the side, was big-time bug-eyed, and was never without his black, felt hat and boots, winter or summer. John loved the Western way of life and day worked for a bunch of folks in his lifetime. He helped us off and on for over fifteen years, and I came to know John real well. I saw a good side of John that a lot of folks never saw. John had a big heart, hard work ethic, was good to little children and good to his or your horses, but he was not without flaws. To say the least, it was an understatement to say John loved to drink, and the more people who were around, the more he liked to drink. When Clark would pay him his wages, he'd go straight to Atoka and head for the bar. If the local police caught a glimpse of him, they'd arrest him on the spot, assuming he was drunk, which he either was or was gonna be. He'd call, and Clark would bail him outta jail; John worked off the fines.

Clark used to ask, "John, why don't you quit drankin' and save your money?"

John said, "That's why I work, so I can drank."

Clark said, "Then why don't you just buy you a fifth and go off by yourself and drink it? That way you wouldn't get thrown in jail, giving all your money to the jailer."

John said, "It's fun bein' in the bar with all the people. Ain't no fun drankin' by myself!"

One morning, I picked John up at his house, and I mentioned it was a little cold this morning. John said, "Yep, I heard on the radio the windshield factory is gonna be worse than yesterday."

> *It's so cold it'd freeze the balls off a pool table!*
> —BILL HAMILTON (CHILLY WILLY)

Junior Edge and Bob Weaver were talking to John one day, and Bob noticed a scar across John's throat. Bob said, "John, what happened to you there?"

John said, "Oh, my first ole lady snuck up behind me and tried to cut my throat with a butcher knife!"

Bob said, "What did you do, John—provoke her?"

John said, "You bet I poked her—I hit her right in the goddamn mouth!"

We were at the roping pen one day, and John said, "Pate, my wife's real sick and is in the hospital."

I said, "What's wrong with her?"

He said, "The doctor said her flyroid was acting up again."

Even a clock that duddin' run is right twice a day!
—DALE ENNIS

One day John and I was eating dinner (that's "lunch" to some folks, but we call evening meals "supper") at Wheelers in Kiowa, and his stepdaughter was cooking. We had been shipping cattle for a couple of weeks, and the best way to keep John on the hook was to not take him home. She came out and told John he'd better go home because the city was about to condemn his house because of the dead dogs in the yard. I had taken John home before and saw his wife Baby Doll, sittin' in the yard in a chair with a dress on, all straddle legged, feeding dogs out of pots and pans from the house, holding the pans by the handle while the dogs ate.

Now, I have a cast-iron stomach, but this whole ordeal kinda turned my stomach, but it was nothing compared to what I saw when I drove John over to his house that day. There were dead dogs lying all over the yard, even one on an outside bed up next to the house. Baby Doll was not there; I guess she decided to thin out the dog population and just poisoned them all. When we pulled up to the house, I rolled up the windows (even though there was no air conditioner in that truck) and told John that I didn't like dogs, especially dead dogs! John, at any given time, could bend over, open his mouth, and puke, and this was a golden opportunity. He would throw these decomposed dogs in the back of the truck awhile and puke awhile.

John told us that the measles dropped on him when he was a young man, so he couldn't have children. I asked him, "John, how big did those nuts get?"

He said, "Pate, they wuz big as bowlin' balls."

One of my favorite Sharp stories is one winter when John hadn't shown up to help feed for several days. After dinner at Chockie, Pap and I were just fixin' to pull off the hill to go feed some more when we saw this old rattletrap of a brown car coming up the hill. It was John and two women. John got out, drunk of course, and Pap opened the truck door and said, "Get in, Sharp; let's go!"

John said, "Oh, I cain't, Pap. I gotta see Clark about borrowing some money to go get married. I done went and got this girl pregnant!"

Pap said, "Oh hell, Sharp, you couldn't knock 'er up with a stomach pump!" Pap shut the door, and away we went, without Sharp.

You may like this one. One day Clark, Pap, and John were eating dinner at a pitch-till-you-win smorgasbord in Stringtown. Clark was talking about somebody getting a divorce. All of a sudden, John said, "Pap, that reminds me: a guy died up at Kiowa, and they sent word to tell ya they want you to be a polar bear at the funeral!"

Clark looked up from his plate at Sharp, and then Pap said, "What did you say?"

John said, "They sent word from Kiowa that they want you to be a polar bear at a funeral!"

Pap said, "Ya say somebody at Kiowa got a divorce?" Clark told us this story at the kitchen table that night, and we all roared with laughter.

Another time Clark had East Lost place leased, about four thousand acres, between Wesley Road and Highway 43. Pap and John Sharp stayed in a house on the place and fed the cattle daily. One day, Clark, Pap, and John were over there working cattle when John stepped on a nail that went into his boot, through his foot, and came out the topside of his boot! Clark looked at his foot and said, "John, don't you think you coulda eased off of it a little bit before it went all the way through your foot?"

Clark got a nail puller off the truck, hooked it at the bottom, and pulled it back out the same way it went in. He went to the house and got some of Pap's rubbing alcohol and poured a full bottle down the top of his boot, and John began dancing a jig. After John quit dancing, Dr. Clark told John to keep the boot on until the next morning. When he took it off the next morning to clean his foot, it was real bloody but never did get sore. I asked John later which hurt the most. Was it when the nail went in or when Clark pulled it back out? He said, "It was when Clark poured that damned alcohol down my boot!"

That's a pregnant idea!
—Jac McEntire

John was killed by a north-bound Texas car, crossing Highway 69 one night, drunk, with a six-pack of beer under his arm. His family called and asked me if I would be a "polar bear" at his funeral. I gratefully accepted. This is one reason why I have very little use for preachers. I sat down the day before the funeral and wrote down a bunch of good things about John. I then took the paper to the preacher doing the funeral and asked him to just read my opinion of John. He reluctantly accepted the task, but when he read it to the congregation, he marked out most of it and put in his version, which didn't resemble what I had written. After the funeral, he walked up to me and said the reason he changed it was because he didn't want to preach John into heaven. I wanted to tell him that was the least he could have done, but I didn't. John's family came up and thanked me for being a polar bear, and that was the only time it wasn't funny.

I'm not worried about dying; I just don't wanna be there when it happens!
—Woody Allen

Chapter 22

GARNER BOYD

Pake and Garner Boyd at Ray Price and Merle Haggard show. 2012—Family Photo

I love to visit with Garner Boyd because he is fun. There are no short conversations with him. He tells good stories, mostly about music and life, and is a good listener. Ever visited with someone who wants to do all the talking and won't let you talk because they don't give a flying rat's ass what anyone else has to say? Garner hangs on every word you say, and you know because he will ask you questions about what you just said. Although our ages differ by about twenty-five years, our visits are like folks of the same age. I think another reason I like talking with Garner is he is a real worker. Today, at eighty plus years, he's up way before daylight, tending to his US mail routes. He will come back to the house around eight or nine in the morning, take a nap till noon, and then get up and go again.

During the time I was dating his daughter, Debbie, I'd come by and pick her up, and Garner would collar me and play something of Bob Wills on a scratchy, worn-out-of-a-gourd record player. I had heard almost every one of those Wills songs because I loved country music too, but I was a Haggard man! I complimented his selections out of courtesy and respect but couldn't wait to get outta there and go be with Debbie.

I fell in love with Debbie at an early age and still am. When we dated during our high school years, the hours flew by like minutes. I kept her out too late, only to find Garner meeting us on the front porch steps one morning about three o'clock. He sent her on into the house, and he gave me a man-to-kid talk, putting one arm around my shoulder and the other on my chest and saying, "Hoss, this thing with you and Debbie is no more. I ain't puttin' up with you keeping her out so late. So the next time you come by to get her, *don't!*"

"Beautiful" Debbie Boyd
—Sue Rhyne Photo

After I got married to Katy, Garner would see us out with her mom, Betty, whom I have always liked for being plainspoken and speaking her mind. Garner would tell Betty, "You know I almost had ole Pake for a son-in-law!"

She got more than an ass full of this statement, and I've heard her reply, "It ain't too late. You can have him!" This was mission accomplished for Garner because he got a big laugh outta that.

Garner loves country music, and his taste changes with the times. I don't know anyone his age that even comes close to keeping up with today's country. In Garner's day, it was all Bob Wills and the Texas Playboys, and he's a big fiddle fan. Garner is a worldly kinda guy. If he so desires, he heads out to Tulsa, Oklahoma City, even Nashville, to hear who he wants, or visits with who he wants to see. Distance is no problem for Garner, and he never meets a stranger. I think he and I share the same feelings—that we like to visit with someone we don't know, as well as someone we already know.

He became good friends with world-known fiddle player Vassar Clements. Garner loves to bullshit, and one night Vassar was playing this club. Afterward, Garner told Vassar, "That was purty good, but ya need ta tune that fiddle!" I cain't imagine how this screwed up Vassar's train of thought, and I'm sure he went off, wondering if Garner was kiddin' or shittin'.

Chapter 23

KIOWA

Kiowa locals donated money for the construction of this
sign just north of Kiowa. 1987—Family Photo

As I read Robin's book, a couple of Kiowa stories came to mind. One was about Oscar Walker. Oscar came into Cason's General Store and seemed to wander around the store until everyone left; he finally went up to the register and said, "Mrs. Cason, my wife, Nettie, sent me down here to pick up a box of Kotex." Mrs. Cason said, "Oscar, what size?" Oscar looked at her kinda dumbfounded and said, "I don't know—big as ya got!"

Is that a gun in your pants, or are ya just so glad to see me?
— MAE WEST

As you may already know, when you check the fluid in the rear-end axle of a pickup truck, you take the plug out, stick your finger in the hole, and if there is oil on it, then it's OK; if not, you add some. This story came from James Maxwell. The Maxwell family—James, Annie, Kenny, and Larry—all owned and operated the Maxwell Station at Kiowa, Oklahoma, north of town, for forty-one years. A nicer bunch of folks you'll never meet. James told my good friend David Hall that he and Annie put the flat's they fixed into a savings account, and those flats shore do add up. James was not the fastest guy on two wheels but was always there and worked steady. He had a nickname: "Speedy." I asked James one day what was the funniest thing he ever heard or saw at the station. He said, "Before I had my station, I worked at Mr. Heath's service station on the south end of Kiowa, and a lady pulled up in the driveway in a pickup truck. She walked up to Mr. Heath and asked, 'Mr. Heath, would you please check the grease in my rear end? Last night my husband stuck his finger in it and said it was bone dry!'"

James Maxwell, Kiowa Apco Station.
1959—Annie Maxwell Photo

James told Garner Boyd that when he was about nineteen years old, a carnival came to Kiowa. Within this carnival was a promoter with a prize-fighter who was about five foot six, weighed about 155 pounds soakin' wet, and was about forty-five years old, with some gray at his temples. The promoter would let locals enter the ring and wager they could whip his fighter, and by looking at him, there were plenty of takers, at first. James thought about the fact that he was nineteen and the old man was forty-five, and that he could knock this gray-haired carny out of the ring, through the ropes, and into the third row of the bleachers. They put the gloves on James and told him that the two fighters were to touch gloves and then start fighting. He walked out to the center of the ring, touched gloves with his soon-to-be-defeated opponent, and the next thing he knew, he was waking up on the ground, and someone was pouring water in his face! Come to find out James hadn't laid a glove on the carny!

In about 1959 or '60, local boys Ronnie Spears, Clark Rhyne, Bob Hensley, and Robin Lacy played a country music dance upstairs at the K-P and Redman Hall in Coalgate, Oklahoma. There was an old piano with the top lid open and the key cover missing. It was very old and appeared to have not been played for a while. Ronnie was a good hand at taking a drink; actually he was really saucer eyed by closing time. Ronnie had mixed some whiskey in a coke bottle (mostly whiskey) and had set it down on the piano front, above the keyboard. He pushed it back against the sound board, so it wouldn't vibrate off of the piano when they were playing. Bob was watching Ronnie, and as they ended a song, Ronnie picked up the coke bottle to get a little drink. A stinging scorpion, a big one, was perched up on the top of the open coke bottle, with his stinger standing at attention! Ronnie was bad, bad drunk by this time. Before Bob could say anything, Ronnie, with his eyes half closed, brought the bottle up to his mouth and *bang*—the scorpion stuck its stinger right into Ronnie's upper lip. Ronnie just blew air and puffed the scorpion off the bottle top! He was so drunk that he didn't even feel it! In ten seconds his lip was swollen as big as a golf ball, and he looked through half-shut eyes at Clark and said, "What do you boys wanna play next?"

Bill Harrington was the Pittsburg County commissioner, witty as they come, and had quite a paunch on him. Never seen without his boots, cowboy hat, and tabacker juice streaming out both corners of his mouth, Bill came into Jones Grocery one morning when Thelma Richardson was at the checkout register. Bill was giving her a hard time, all in fun, when she walked up to Bill and poked him on the belly and said, "If that was on a woman, I'd know what would be wrong with it!"

Bill said, "Why hell, Thelma, this morning it was on a woman—what's wrong with that?"

Stouter than stud horse piss with the foam farted off!
—BILL HARRINGTON

Bill Harrington—Polly Hamilton Photo

I think of all the coincidences I've heard about in my lifetime, this one is the biggest, and it happened to Kenneth Jones. Kenneth is a very unique musician. I've been around a lot of pickers in my time, but I don't know anyone who knows more chords on a guitar than Kenneth. One time Kenneth was in downtown Los Angeles with some friends, and they had driven around for several minutes looking for a parking place. When they finally found one, Kenneth got out of the car on the passenger side, and there were like thousands of people milling like ants, and the first person he looked up and saw was Earl Rhymer from Kiowa—now that's a coincidence!

Jimmy Gene (better known as "Hog Man") used to borrow money from Kenneth and anyone else who would loan him money and was slow about paying them back. Kenneth would have to hit him up repeatedly before Hog Man would pay him. Kenneth got tired of this process, so when they came to an even point, Kenneth waited about a month until he saw Hog Man on the street one day. Knowing Hog Man didn't owe him, Kenneth said, "Hey, man, where's that twenty dollars you owe me?"

Hog Man said, "I don't owe you—we're even!"

Kenneth said, "Noooo, you owe me twenty dollars!"

Hog Man faintly stood his ground until he finally said, "Man, I don't remember this one, but if you say so, I'll go get it." Later Hog Man showed up and paid Kenneth twenty dollars! From then on, Kenneth was never worried about Hog Man borrowing twenty dollars because he paid it back before he borrowed it!

You cain't shit an old shitter!

—JOHN BARNES

One of my favorite people at Kiowa was shoe cobbler Don Adams. He was a big guy with a round, red face and was a good boot man and storyteller. If you walked in with a pair of boots that needed to be half soled and left them with him, you may come back a week later and find them right where you set them down and hadn't been touched. I figured out that if you take them off your feet, tell him that you will wait on them, and sit and visit with him, he'll drop what he's doing and do yours.

Don said that when he was a young man, local men would go up into the hills southeast of Kiowa and cut crossties for the railroad. These ties had to be oak and meet length and width requirements made by the railroad, and if not, they'd have to take them home with them. These men were called "tie hackers." Mama used to call water gravy "tie hackers' honey." Anyway, Don said that one hot summer day he decided to walk up into the hills and watch the men work. Because it was so hot, the men would all strip off and work naked. Don didn't warn the men he was coming, just walked up on them, and he could see the grown men standing over the cut-down trees with their nut sacks just a hangin' and a swingin' with every swing of their axes and split molls. When they heard someone coming, they ran for the bushes, grabbing for their clothes, until they saw it was just Don.

Chapter 24

MONEY

I have run across many types of money people. You, too, know of folks that live from paycheck to paycheck, run up large amounts of money on credit cards at high interest rates, or float or kite checks, but I want to talk about the other side of money people.

The first one is Robert Gray from Wardville, Oklahoma. If five years ago I would have sent you to Robert's house and told you to look for a millionaire's house on the left-hand side of the road coming from Highway 69 into Wardville on Highway 131, you probably would go past it several times. Robert lived in a white house badly in need of paint and upkeep. When you went to visit him, he wouldn't invite you in. He worked at the army base and occasionally carpooled with J. V. Newberry, who said sometimes Robert picked up pecans and took them to work for his dinner that day. When it was time to take his rig, he would put just enough gas in it to get to Wardville but would run out before getting back to Kiowa.

One day J. V. said, "Robert, you need to get you a woman to help take care of you!"

Robert said, "All a woman will do is spend my money!"

Robert had no television but did take the paper, so he could figure out where to invest his money wisely. About three years ago, they found Robert dead in his house, and I never did know what from. Word was he was worth well over a million dollars.

James Holder from Coalgate has worked for Coal County for over twenty-five years. James grows a garden every year and, until recently, has been single all this time. He has over eight hundred acres of land and

180 mama cows paid for, all from working for the county. Someone said, "Hell, if old James had worked at the post office, he'd been a millionaire by now!"

Clark McEntire likes to talk about Irvin Featherston. He, like Robert, lived around Wardville and was more than conservative. When he went into the Wardville store, the men there socializing would offer to buy him a sodie pop, and he'd say, "No thanks, I don't wanna get used to drinking them, but I'll take your nickel!"

> *When it comes to money, spend some, and save some.*
> *Don't try to save it all, but don't spend it all.*
> — GARNER BOYD

Irvin was a rough-looking customer; he always needed a bath and skimped on just about everything, including soap. One time he sent several boxcar loads of steers to Kansas City, to the cattle sale. He was going to ride with the train and had packed a sack of goat meat for the trip. Clark was pretty young, and Irvin had Clark holding his sack until it was time to go. When Irvin went by on the train, Clark pitched the sack, but Irvin missed it. Three days later he showed up back at Limestone Gap and came into Pap's house. They were eating and invited him to sit down and eat. He said, "You bet; I haven't eaten since I last saw y'all."

When Irvin arrived in Kansas City, he slept in the hay mangers at the stockyards where the cattle were. One day he decided to take a walk downtown and just look around. The police found him and arrested him for vagrancy. He told them he had several loads of cattle at the stockyards, and he was just looking around town. They didn't believe any of this, so he told them the name of the commission men at the yards and said to call them. The police did and got this answer: "You boys turn Mr. Featherston loose; he is a good customer of ours, and yes, indeed, he has several pens of cattle out here!"

Clark had gone with Peeler Beal to Kansas City before, on the train with cattle. Pap sent Clark as a youngster, around twelve or thirteen years old, by himself to make the business transaction. Obviously Pap expected a lot out of his son at an early age. Clark liked it because he got to ride up front with the conductor.

> *Successful people are willing to do the things that unsuccessful people simply refuse to do.*
> —UNKNOWN (BUT BRILLIANT)

Chapter 25

KIOWA HIGH SCHOOL

Jac worked at the school as the school secretary, which often was not good for me. One day I got into fisticuffs with a kid named Sylvester, and Mrs. Richardson sent me to Mama's office instead of Mr. Neal's, the principal. Jac said, "Pake, you don't have to come to school at all; you can just stay home. Clark needs help, and you can just help him." It didn't take long to answer that statement. I was already getting all I wanted from Clark on mornings before I went to school, after school, and on weekends. Clark had the knack of working the dog shit outta ya and making you feel lower than a snake's belly in a wagon rut! The summers weren't too bad, but the winters were real busy, and he was always shorthanded. I thought about what she'd said, looked at Jac, and said, "You won't have any more trouble outta me!"

Jacqueline McEntire as Kiowa High School secretary. 1967—Family Photo

Looking back, I would have been better off financially if I had gone home. I was fourteen then, and by the time I was eighteen and out of school, I would have had a financial statement larger than most of my teachers. But I would have missed the Kiowa Cowboy Country Music Band Class.

I really did like school, especially being around all the kids, teachers, bus drivers, janitors, and cooks—the whole nine yards. I liked FFA, 4-H Club, basketball, and, of course, our country music band class.

I think keeping kids home for homeschooling is depriving them from socializing with the rest of the world and is shamefully cruel. I've heard of parents keeping their kids home, so they won't be exposed to all the bad things they learn from other kids, but I think this is asinine. They are gonna see the bad things eventually—just teach them to not go down that losing road. Teach them right from wrong, plain and simple.

About the only thing I didn't like at school was studying. Hell, who does like to study about something completely uninteresting? But like most of us, I used these things later on in life.

Doc Coker and Irvin Jewell presenting Pake an FFA award. 1971—Family Photo

Pake, since starting to proofread your book, several hours ago, I've not gotten up from the computer once. I love it. Here are a few suggestions: Tell more about your mother's qualities, her brains, her wisdom, her beautiful voice, how she taught you kids harmony, and how she made the Kiowa School a much better place when she was there, how she was loved by all, and how badly she was missed when she quit. Not enough credit was given to her for ideas that she helped develop. The teachers, bus drivers, custodians, children, cooks—everybody respected and loved her. When she left, it became a cold and sterile place.

— CLARK RHYNE

When we were in the eighth grade, we were in Mr. E. V. Roberts's class. This was just after dinner and anybody who wasn't in class when the bell rang had to go see Mr. Roberts and get an admit to return to their class. Here came high school boys Claude Lackey, Roy Roberts, and John Lewis, who had gotten back from the smoke shack a little late for class, requesting an admit. This day Mr. Roberts was not in a very good mood, so he angrily told them to grab a seat in the back of the class. At the end of the hour Mr. Roberts walked back to the boys, and by this time he had begun to get in a little better mood. He said, "John, what kind of cigarettes do you smoke?"

John said, "OPs."

Mr. Roberts said, "What kind is that?"

John said, "Other people's!" We all got a kick outta that, even Mr. Roberts.

Although our basketball team sucked out loud when it came to winning, we all had fun, maybe even more fun than the teams that won games. For example, at the beginning of practice, we would all be shooting basketballs at once; the coach would blow his whistle and holler, "Hold your balls!" At that moment everybody would stop shooting and grab their nut sacks!

I told you earlier that I hoped I would tell more things about my shortcomings than others', so here comes a good 'in. In the eighth grade, we didn't have desks to sit at; instead we had tables. I was sitting next to a real pretty girl, and we became quite comfortable with each other. One day I decided I would place my hand on her leg under the table. I enjoyed it, and she seemed to put up with it. The next day I did the same thing, but this time her hand was on her leg right where I had mine. I glanced over at her and saw both of her hands on top of the table. I looked past her and saw sitting next to her was Willie Tucker, looking directly at me! At the same time, we both pulled our hands back. I don't know about him, but I didn't do that again.

Harold A. Toaz (Supt.), Floyd R. Neal (Prin.), Francie Corey (Spon.), Royce Casey (Spon.), Gary Hall (Pres.), Ronald Wilkins (V. Pres.), Glynda Williams (Sec.), Becky Tatum (Treas.), David Jewell, Carmen Evans, Gregory Caldwell, Rickey Fender, Patricia Smith, Linvel Powell, Jr., Sally Williams, Buddy Lewis, Juanita Griffin, Janie Griffin, Larry Kinman, Donna (Scott) Harrington, James Frazier, Sandra Lane, Pake McEntire, Jeanie Hatridge, Charles Patton, Floyd King, Maria Hargrave, David Turner, Judy Watkins, Donald Smith, Joyce Clifton, William Tucker and Joni Frazier.

Chapter 26

MR. HAROLD TOAZ

Besides basketball, Vo-AG (Vocational Agriculture), and music, one of the most interesting classes I attended was superintendent Harold Toaz's US history class. He was a real intimidating man—big ears, long sharp nose, and tall in stature—and he usually thought outside the box. For example, he'd get his grade book out, start down the row, ask one question, and if you got it right, you got a 100 in the book. If you didn't, you got a 0! If you gave an educated guess, he would sometimes be generous and give you a 50. Now this just scared the hell outta all of us. So when he'd start this game, everybody's asses began to pucker up real tight, nervous as a dog shittin' peach seeds, trying real hard not to get a 0. One day at the first of the semester, he made assignments for us to get up in front of the class and do an oral report on anything of our choice. You guessed it: I chose rodeo. I went home, got some big cardboard charts, pasted rodeo pictures of all the different events, and explained each one precisely. He was impressed and gave me a 94 on the project.

He picked the topic on the next one we had to do, and mine was copper. As you can probably guess, I didn't give two hoots in hell about copper, but I got out the Britannica Books of Encyclopedia Jac had bought for just these occasions and got what I needed to pass. When I got through, Mr. Toaz asked me, "Pake, what did the Indians use copper for?" I didn't remember seeing anything in the book about Indians and copper, so I said I didn't know.

He said, "They wore it on their bodies to help them with arthritis."

When Alice was in his class, he made an incorrect statement on history, and Alice contradicted him. He said something to the effect, "Well, Miss McEntire, if you'll look it up in the history book, you'll find I'm right!"

Alice said, "I did, Mr. Toaz; it's right here." She began to read it from the book, proving him wrong. Later he came back into his office and told Jac, "Your daughter just set me straight in our history class!"

One noon hour, when all the kids at school were in the halls or outside, I was standing in the hall next to Mr. Toaz's office window. Joe Clifton and I were horsing around when I slung my elbow, sticking it right through the plate-glass window of Mr. Toaz's office. I immediately thought, "Oh shit!" We stood there waiting for a teacher to come and hang us up by our nut sacks, when Mrs. Toaz came by and said, "Boys, you'd better go to the lunchroom and tell Mr. Toaz what you've done." We headed down there and discovered our worst nightmare. There was Mr. Toaz, sitting at a table eating lunch with about five or six teachers and Mama. This meant we had to confess our bad judgment not only to Mr. Toaz, but to all the teachers. After we told them all what we'd done, he said, "Well, you boys go get a broom and a dustpan and clean it up." Right before we turned and walked away, Jac said, "Pake, I guess you know you'll have to pay for that window." I said, "Yes, ma'am." Mr. Rhyne told me later that after we left,

Mr. Toaz looked down the table and said, "Mrs. McEntire, I'll decide who pays for what around here!" That was the end of that, which meant I didn't have to pay for the window.

Mrs. Healion Toaz. 1970—Family Photo

I don't care who is in charge of any organization: it ain't possible for them not to make mistakes, and it's real easy for the shade tree section to criticize up one side and down the other. It is only human to make them, and I'm sure Mr. Toaz made plenty along the way of thirty-some years as superintendent. I'm guessing he would like to have taken back some decisions but couldn't. I liked him, plain and simple. He had the balls that if he told you something, that was the way it was gonna be. No fence-straddling, wishy-washy political stammering, tell you what you wanna hear and then turn around and tell someone else the total opposite, as long as that's what they want to hear. He had the respect of all us kids at school, and we all liked it that way.

This story comes from Warren Casey. I was at his house, selling insurance one night, and he told me a story about one of my favorite people, Harold Toaz. Mr. Toaz was the superintendent at Limestone Gap back in about the midfifties. Mr. Toaz had a rule that if a teacher was smoking a cigarette during school hours, the students could too. Mr. Toaz sent for Warren and another boy to come to the office, to tell them to go change the light bulbs in the gymnasium. They had done this many times before, but when the boys walked into Mr. Toaz's office, he had his back to the door; he was sitting in a chair and talking on the phone. His feet were propped up on the windowsill, and he was smoking a cigarette. The boys looked at him, waiting for him to get off the phone, looked at each other, reached into their shirt pockets, pulled out their packs of cigarettes, and lit them up! When Mr. Toaz got off the phone, he turned around and saw the boys smoking. He had a look of surprise on his face, put out his cigarette, and said, "All right, boys, go change those burned-out light bulbs in the gym."

CHAPTER 27

KIOWA HIGH SCHOOL BAND CLASS

When we were real young and rodeoing with Clark, Jac used to get all of us kids to sing in the car going down the road, mainly to keep us out of trouble from a-fussin' and a-fightin'. She could hear and separate harmony parts from lead parts from singing in church back at Tipperary, the country church on the corner near Boggy Creek. She soon found out that we took to it like ducks to water. While singing our part, we would put our finger in our ear next to the kid she was trying to stack another harmony part on, and concentrated real hard to stay on our part. Some of the first songs we learned were "Walk Right Back," a Phil and Don Everly (The Everly Brothers) hit, and "Heart Over Mind," which has been recorded by greats like Mel Tillis and Ray Price.

Clark Rhyne played guitar and sang at the WH Corral every Saturday night and did other music jobs to make extra income. He had been playing fiddle and guitar most all his life, and he and Jac got together and asked Mr. Harold Toaz if the school would fund a country music band class. Nine students with very unique talents enrolled in the class, and it was the beginning of something really special: one hour a day, four days a week (not five because of the floating class—this meant every day one subject in school was skipped). We even got a grade for it on our report cards. The class consisted of singers Dianna Kay Smith, Carol Johnson, Susie

McEntire, Reba McEntire, drummers Kelly Rhyne and David Jones, bass Roger Wills, lead guitar Gary Raiburn, and me playing rhythm guitar and singing. We played for everything the school wanted us to play for, similar to what a marching band did.

Pake and Carol Johnson. 1970—Carol Johnson Photo

Kelly Rhyne, Gary Raiburn, Pake, and Reba. 1969—Family Photo

Raiburn was a wiry kinda kid, witty, and real thin; with his veins showing through his skin, he looked like he needed to carry around a bottle of Geritol in his back pocket. He wrote on the bulletin board in the hallway of the school: "Due to rain, the annual Navajo Indian rain dance has been cancelled!" Mr. Toaz failed to see the humor, but Mr. Rhyne liked it.

We first began our Kiowa High School Band practice at the fairgrounds, in the Home Demonstration Building. Mr. Toaz put us there because it had a stage, and he didn't want us interrupting classes. Roger Wills came to class strumming on a beat-up electric guitar. No kid wanted to play bass, so Mr. Rhyne did. After we moved the class to the cafetorium at the school, one day Mr. Rhyne took off his bass and walked over to Roger and said, "Here, Roger, you play this." That day began Roger Wills lifetime career as a bass player (and a great one he is). Today he plays for Alan Jackson, as he has for the past twenty-two years.

While out on the road, one night Roger and Alan were in this club. Alan got up to play the jukebox; Roger yelled out, "Don't rock the jukebox!" This gave Alan the idea to write the hit, "Don't Rock the Jukebox."

1969-1970 Kiowa Cowboy Country Music Band Class: Gary Raiburn, Kelly Rhyne, Pake, David Jones, Carol Johnson, Reba McEntire, Dianna Kay Smith and Roger Wills - Carol Johnson Photo

CHAPTER 28

BALLAD OF JOHN MCENTIRE

One Monday morning, Mr. Rhyne came into the class and said, "You McEntire kids—yesterday I wrote a song about your grand pap." Now, Mr. Rhyne, his dad, Todd, and Pap were all real good friends. We sat down and listened to the song that morning and fell completely in love with it. To this day I still do it on most all my shows, and it goes like this:

Gather round me, boys, I gotta story to tell
About a friend of mine that you all know well
He's an old cowhand he's known near and far
He goes by the name of John McEntire
1897 was the year he was born
In Lula, Oklahoma, on a small dirt farm
Some say John was born with a rope in his hand
He wanted to be a Rodeo Man

A friend, a companion, and a Rodeo Star
There's none greater than John McEntire

His father said, "Son, you must change your plans
There's work to be done farming the land"
He wouldn't give in to his father's advice
Roping and Rodeos was his whole life
You've heard it said, and so often it's true
Behind a great man, there's a good woman too

He had a great wife—Alice was her name
She helped him to ride a long road of fame

A friend, a companion, and a Rodeo Star
There's none greater than John McEntire

He traveled the land from the east to the west
Just a ropin' wild steers—he was the best
He worked mighty hard, and his dreams came true
He made Worlds Champion, and his son, Clark, did too
His friends they number a million or more
John turns no one away from his door
Whenever you're down and all out of luck,
He'll give you his shirt or his last buck

A friend, a companion, and a Rodeo Star
There's none greater than John McEntire

Yes, there's none greater than John McEntire

We worked on the song that hour of class, went home and worked on it that night, and went back to school the next day and worked on it in class again. That night, on November 20, 1970, we went to Oklahoma City, to Benson Studio and Boss Records, and recorded the very first record Reba, Susie, and I ever recorded, called, "The Ballad of John McEntire." Other pickers on that cut were Clark Rhyne on rhythm guitar, Kelly Rhyne on drums, Benny Kubiak on fiddle, a staff studio bass player whose name I cain't remember, and Doug Campbell on steel. We took Pap with us up there, and Mr. Rhyne suggested that Susie, Reba, and I sit down and do an interview with him. This is kinda the way it went:

Reba said, "Grand Pap, when were you born?"

He said, "February 19, 1897. I'm seventy-three years old."

Susie said, "Grand Pap, what were some of the pranks the cowboys played on you when you were rodeoing?"

He said, "Well, they played so many on me, I cain't hardly remember."

Susie said, "What about the one they played on you at Burwell, Nebraska?"

He said, "Well, this guy was fixin' to mow the churchyard, so I asked the guy if it would be OK if I let my horse graze it before he cut it, and he said sure. Well, the boys called the law and had me arrested for it—all a sham deal."

I said, "Pap, what advice would you give to a young, up-and-coming rodeo cowboy?"

He said, "Well, I'd tell him it's the greatest lick they are and to master three licks." (A "lick" refers to a well developed skill or talent)

I said, "Pap, I've heard you do it at dances and at cafés, but give us that McEntire yell."

He laughed and said, "It's been so long don't know if I can!"

At that point he let 'er go, and it was loud and long. So loud we had to do it over because it maxed out the microphone to distortion. After we were done that night, he walked out of the studio, opened up his arms, and gave the girls a big hug and said that was the greatest day of his life.

Clark Rhyne remembers he ordered one thousand copies, and when we got them back, he began to sell them for one dollar apiece. He went around Coalgate, Atoka, and Kiowa and put them on jukeboxes. I remember one day Pap and I was eating dinner at the Chuck Wagon in Coalgate, and somebody played it, and Pap lit up like a Christmas tree.

Later on, Clark went to Pap and said, "John, I have most of my money back, and I want you to take a couple of boxes of these records and go anywhere you want and give them to anyone you want to have one."

Pap said, "OK, but let me pay you for them first."

Clark said, "No, I won't take any money for them. I just want you to have them."

Pap loved to give things away, and he had a real good time with these records. Later he saw Clark and asked if he could buy some more, but

Clark said again, "I'll give you all you want, but I won't sell them to you." So he did.

The school let us take their PA (public address sound system), bass, and amps out on weekends and play music jobs. Hell, why not? Not letting us take those instruments would have been like telling a kid in English class he couldn't take a book home! Jac got us several gigs at Antlers, playing at a community hall for a percentage of the door, which was usually about fifteen to twenty dollars apiece, which was great for us. They let Jac sit and take the money at the door, and the lights were down real low. We noticed the crowd was really rockin' and liking our deal, and the more energetic they got, the harder we tried. After the first night, on the way home, we commented to Jac how much the crowd seemed to like our music and how rowdy they were. She said, "I guess so. I counted fourteen fights all night long."

Mr. Rhyne came up with the idea of sending out letters informing surrounding schools that we would come and play their junior and senior proms. Wapanucka and Pittsburg, Oklahoma, responded, and we made a deal and played them.

Thank y'all for coming out to see me here tonight and supporting my show; it costs a lot to look this cheap!
— DOLLY PARTON

Chapter 29

MY RED FORD PICKUP

I was approaching sixteen when our neighbor Vernon McCormick had a four-hundred-dollar motorcycle for sale, and I wanted it badly. I asked Clark and Jac if they would buy it for me, but they had a better idea. They would pay half for a 1970 model half-ton, solid-red with a white top Ford pickup from Harmon Jones Ford in Atoka that cost $2,400 brand spankin' new. A real cat's ass! It was a three speed on the column with rollup windows and no air conditioner; it would barely pull the hat off your head, started and showed up for work, shined like a diamond up a goat's ass, and I liked it a lot. The doors shut with very little effort, so I felt it necessary to remind passengers not to slam the windshield and windows out of it. (They don't call me "Picky Pake" for nothin'.) I even ran Donald Fred Smith a car race down old Highway 69, south of Kiowa one night, and we did purty good—we came in second place! I had a note just above the radio that said, "These buttons are set to country music—don't change them!"

Smoking and rock music were not permitted in the little red truck. I took it to a steer roping the first weekend we had it and won my twelve hundred dollars back. We fed cattle in it, and then I would clean it up and drive it to school. On weekends I took beautiful Kiowa girls out on dates. I refrain from naming names to protect the innocent.

If McEntires kept the oil checked, the sticks from dragging under it, and baling wire off the drive shaft and rear end, then we were doing good for us on the upkeep. Maybe since we always let it go way past the oil change and grease date, after about a hundred thousand miles, the truck sounded like it needed a tune-up. I drove it back to Jones Ford one day and told them it wuddin' runnin' right and to fix it. Without calling Clark for the OK, they overhauled the whole engine! We got a tune-up all right, to the tune of five hundred dollars. Clark liked to have shit a brick 'cause back then that kind of money was hard to come by, but things turned out good in the long run. We kept on driving it until it was completely worn out. Ya see, Clark and Jac rarely throw anything away if there is just even a dab of good left in it. I'm not as much, but I am a lot that way and proud of it.

A penny saved is a penny earned.

—BEN FRANKLIN

Jac donated a small camper with a bed in it, and we took the truck rodeoing. In three out of four years, Clark and I won the average at a roping at Post, Texas, totaling over twelve thousand dollars.

After we put the camper on it, Jac repeatedly told me to be careful with the camper and not back into anything. One day we were down at the lots, and she backed into a bois d' arc tree limb that went all the way through the back of the camper! We stuffed some paper towels in it and left it at that. Because of the camper, we rarely fed cattle in it after that, until Pap and I had the cattle up at George Coop's.

Jones Ford in Atoka had a promotional contest, and Reba entered it and won a car for a year. Like Robin Lacy would say, "We drove the doo-dog out of that thing." Everywhere we went that didn't require a trailer or a camper, we went in that car with a big poster on the side of the doors advertising Jones Ford.

Chapter 30

HARDCORE COUNTRY

I was so hardcore country it made a few younger people hate me. I have tried to like other kinds of music—like classical, with all the strings and horns, even rock—and can listen to some, but the hardcore heavy metal just doesn't do it for me. I like the rock stuff after it's become a classic and everybody else is sick to death of it. I wish I did like other music because I feel I am missing out on entertainment.

You would think that getting to play country for one hour a day in our country music band class, being a school hero, getting a grade for it, playing for football games and pep rallies, and taking the instruments out on weekends to make extra money playing jobs would be enough to make anyone happy. Right? Wrong! There was a lot of friction in the band. Kelly, Roger, Gary, and David wanted to play rock. We were all supposed to play country music in the band class because Mr. Toaz hated rock-and-roll, and I did too. We would be in class playing, and Mr. Rhyne would leave the room to go tell Mr. Toaz or Jac how good we were doing, when the rock boys would stop in the middle of a country song and start playing acid reaction or some shit from Led Zeppelin (whoever the hell he was). The rock boys usually played way too loud!

Buttermilk Sky—Sue Rhyne Photo
David Jones, Gary Raiburn, Kelly Rhyne, and Roger Wills

One day Mr. Rhyne suggested I go ask Mr. Toaz if we could play for the students while they ate lunch. I walked into his office, reluctantly, half scared of him and half intimidated, but I conjured up the courage and went anyway. I put the deal to him, and he agreed, with two conditions. One was that we played quietly, and the other was that we ate lunch first. Who in the hell wouldn't want to eat instead of the last fifteen minutes of English class? I walked out of his office feeling prouder than a peacock of Mr. Rhyne for suggesting such a great idea! I told Mr. Rhyne and then told the class the conditions, and we were all excited.

The first day we started playing, Mr. Toaz walked to the table with his plate of food, looked at me, and raised his hand and then lowered it. I knew we were too loud. I turned down my guitar and told everybody else to do so, but they didn't. To tell them to turn down the sound was like throwing a bucket of hot piss in their faces. Mr. Toaz stopped the playing during lunch hour, and the rock-and-roll boys cussed Mr. Toaz for it.

It was real hard for me to like those boys, and they really didn't like me either. To them I was a stiff, country redneck shitkicker that didn't do drugs like they did. I didn't run loose like a wild coyote doing whatever I pleased, like they did. Guess if Clark hadn't worked the line back shit out of me, I'd have been like them, but he and Jac wuddin' gonna let that happen. My hair was cut short, and they wore theirs as long as the school would let them. Roger used to ride a motorcycle up and down the streets of Kiowa with his hair blowing in the wind. We had almost nothing in common, but I tried to get along with them. Later after we all graduated, we became great friends because they all turned country. They were all just good old country boys; they just didn't know it.

The first time I saw Kelly was at Cairo, where I live now. He was about six or seven years old, helping someone carry his drums up the steps at the Cairo schoolhouse. I think they were having a Coon Hunters Ball, and Kelly was the drummer in the band. I remember he had a proud air about him. Another time, they had this same ball; we didn't go, but Louie Sandman did. He came back, saying, "Boy, you kids should have been there last night. Your uncle Peck offered Molly [our cousin] five dollars to get up and sing a song, but she wouldn't do it." Hell, we would have sung all night for five dollars.

> *"Pake, do you know why that amp's a hummin'?"*
> *I said, "Why's that?"*
> *He said "'Cause it don't know the words!"*
> — RICKY "BEAVER" SOLOMON

Eventually Kelly and I became real close. I missed out on the drug scene, so Kelly did his and mine too. Leon McClendon once told me, "The only way for friends to remain friends is to overlook each other's faults."

Kelly had to overlook a bunch of mine, so we remained friends. Kelly would tell me all about his wild—and I mean *wild*—drug experiences, and he liked to hear rodeo and music stories from me.

Chapter 31

WARDVILLE BOYS

J. V. Newberry, Sam Rhyne, Tod Rhyne, Jim Rhyne, and Tod Rhyne—Sue Rhyne Photo

Far as I'm concerned, James V. Newberry was Wardville, Oklahoma. If they had taken the sign down at Wardville and put up one that said, "J. V. Newberryville," I wouldn't have thought anything about it. J. V. was the one you called when your car broke down, you were putting electricity in your self-built house, your washer broke down, you needed help working cattle, you needed gettin' pulled out of a mud hole—just call J. V.! Now, there is no reason to call someone if they ain't gonna show up, but he would show up.

Folks ask me many times who got me started in country music. Well, Mama bought me, like Jerry Reed said, my first guitar, and Clark Rhyne gave me guitar lessons. But who got Clark started on the fiddle at an early age? Yes, J. V. Newberry. When asked a question, you may not always like his answer, but J. V. would shoot it to ya straight.

One time, he called and wanted me and Reba to help him do a music show at Coalgate. We brought Susie along. Now, Susie was pretty young—I'm gonna say about eleven or twelve years old, and at that time she didn't know very many songs. At the end of the night, J. V. gave Susie his night's pay! That, my friend, is integrity. Never pass up a chance to build integrity, and that night J. V. didn't! All the show money J. V. and Helen made over the past fifty years went toward them and their family. Every dollar was counted and needed. His decision to give a little girl his night's pay was the kind of integrity that needs to be passed on for generations after generations, and you can do the same for someone someday. You'll feel real good about yourself and make others do like you, just like J. V.'s night of integrity affected me!

That's a humdinger!

—UNKNOWN

John Pratt (Corky) Hooe also lived at Wardville all his life, and most everyone around the Coalgate area knew him. Eula Kelly was the teacher at Wardville and had Corky in school in his early grades. One day after recess, Corky didn't come back to class, when a student told Mrs. Kelly that Corky was at the outhouse. She asked the boy if Corky had messed in his britches again, and the kid said yes. Mrs. Kelly went down to the outhouse, and there was Corky, and sure enough that was the case. She scolded him and said, "Corky, you've got to quit doing that, and I mean it!" (Or something to that effect.) Corky said, "I did not do it. Bobby Joe Witherspoon did it!"

He was a lot of fun because of the way he talked. He liked to visit and was usually very entertaining. Corky loved to talk about women. He usually claimed to have a girlfriend, but I cain't recall ever seeing him with one. I did a show at the park in Coalgate one Fourth of July. I pulled in early, and Corky was there. He came over to the truck where Katy and I were sitting. Katy and I had been arguing about something (but really over nothing). I asked Corky if he had a girlfriend. Corky said, "Yesh, I jot shew ushem."

I said, "Are either of 'em purty?"

Corky said, "You jod jam wight dey shore are!"

I said, "How 'bout you swappin' one of 'em to me for my wife, Katy, here?" I pointed to her sittin' in the truck. Corky looked at me, then looked at her, and took off walking away from us. About ten feet away, he stopped, turned around, and walked back to us and said, "O'chay!"

Katy said, "You shouldn't tease him like that—it's cruel!"

My intention was to have fun with Corky, not make fun of him; besides he loved the attention. A couple of weeks later, we got a call from a lady at Mr. Quick at Kiowa, saying a big guy was there wanting to know where we lived. I said, "What's his name?" She turned and asked him, and I heard him reply, and I knew it was Corky. He had come to make the swap. I told her to tell him we were not gonna be home, and we'd catch up with him some other time. Katy still was not enjoying any of this.

Corky called up J. V. Newberry one time and said, "J. V., shum shum bitch jot in my jod jam housh [house] and shtolde [stole] my jod jam retchnerds [records], shtolde my booch [boots], and shrewed [screwed] my jod jam joat [goat]!"

I don't know if it upset some of his relatives or not, but they asked me to sing and play at Corky's funeral. I played "Milk Cow Blues" and "Orange Blossom Special." I am sure Corky liked them real well.

Corky Hooe—Sue Rhyne Photo

Last, but certainly not least, is Joe Mike Smith, who also lives at Wardville, Oklahoma. He and his wife, Daisy Mae, were born and raised there, and rest assured, they will remain there until they die. Daisy is in a wheelchair, and Joe takes care of them both. Recently a government provider came to help with Daisy, but before then, Joe provided all the assistance. If everyone was as dedicated to their marriage as Joe Mike, there would not be any divorces. He has a knack for knowing who is kin to whom—just ask him. He is the last of the real, old-time cowboys, a dying breed, with hat, Levi's, and spurs, and he rides horses that he loves to hang the hoo gals (spurs) in. Joe also loves to pick things up on the highway, such as angle iron, short or long chains—you name it. If it's on the highway, it's fair game. He and Daisy love to eat at the Sonic in Coalgate, and one day he was helping us ship cattle, when he said, "Steph, you'll never guess what happened! The other day Daisy and me was at the Sonic Drive-In. I ordered a hamburger with French fries and a cherry Coke, and Daisy ordered a fish sandwich with onion rings and a Dr. Pepper. I looked out my window, and there was a nickel on the ground! I got out, and there was a penny beside it, and I looked a little farther to my left, and there was a dime! Before they brought our sandwiches, I had picked up twenty-seven cents! They gave us some free mints with our meal too. It was a good day at Sonic!"

What a great country we live in today, with people throwing money on the ground and all you have to do is bend over and pick it up. As of late, he hit the jackpot for $1.65. Guess there'll never be another poor day!

Another time, he was helping us work cattle, and he said, "Steph, you'll never guess what happened the other day!" He always talks to Steph because she pays him more attention than I do, and his tone of voice is always full of excitement. "I was down at the Choctaw Plaza gettin' gas. I looked over at the west end of the building, and there was two security guards in the parking lot, chasing a chicken! They chased it until it finally ran in between two buildings, so they gave up! They went back inside. I got my gas, and I went over to those buildings—and guess what! I got that chicken! I took that chicken home, and you'll never guess what happened! It laid an egg!"

One day, Joe and I were fixing the Buck Creek water gap at Jr. Edge's. Jr. had a boat we used to take the wire across. Joe took his billfold out of his pocket and laid it on the fender of the trailer, to keep from losing it in the water. When we finished, we came back to Limestone Gap, and Joe grabbed his pocket and said, "Oh shoot, I forgot to get my billfold off the fender of the trailer; it must'a fell off when we left. I'll go back and get it."

There is a train underpass for the traffic to go under the tracks about seventy-five yards from Junior's house. Many times, people will come off the highway and stop under there to have a piss or dirty break.

I waited for Joe back at Limestone Gap at the mailbox and saw him coming in a panic! He drove up behind me, skidded the tires (with the gravel just a flyin'), jumped out of his truck, and ran up to me with his eyes big as silver dollars, like the whole world was coming to an end, and said, "Pake, you ain't gonna believe what I just saw!"

I said, "What, Joe?"

He said, "When I pulled up to the underpass there at Jr.'s, there was a car parked under the train track where I couldn't get by, and this man and woman wus in the backseat. And they wus a-fuckin'! When they looked up and saw me, they jumped over from the backseat to the front, and I saw her butt and everythang!"

I looked at him and realized Joe lives in an exciting world.

Joe Mike Smith—Joe Mike Photo

CHAPTER 32

MISCHIEF

At Chockie, we had a rollaway bed that I liked to sleep on in the living room at night for the south breeze. One night, Alice came in late from a date and didn't want Jac to know what time she had made it in. So unbeknownst to me, she just got in bed with me on the rollaway.

The next day, she said that sometime in the night, she had her back to me, and I rolled over next to her, threw my leg over her, reached around her with my arm, and grabbed a handful of boob. She said she elbowed me and said, "You son of a bitch, move over!"

She said I said, "Oh baby, don't do me this way!"

Alice got married at the house at Chockie to Bobby Stewart from Wilburton. Jr. Edge asked Pap, "John, what does Alice's husband do?"

Pap, being all cowboy, said, "Well he…uh…he, well…he…He duddin' rope!"

Bobby Stewart and Alice on their wedding day at Chockie.
I wish Alice had married a veterinarian and great friend,
Calvin White. They dated, but it didn't work out. Guess ya
cain't choose husbands for ya sisters—Family Photo

On occasion we took the International Scout up through the hills northeast of Limestone Gap and climbed the three-hundred-foot communication tower. The first time was Bill Hamilton and me. We had such a thrill that we had to get others in on the fun. So the next time, we took Sally Williams and Debbie Boyd. The ladder was straight up, with about three rest intervals to the top, where there is a fifteen-by-fifteen-foot platform and a huge, red flashing light in the middle. On the way up, the girls needed encouragement to continue from vapor locking. Debbie climbed it wearing moccasins, and her feet were sore when we got back down. The whole ordeal was kinda scary because the tower swayed back and forth, and the wind picked up and made a draft up through the center where the ladder was. We took our light jackets off and dropped them, and they flared out like a man falling. I climbed it again later with Alice and Flip.

This was all kept secret from our parents at the time, for obvious reasons, but we told them later. It was really a lot of fun, but unless someone was after me with a sharp stick, I wouldn't want to climb it again. I did some things back then that some folks would call "risky," "out of character," or "just plain eat up with the dumbass"!

One shore 'nuff dumb incident occurred with Steve Phipps, sometime around 1980. Steve and I boarded a single-engine plane at McAlester and headed to Nashville—with a student pilot in turbulent weather! To top it all off, Steve brought along some Sprite, Pepsi, and a fifth of Old Charter whiskey! Steve was in the back, mixing the drinks for him and me, and he kept offering the pilot some; but he wasn't haven't any, so Steve started flipping him on the ears. This young pilot was having lots a hell flying this puddle jumper, just a-jumping and a-buckin' up and down and sideways. He had a pencil in his mouth and a roadmap in his lap, with Steve and me hollerin', "Powder River, let 'er buck, a mile wide and an inch deep!"

When we got to music town, we fell out of the plane and wobbled into the terminal, while our nervous wreck of a young pilot headed back for McAlester.

Chapter 33

MATCHES

Steve Phipps and I were in Nashville, looking for songs to make my first album. At the time, there were about three hundred publishing companies in Nashville; now there are nearly one thousand. A publishing company is where songwriters put their songs, and the publisher pitches the songs to the record labels or artists, to be recorded. The writer and publisher usually split the royalties from the sales. They get paid when the song is played on a jukebox, radio, or a movie. Back then, Tree Publishing had over twenty-five thousand songs in their possession. They were more than willing to show these songs by letting you hear them, but they only showed you what the major record companies didn't want. We listened but didn't find anything we liked.

We walked into Combine Music Group, when a guy pitching songs to us pulled out a list of about ten nationally known recording artists that had turned down Johnny Lee's big hit, "Lookin' for Love in All the Wrong Places." This goes to show that nobody knows what is gonna be a hit. We walked down a sidewalk on Music Row and looked up to see an old house turned into a music publishing company called, "Three Kings Publishing." Inside, a real nice guy met us, and we all sat down and listened to songs, but to no avail.

We thanked him and began to make our way to the door, when he said, "I've got one called 'Matches.'"

We said, "Pardon me?"

He sorta struck the door facing, like striking a match on it, and said, "You know, like a match." We sat back down and found what we had been looking for days for. This was the second one, after "The Ballad of John McEntire," that was played on the radio. Billy Parker from KVOO radio in Tulsa was the first one to play it, and it helped boost my little career at the time.

Steve got the idea of heading over to Leon and Vicki Adams of Stuart, Oklahoma, for some promotional pictures. Leon and Vicki had traveled the United States and foreign countries to perform a great specialty act with their horses and steers. Many times they were voted "Specialty Act of the Year" by the Professional Rodeo Cowboys Association, the group that Pap, Clark, and I have been a part of all our roping careers.

Leon always kept at least two grown steers that had been castrated at a later age and did stunts like roman riding, jumping them through hoops of fire, and so forth. Steve thought it to be a great idea to do a photo shoot with me sitting on one of Leon's steers! I was hip with the idea, but a little skeptical, and had to build myself a little courage for the event. I think if I hadn't been raised up around cattle and had instead gone in blind, it would have been easier, but I had been around cattle all my life and knew the kinds of bad situations they can get a feller into.

Leon had his steers turned out, running with some cows in the pasture. He informed us that he had to do that on occasion because keeping them confined in a pen or trailer on the road was not healthy for them. Also it sorta took them back to their wilder nature side.

We watched him go out and sook them into the corrals and put a snap that hooked onto their nose rings, so he could lead them around.

He said, "Now this one is purty stubborn when it comes to training, but when the chips are down and the lights come on in front of a crowd, he performs great, even better than the other one."

He led the steer to a pond down under a hill from the pens. Steve, the photographer, and I all went down there, and I climbed up on him. We were up on this pond dam, almost ready to say "Cheeeese," when this huge steer of fifteen hundred pounds wheeled to the left and headed right toward the water, looking like he was gonna run into the pond with me on him!

This all happened in less than a few seconds, so just before we got to the water, I jumped off, hitting the ground just at water's edge. Being the wild bull trainer, this upset Leon, and he said I should have pulled his head around and stayed on him. Knowing then what I know now, I would have. The big steer ran back to the pens, and Leon gathered him up. By then, we all got a big laugh out of the ordeal, but I really had to reach down in my courage sack and pull out a bunch to finish what we all started. Leon suggested we try the other steer. (Whew, OK by me—this did help my courage factor!) The second steer did everything we wanted, so we got our pictures.

Pake on Leon's Steer—Steve Phipps Photo

Chapter 34

WH CORRAL

While trying to chisel out of my dead-note debt in the cattle business, I met my soon-to-be wife, Kay Gwinn. Danny Hamilton and I were roping calves at Paul LeDoux's house east of McAlester. It was too wet to rope at home, and his pen was real sandy. Paul was a podiatrist, and Kay was his assistant for over eight years. He introduced me to her and her girlfriend, Tinny Bell Harmon, at his house. I had to see Paul about some foot problems and saw her at the office on occasions. We began to date, and a year and a half later, I asked her to marry me.

She wanted to get married in Muskogee, at a preacher's house she knew, and so it wouldn't make the McAlester papers. We drove up there and waited for over two hours, when he showed up very apologetic. The ceremony consisted of me, her, and the preacher. His daughter showed up later to witness the whole ordeal. We lived in her house at McAlester for a year and then built a house southeast of Pittsburg, Oklahoma, and lived there for the next twenty-three years. We had three girls: Autumn Kate, Calamity Jo, and Chism. I'll admit I wanted all boys, but my girls and I were all real close. We had fun after fun in those twenty-three years; seemed like all of a sudden, they were all grown up, and we grew apart. All are great kids—never had any problems out of them. I have no regrets, but life moves on.

Every old Crow thinks hers is the blackest!

—Harold Toaz

While living in McAlester, I had a music gig in downtown McAlester one day, playing hollow-body guitar and singing on a flatbed trailer. It was a hot, sunshiny July morning, and I was sweatin' like a feller in a cotton patch, all for about twenty-five bucks. Robin Lacy was in town visiting his mother-in-law, Jewell Wilson, and he came downtown to the festival I was playing. He walked up to me and said with a big grin, "It's tough everywhere!" A couple a days later, he called me and said, "Jerry Holcomb has hired me to run the band at the Corral in Sulphur. I have Roger Wills playing bass guitar, Wayne Guinn on fiddle, Darrell Romine on guitar, Jerry Hall on steel, and me on drums. The problem is, Wayne is the only singer, and we're about to work him to death. I need someone to play bass that sings also: can you play bass?" I told him I hadn't much experience playing bass, but that didn't deter him even a little bit. He said, "Practice your ass off, and be over here in two weeks for a tryout."

I did as Robin said. I worked on the bass as much as time would allow and loaded up the Japanese bass I had bought from Smiley Weaver at his Guitar House in Ada. I remember Smiley told me, "Don't buy this bass on the pretense you will keep that job over at the Corral." I bought it anyway because for some reason, taking chances excites me.

The four-hour dance went by *real* slow; playing bass and singing at the same time felt like I was patting my head with one hand, rubbing my stomach with the other in a different direction, jumping up and down, and chewin' double-bubble chewin' gum—all at the same time with an anvil tied around my right shoulder! Other than that, it went off purty smooth.

I kept noticing that Robin wasn't diggin' it some. He was trying to teach me bass and playing his drums at the same time by telling me to lock into the kick drum. I tried my best, and at break time, I asked him, "How'm I doin'?" He said, "I'll tell ya after the job's over."

He waited till everyone was gone and Jerry had locked up the place, when he said, "Pake, come over here and sit down."

He reached for the tailgate on his pickup truck and pulled it down. We sat there for a minute or so, and he stared out over the horizon, with a faraway look, studying about how he was gonna put this. Finally, he said, "You played behind the beat all night long!" Then he said in a calmer voice, "Take that bass home and put on some songs and play right on top of the beat, not behind it or in front of it—right on top of the beat; and play that thing till the world looks flat!"

He didn't fire me because he needed my vocals. So I did as he said, and the next Saturday night was a little better, and the next was too, until I began to see the strain leave Robin's face.

I stayed there for about a year and a half and learned a bunch. Robin played there for sixteen straight years, every Saturday night and on special occasions.

Pake and Wayne Guinn at
The Corral—Family Photo

A guy named Kenneth "Spider" Woodard used to come to the Corral. A couple of years earlier, Clark Rhyne took a white shirt and a magic marker and drew a big spider with little spiders and spider webs on the back of this shirt, with a caption at the bottom saying, "Black Widows Beware!" Spider wore this shirt to the Corral every Saturday night until it nearly rotted off of him. Spider liked to get all boozed up and then ask to sit in and sing "Fraulein."

The bandstand at The Corral was about four feet high, and on the west end were the steps. One night they gave Spider this huge buildup, introducing him to come up and sing. Spider got way back about ten or fifteen feet from the steps and got a big run at the stand. So when Clark Rhyne said, "Folks, let's hear a big round of applause for our very own Spider Woodard!" Spider took off in a dead run, made the first step, but hung his toe on the last one and hit on all fours on the bandstand, right in front of Wayne Guinn. Wayne was taking a drink and looked down at Spider and said, "May I offer you a drink, mister?"

I sold insurance for ten years; one of the insurance managers and I wound up eating supper at the Savanna truck stop. I asked him, "Are you a country music fan?"

He said, "No, but my wife is. She and some friends of ours used to go down to Sulphur at a huge dancehall. It was the type where you bring your own bottle, and they sell you setups like ice and pop and so forth. I wouldn't go with them because, first of all, I don't dance, and I don't like country music all that well. They kept on at me until I caved in and decided to go with them one Saturday night."

All the time he was telling me this story, I kept quiet, not revealing I had worked there for over a year, when he said, "We got there, paid our way at the door, bought the setups, found us a table, and they jumped out on the dance floor and began to dance their asses off. Not me—noooo, I just sat there all swelled up, nursing on my salty dogs of vodka and grapefruit juice, wishing I was anywhere else. After a while I was starting to have a good time, like they were, until I had to get up and go to the bathroom. I walked to the back and was in the restroom, standing at this long metal urinal with water running into the trough and leaking onto the floor."

I knew this place to a T. He said, "I was standing there shaking the dew off my lily when the next thing I knew I had passed out and was face-down, soaking up all the water and piss on the floor! I somehow managed to roll over, soaking up more with the backside of my shirt, when some guy began to help me up. I got my business back into my trousers; the man pointed me back toward my table, with my shirttail hanging out, with water and piss all over me! With great effort, I made it back to my chair when my wife and the couple we were with saw me and decided it was time to go home. Because of the odor, they all three sat up front, and I was lying down in the backseat. This was in the cold wintertime, and the next thing I knew, I had my head out the window, puking down the outside and inside of my friend's car. They were all giving me hell, calling me these terrible names, when I finally got the window rolled back up, laid back down, passed out, and woke up, realizing someone had shit my trousers! Now I had piss on my clothes, front and back, puke down my front and all over the door and backseat, and shit in my trousers! They soon decided the cold was not nearly as bad as the smell, so they rolled all the windows down all the way back to Oklahoma City, cussin' my city ass every step of the way! I said, 'I told you sons a bitches I didn't wanna go in the first place!' You know, after that they never did ask me to go out with them again."

Liquor by the drink and Mothers Against Drunk Drivers was the downfall for The Corral and other local dancehalls, bringing the curtain down on big ballroom dancing. In a way, it was a shame, ending all the fun to be had, but like Randy Travis said, "On the other hand," something had to be done about all the drunk driving because lives were wasted. It didn't completely stop the problem, but it slowed it down tremendously.

In our area, just last week, two young couples, twenty and twenty-one, were drunk out of their minds, going in excess of eighty miles an hour on a country back road, and hit a tree, killing both. One may say the liquor killed them, but I disagree. The decision to drink and drive killed them. Same way with guns. Guns don't kill people; people kill people.

The big deal now is senior citizen dances, better known as "Granny Grabbins." A picker can play four or five nights a week if so desired, only playing up to two hours, usually an hour and a half, and most all on a percentage of the door. Small venues, upward of about a hundred fifty people, with no drinking or smoking (at least inside the building) but plenty of dry hunching by the elder patrons, with them mating up after the dance just like in the old days. The pickers I know who play these on a weekly basis are Sid Manuel, Dusty Rhodes, Curt Canada, Jerry Duncan, and Benny Kubiak.

Chapter 35

WAYNE SEXTON

Wayne Sexton was teaching fourth grade at Limestone Gap in about 1961, and my sister Alice was in his class. Wayne was always a good friend, but for some reason, Alice slapped his face in school one day. He gave her an old fashioned school spankin'.

Wayne lives in Kiowa, near Bill Hensley. On occasion, they get together and fix up a batch of homemade ice cream. Bill is a big eater and has a big, square frame, and Wayne is tall and slim. Bill usually ate more ice cream than Wayne and often boasted about it. One night Bill came over to Wayne's, and Wayne was ready for him. He fixed up two batches of ice cream, one was very bland—light or fat-free, you might say—and the other was richer than two foot up a bull's ass!

Wayne said, "Bill, you sit here in the living room, and I'll go get the ice cream." He served Bill the rich and himself the bland version. They both ate about three bowls, and Wayne said, "Ready for some more?"

Bill said, "I think I've had about enough!"

Wayne said, "I think I'll have another'n!"

Wayne went back and had two more bowls, with Bill sitting there watching him in complete amazement.

Wayne didn't tell Bill what he'd done until Wayne heard Bill telling the locals all over Kiowa that he'd match Wayne at eatin' ice cream against anyone!

Wayne and Joyce have four grown kids: Michael, Greg, Rod, and Vicki. When Michael was in the first grade at Kiowa, there were three Michaels in the class. Every time Mrs. Eula Kelly would say "Michael," all three looked up. One day Michael Sexton said, "Mrs. Kelly, I know how we can fix this Michael problem."

Mrs. Kelly said, "How's that, Michael?"

Michael said, "You can call him 'Michael,' you can call him 'Mike,' and you can call me 'Mr. Sexton'!"

Vicki married Milton Clonch, and they had three boys and one girl. When the kids were little, Vicki took a nap one afternoon, and the boys took the scissors to her and gave her a haircut and left the hair sittin' on her head. When she woke up, her hair began to fall to the floor. By the time Milt came home, she had a towel wrapped around her head and was mad, fit to be tied! She said, "Milt, I want you to look at what our kids did to me!" She pulled the towel off her head, and Milt began to giggle. One of the boys said, "Don't laugh, Milt. You're next!"

Chapter 36

JOHN MCENTIRE MEMORIAL STEER ROPING

Along about 1989, Wayne and I went to Cheyenne together, when he said, "Pake, we ought to have a John McEntire Memorial Steer Roping." We decided to have it at the Kiowa School Rodeo grounds that were built by local folks under the superintendent Harold Toaz administration. Our main goal was to have fun with it, keep it nonprofit, not have to go to the bank to keep it going, and not piss anybody off. We donated money to the Kiowa FFA Chapter and 4-H Club. My oldest daughter, Autumn, was twelve in 1990, and she sang the national anthem at the first one. We agreed the date would always be the second Saturday of May, beginning in 1990.

Autumn singing the national anthem at the first John McEntire Memorial Steer Roping. 1990—Family Photo

Wayne had torn his knee a couple of weeks before and was in the hospital. He told the doctor, "I've got to get outta here and go to a steer roping at Kiowa I'm supposed to help with." The doctor said, "OK, go ahead and get up."

When Wayne started to get outta bed, he got sicker than hell and knew the doctor had just made his point.

Free BBQ being prepared by local friends—JMSR Photo

Terry Canida, Clark Rhyne, Pake, Kelly Doolin, Kelly James, Lloyd Rush, George Ellis, Lonnie Bartmess, and Kenneth Jones—JMSR Photo

A bunch of close local friends prepared a free barbeque and had a live band of locals, like J. V. Newberry, Clark Rhyne, Royce Sparks, Michael Gilliam, Jeff Gilliam, Kenneth Jones, Robin Lacy, and Kelly Rhyne. There were even friends from farther away, like Kenny Surratt, Bill Roberson, Lloyd Rush, and many more.

Clem McSpadden—JMSR Photo

Our announcer and longtime friend, Clem McSpadden, introduced dignitaries, who would either ride into the arena horseback or were brought into the arena in a surrey (a very sophisticated wagon). It is real difficult to get folks to come out for a deal like this, but we had a decent crowd. It was tournament style, where ropers drew for positions and had two head matches, with the winner advancing until it came down to the final two. We had about fifteen ropers, and everything went fairly smooth. We had five hundred dollars left over when the dust settled. We decided to make it an annual event and made up a committee of about ten of us, like Vo-AG instructor Brian Craig, Joe and Judy Chapel, Wayne and Joyce Sexton, Katy and me, Bear Gilliam, Pam and Barry

Horsley, Mark Sandman, and Pat and Rupe McEntire. We all gathered at each other's houses and had meetings and social gatherings. At the end of a roping, we would have a cream-can appreciation supper, usually at Wayne and Joyce's.

Mark Sandman at the John McEntire Steer Roping—JMSR Photo

Mark, I appreciate the extra-hard work you put into the JMSR. Thanks, too, for all the fun.

— PAKE

We had a Calcutta pool at the Holiday Inn in McAlester and served a real nice hors d'oeuvres table and had music there also. A Calcutta is where we auctioned off the ropers to the highest bidder and split the money to the person who bought the winners of the roping. The committee took out 15 percent for expenses on the party and the roping. We even sold chances on a stock trailer to be drawn out at the Calcutta, with the last one drawn being the winner. We had caps printed with the logo on it and gave all contestants one, each year, for free. I still see some of these caps around today. Not only did we have fun, but it brought outside money to the local

McAlester and Kiowa merchants, who in turn donated back to the roping to help keep it going.

For a couple of years, we invited Billy Lee Hamilton and Shane Slack to rope a six-head match, roping at their young ages of eighteen. That was extremely popular because the matches were real close.

The two boys had matched before they were in their teens, and Steve (Shane's dad) tells, "It was the cutest thing you ever saw; they were so young. Billy Lee won the match, and on the way home, Shane said, 'Dad, does this mean he's better than me?' I said, 'It means he was better than you today.'"

One year we had two retired world champion steer ropers, Shoat Webster and Clark McEntire, team steer rope a steer for exhibition. Because of his knees and back ailments, we stood Shoat on the fender of a nearby trailer out back and led James Allen's horse up to it, so he could easily get on. Clark hadn't roped a steer in years but could still get on and off. Shoat roped and tripped the steer and stayed on his horse while Clark loped behind, got off his horse, and tied the steer. I don't recall who invented this event, but it sure went off well. It brought back the fans' memories of two past steer roping greats we all have enjoyed throughout our lifetimes. These two family-oriented, fiercely competitive, clean-cut, hardworking ranchers were every steer roping fan's hero. In the fifties, Shoat and Clark were always going head-to-head in steer roping. If one didn't win the roping that day, the other would. These hungry, former calf ropers were eager to step up into the winner's circle of past champions like John McEntire, Everett Shaw, Dick Truitt, Ike Rude, and Bob Crosby, carrying on the steer roping tradition by winning a combined seven steer roping world championship titles.

At Clark's induction at the Cheyenne Frontier Days Hall of Fame, he pointed to Shoat, who was in the audience, and said, "I'da won a lot more championships if it had'na been for that short guy right there."

We even had a senior steer roping that involved ropers fifty years of age and above. The ground rules for the entire steer roping were more than unique. There was no barrier for the steers' designated head start, but instead a chalk line about ten feet to flag started the time. Then we put a chalk line about one hundred feet from the roping chute, and the steer was not to land inside the chalk line or a ten-second penalty was assessed. There was no six-second time limit for the steer to kick loose and no wrap or hooey. When the roper threw up his hands to signal for time, and the flagger dropped his flag, the time was official. Jim Clark said, "Pake, give me the job nobody else wants." So I asked him to flag, and he did an excellent job for eight years. Kelly Corbin flagged the last two. Steve Slack, from Idabel, flagged the starting line for the first eight years, and Bradley Hamilton flagged it the last two.

Jim Clark flagging a roper at John McEntire Memorial Steer Roping. 1990—JMSR Photo

Pake ropin' a steer at John McEntire Memorial Steer Roping. 1990—JMSR Photo

We videotaped every roping we had, which was a little costly, but I'm glad we did. When I watched the videos from the previous roping, I noticed the ropers would jack around in the box. By this I mean, they would get in the box, get into the corner, ride their horse up and back, wait while he took a shit (the horse, I mean), turn right, turn left, swing their rope, move around in the saddle, and take *forever* to nod their heads and call for the steer. This meant the fans had to sit and wait for the action to begin.

H. L. Todd, senior champion, and "Doc" T. K. Hardy, super senior champion. 1992—JMSR Photo

I thought about the "delay of game" rule the NFL had that required the players only so many seconds to get out of the huddle, get on the line, and snap the ball. I inserted a rule where the roper couldn't call for the steer until the previous steer had left the arena, but then the roper had five seconds to call for his steer, or the line judge would say, "Turn him out!" I had some ropers say, "Pake, what if my horse is taking a shit?" I said, "Well, he's gonna have to pinch it off or string it!"

Longtime friend C. A. Lauer getting ready
to rope. 1991—JMSR Photo

Upon the previous steer's exit, Bradley raised his flag and began to count to five. I only remember him having to turn out a couple. I thought it was funny that in previous ropings, I had to have someone tell them, "You're next. Please, hurry up and get in there." But this time, just as soon as the roper left the box, the next one was in there, fearing his steer would be turned out before he was ready. This idea cut forty-five minutes off of the entire day. Fans saw more roping, without dead time, and the ropers loved it because they got home earlier.

"Crowd Thriller" Robin Bland unloading horses at John
McEntire Memorial Steer Roping. 1992—JMSR Photo

Fred Meyers getting ready to "rope 'em when they're up, tie 'em when they're down." 1995—JMSR Photo

Some of the champions winning the John McEntire Steer Roping included Rocky Patterson, Gip and Guy Allen, Tee Woolman, J. Paul Williams, Gary McNair, H. L. Todd, Doc Hardy, and Jack Lucas. Reba donated a real nice Gary Gist belt buckle to the champion of the open steer roping each year. Butch Mellor of Mellor Chevrolet donated a saddle, and Pat and Jim Bob Winslett donated a buckle in memory of Junior Winslett. Other donors donated buckles to other events. The hard work involved was the reason all of us decided to stop having it. Still, I miss having the roping, and if the time is right, maybe someday I will resume it and begin on the eleventh John McEntire Memorial Steer Roping.

Randy Ward and grandsons, with Gary Coffee—JMSR Photo

JOHN McENTIRE MEMORIAL STEER ROPING

Butch Mellor, Pake McEntire, Tee Woolman (winner of trophy saddle and trophy buckle), Walker Mac Woolman (Tee's son), Shelby Blackstock (Reba's son), Reba McEntire (presenting buckle), and Wayne Sexton—JMSR Photo

Calamity McEntire, Garrett Beck, Autumn McEntire, Chism McEntire, Luchesse Luchsinger, Katy McEntire, Trevor Foran, Ep Luchsinger, Pake, Alice, Susie, Clark, Jac, and State Senator John Dahl. The Oklahoma State Legislature declaring the second Saturday in May "John McEntire Day." 1991—Family Photo

Chapter 37

BIG MULE

I take pride in my driving—disregarding the night that I was about eleven or twelve years old when I was gonna move the family car and had it in the wrong gear, and my foot slipped off the clutch and caved in the left front fender of Uncle Slim and Aunt Jeannie's brand spankin' new car they had just driven up to the house to show us. Oh shit.

Some folks have trouble backing trailers, and after I wore out my one and only inline trailer (this is a four-wheel trailer with one horse in front of the other and a fifth wheel under the front), any other trailer is real easy to back into places. The secret to backing an inline is you have to be able to see the front tires on the trailer. One time Katy and I were coming back from San Antonio, and she woke me up from a deep sleep. Seems she had gotten off on a service road and came to a dead end with no turnaround. She held a dim flashlight on the front tires of the trailer, and I backed it half a mile! Almost burned the clutch out, but I got us out of there.

Speaking of inlines, these cowboys pulled into a gas station, and this service station attendant was gassin' them up while they went inside to the restroom. The attendant walked to the front of the trailer and looked at the front horse's head, walked to the end of the trailer and looked at the ass of the back horse, and scratched his head. When the cowboys came out of the station, the attendant said, "Mista, I've seen a lot a horses in my time, but that horse is the longest mutha fucka I eva did see!"

I can back a big mule up a little mule's ass!

—ROBIN LACY

Once, when Katy and I were rodeoing and playing music at the same time, we had a lot of all-night drives, like doing a night show and then loading up afterward and being at a steer roping the next day five hundred miles away by 1:00 p.m. I had to do this because back then I didn't think they could have a steer roping without me.

We had a clock in the dash of this particular truck, so we agreed to each drive two hours and then wake the other up for his or her turn. She had done her part, when she pulled over at about three in the morning. I was sleeping dead away in the camper, just past the boot, jumped up behind the wheel, and she hit the bed, soon fast asleep. I went about twenty-five miles and could hardly hold my head up. That's when the cowboy came out in me. I turned the stem on that dash clock and rolled it up two hours, pulled it over, and hollered, "Man, that was a hard turn. I fought it all the way, but I finally made it."

She dragged out of that camper through the boot, saying, "Damn, feels like I just dozed off!"

My plan would have worked if she hadn't turned on the radio. All of a sudden, I felt the truck come to a skiddin' halt, when she hollered, "You shit ass! You rolled up the clock, didn't you? You get your ass back up here!"

Clark bought a horse from Freddie Wafford. We called him "Badger," and he had been turned over or handled recklessly in the trailer. We knew this because when you put him in there and rolled the tires, he'd start fighting the trailer, panicking from claustrophobia, trying to get upside down. Someone told me if we put him in backward and let him hang his head out the back, then he might ride OK. I had Katy out there one night to help me back him into the trailer, and the son of a bitch stepped on her toe. She limped on it for a couple of days. It wuddin' easy getting him in there, but we finally did—and shore 'nuff, it worked! You could circle the rig, whip it, and nothing could make him fight the trailer.

I had a CB radio in my truck at the time, and a trucker pulled up behind me one day and said, "Hey, cowboy, your horse done went and turned around in your trailer!"

When I got to the roping, some of the cowboys asked me why I loaded him that way, so I said, "He duddin' give a shit about where we're going; he just wants to know where we've been!"

Bob Christopherson and I picked up Jerry Beagley at McAlester on our way to Guymon to the rodeo the first weekend of May. After we loaded Jerry's horse, Bob noticed while going down the road that the horses were fighting in the trailer. He pulled over, and all of them looked as innocent as newborn children. We tied all of them all a little shorter, especially my horse, Robin, who was a spunky little sorrel. We got back on the road, and it was the same thing, only worse. They were fighting and making the trailer swerve back and forth. We stopped again and went back there, only to find everyone calm and looking at us like, "What's wrong?" We got back on the road, and Bob called this trucker behind us on his CB radio and said, "Hey, trucker, one of our horses is causing a commotion in our trailer; pull up beside us, and tell us which one is causing all the trouble."

The trucker pulled up beside the trailer and came back, saying, "No doubt, it's the little red horse in the middle; he's biting the front horse on the neck!"

We stopped, and this time I tied ole Robin's head right up to the side of the trailer, almost to his cheek! We got back on the road, with no trouble from the back—problem solved.

Bob said, "I bet your horse is wondering, 'Now, how in the hell did they catch me doing that?'" With bite marks on Bob's horse's neck and back thanks to Robin, Bob nicknamed him "Pirana."

Chapter 38

WILD TRIPS

The one thing that you rarely hear on Sports Center or read about in newspapers or Pro Rodeo Sports News is some of the almost suicidally maniacal trips cowboys make to get to rodeos. A few come to mind: like the time my cousin Don Wayne Smith and I left Douglas, Wyoming, about five o'clock in the evening and had to be in Ellensburg, Washington, to rope in the slack the next morning. Except for the speeding ticket we got for going seventy in a thirty-five miles per hour zone in downtown Brigham City, Utah, it went off without a hitch. We drove twelve hundred miles in seventeen hours, saving seven hours, pulling two horses.

Longtime friend, restaurant entrepreneur, and steer roper Flip Miller and I left Silver City, New Mexico, after the performance one night and was up in the slack at Lusk, Wyoming, the next morning. I started out driving Flip's brand-new Dodge dually, pulling two horses in his side-by-side trailer, and we had to go about forty miles on a two-lane road before hitting the interstate. I had the ears pinned back on that Dodge Ram, cruising at ninety, when I looked over at Flip, and he had his coat over his head. I said, "What'sa matter, Flip?" He said, "We're gonna die, and I don't wanna see it!"

Philip "Flip" Miller ropin' at Pendleton, Oregon. 1997—Hubbell Photo

We averaged seventy-eight miles per hour but were ten minutes late to run our first steer. We ran our second one without doing any good and then headed on to Union, Oregon. We pulled into a truck stop at Douglas, Wyoming, to eat dinner and gas up; when we got back on the road, I said, "Flip, did you pay for the gas?" He said, "Nope, I thought you did." We turned around and went back twenty-five miles and paid for it, when the lady at the register said, "I saw you guys pull out, and you looked like you forgot it."

Steer roping is like masturbation: everybody wants to do it, but nobody wants to watch!

— BUTCH MELLOR

The wildest trip was the summer of 1997 when I took a run for the National Finals Steer Roping for the first time, roping right handed. The top fifteen money winners in the PRCA for the entire year get to compete at one event called "the finals," which has been going on since 1959. That first year it was in Clayton, New Mexico, and I was there with Jac and Clark, and I was six years old at the time. It was so windy and cold, Jac and I didn't get out of the car, but I remember being in the backseat, looking at all the steer ropers wearing cap earflaps that tied under the chin. Clark was down in his back and couldn't rope.

I made the finals twice, once in 1974 and then in 1982, both left handed, when they had it at Laramie, Wyoming. The finals have been at numerous places because it has trouble making a profit. (Remember what Butch Mellor said?) It's been in places like Clayton, New Mexico; Pawhuska, Oklahoma; Vinita, Oklahoma; Guthrie, Oklahoma; Amarillo, Texas; McAlester, Oklahoma; Hobbs, New Mexico; and now back at Guthrie, Oklahoma. It is now named the Clem McSpadden National Finals Steer Roping—and rightfully so.

Rod Hartness, Jason (Rook) Cooper, and I roped at Burwell, Nebraska, and then went to a small airport at North Platte. We waited for about two hours for a small plane to take us to Denver for a commercial flight to Seattle, Washington. There we took a rental car to Joseph, Oregon, for another rodeo.

We were running out of time in North Platte when a retired bulldogger with a rental car showed up, waiting on the same plane. He dropped the keys in the rental car box slot, built to be irretrievable because of the depth. Rod decided not to go because he had his two little girls with us, so Rook and this guy with the car decided to fish out the keys with a coat hanger I got from the kitchen and head for Denver in the car. They were driving like a bat outta hell through pouring down rain, but we barely made it to Denver. When we got to Seattle, Washington, we rented a car to Joseph, making it in plenty of time. Jason Evans left Joseph with us, riding back to Portland, Oregon. We needed to be in Fredonia, Kansas, the next morning for the roping slack. We got a $140 ticket for speeding through a work zone and were running late big-time. They were driving at speeds of eighty to one hundred miles per hour. I noticed when traveling through some towns that several cars of people were trying to keep up with us for fun, obviously lacking anything else to do on a Sunday afternoon. They pulled up beside us as if to cheer us on. Jason had a girlfriend who was a travel agent, she held the plane at Portland and put us in first-class seats for the cheap-seat price. When we got to Wichita, Kansas, the car rental place was closed, so we had to rent a cab the last one hundred miles, which cost us each about a hundred dollars.

> *I'm the luckiest guy in the world when it comes to roping, but the more I practice, the luckier I get!*
> — SHOAT WEBSTER

Shoat Webster ropin' on Milligan Roany at the '63 NFSR, Pawhuska, Oklahoma. 1963—Ferrell Photo

Chapter 39

CHEYENNE

Jac said, "Clark and his family stayed at the Edwards Hotel in Cheyenne before we were married. The owners wouldn't take reservations, in fear of getting undesirables, but saved the rooms for Oklahoma contestants. I went with Clark the first summer we were married and found it a wonderful place to stay. As well as watching the parades, of which there were two during the week of the rodeo. There was no air conditioning, but with lots of windows and up on the second floor, it was very comfortable. The Okies stayed there every year until the man and wife got too old to operate it and sold it."

We used to stay at the Edwards Hotel when Mama and the girls would go with Daddy and me to Cheyenne. Different from now, we didn't go to the night shows and pay forty to seventy-five dollars to see top music entertainers. Instead we'd hang around the lobby and visit with the other contestants and their families.

I was about five or six years old, and I can barely remember when one night someone asked me to sing "You Ain't Nothin' but a Hound Dog," and they began pitching small change on the floor. Reba saw she could cash in on a deal like that, so she sang "Jesus Loves Me." This was our first paid music show. For the past three years, I've played at the Old Train Depot, just across the street from where the old Edwards Hotel used to be, and the pay has gone up quite considerably. Reba has played the night show many times, and her pay has stayed the same. (Gotcha, didn't I?)

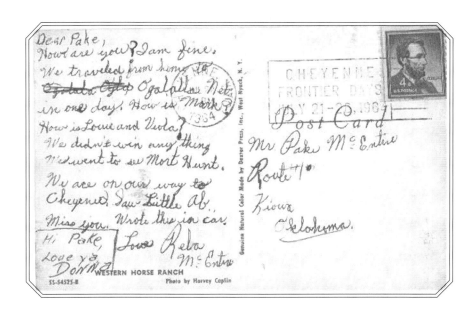

Reba sent me this postcard on their way to Cheyenne in 1964. Clark, Jac, Alice, Reba, Susie, and Donna Wilson all went and left me at home with Louie Sandman to build a split-rail fence around a hay barn. I was used to going to Cheyenne, so I took this hard but liked the postcard.

In about 1992, the rooms in downtown Cheyenne, even at the Motel 6, were ninety dollars a night. So six of us stayed in our camper in the Frontier Park parking lot, where all the contestants stayed. My youngest daughter, Chism, was about seven and loved Alan Jackson. Jackson was doing the night show for two nights. I ran into Roger Wills, who plays bass for Alan, and he checked out the comp tickets, but none were to be had—the show was completely sold out. I just couldn't take the disappointment on Chism's face.

We waited till the show started and everyone who had tickets got in and got seated. Chism and I went to the place where they took the bought tickets, tore them in half, kept half, and gave the customer half to find their seat. I told a huge whopper of a big fat lie! We walked up to them, and I pointed to the concession table up this long ramp and said, "We don't have tickets, but can I go up this ramp and buy my little girl an Alan Jackson T-shirt?" They looked at both of us and said, "OK."

We walked up the long ramp, and I told Chism, "Take your time looking for your shirt." She did, and after about five minutes, she had one picked out. I paid for it and said, "Now look around me down the ramp at the ticket takers, and see if they are looking at us." She looked around me and said, "They're looking right at us." I said, "OK, just keep looking at the souvenirs like you are still shopping." She did, and after another minute, I said, "Look again at them." She said, "They're turned around and looking the other way." I turned and said, "Let's go!"

We turned and walked toward the stage area and headed toward the top of an eleven-thousand-seat grandstand, all the way to the top, where I thought there might be standing room. I wondered if they would come after us, but they didn't, and we watched the whole show! (The things a guy will do for his little girl.)

Calamity, Pake, Chism, Katy, and Autumn,
taken at Cheyenne—Jan Spencer Photo

When listening to rodeo stories, especially steer roping stories, most of them begin with, "One time at Cheyenne," and, "This ain't no shit!" Well, guess what? This one starts out the same damn way!

One time at Cheyenne, in about 1978, I was out back of the east grandstand waiting on my turn to rope, and I met all-time calf and steer roping great Dale Smith, from Chandler, Arizona. He said, "Pake, every time I rope here, I remember one year in particular that I had a steer roped and on the ground, right across the score line. I ran down there and had my string on him, when my horse walked off, so I couldn't tie him, costing me at least first in the go-round. Afterward, I was right about where we are standing now, uncinching, and I was really disappointed with my horse, when Ike Rude walked up and took a look at my horse and said, 'Dale, you'da been better off if that son of a bitch had'a fell over dead!'"

I'd rather hear the band play at Cheyenne than to win a smaller rodeo!
— IKE RUDE

Prison Rodeo in 1943. Left to Right: Ike Rude, Ace Soward, John McEntire, Keith Underhill and Floyd Gale

This photo was taken at the McAlester Oklahoma Prison Rodeo, where professional cowboys roped steers and calves and steer wrestled, and the convicts rode the broncs and bulls.

After seeing his first steer roping in about 1920, Ike Rude told his dad how exciting it was watching the great ropers tie down those big steers, and he just had to do it. His dad told Ike that they had a fat heifer in the lot they were fixin' to butcher, so he could tie her down. Ike got his pony all cinched up; his dad turned the heifer out, and Ike took to her. Ike said later, "I'd been OK if I hadn't gotten my horse over the rope."

Ike was waking up, lying on the ground, and his dad was standing over him, fanning him with his hat. Ike heard his dad say, "Is that how they did it?"

One year at Cheyenne, Mark Sandmann, Bob Christopherson, and I all shared a room at the Motel 6. Bob was an early riser and got up way before Mark and me to go feed his horse. One night Mark asked Bob to go downtown and get a drink and listen to this band play. Bob said, "OK, but I want to get in early; so one drink, and we come back to the room, OK?" Mark agreed, so off they went.

Mark liked to drink tequila and chase it with Coors Light. They had one, and Bob mentioned that one tasted fine enough to order another. This went on until they closed the place down, when Bob asked Mark, "Recon there's another place we can go?"

Off they went to another bar and closed it down. They finally got back to the room around three in the morning, and Bob and I woke up at the same time about seven the next morning. Bob and Mark were in the same bed. Bob was nearest to my bed, when I noticed that Bob looked like he had inherited about twenty-five new face wrinkles in the night. He raised up on one elbow and gazed off into the distance and said, "Mark, you evil bastard!"

Bud Tillard overheard two wives of bull riders who were sitting up in the stands, visiting at the Cheyenne Rodeo, when one said to the other, "How have y'all been doing lately? Been winning?"

"Oh no," the other wife said, "he's been bucked off every time he gets on a bull. As a matter of fact, when we make love, I don't dare move. I just know he'll fall off!"

Clark McEntire ropin' a steer on Hugh Posey's horse Dunny.
Winning first in the average at Cheyenne. 1954—

Chapter 40

OS RANCH

My big win didn't come until 1972. Clark and I entered a new roping at Post, Texas. Steer roper Jim Prather was a son-in-law to the man who owned the beautiful ranch just outside of Post. When I was in the fifth grade, Jim came and stayed with us between rodeos at Chockie, and he'd help me with my arithmetic thought problems (word or work problems). Benefiting the West Texas Boys Ranch, the first roping at OS was in 1971, a three-day event with team roping one day, calf roping another day, and steer roping the last day, on Sunday. Each night they had music entertainment, like Johnny Bush. They had celebrities at the roping, like Ken Curtis from *Gunsmoke*, mingling through the crowd, dressed up like Festus Hagen. After watching a bunch of *Gunsmoke* later, I wish I'd spent more time visiting with him, but all I could think about was roping.

The first year, Clark won the steer roping! I remember he roped last and had to really hustle because top steer roper Randy Burchett, from Pryor, Oklahoma, was close on his heels, winning second average. The first saddle Clark won was in 1947, at Pendleton, Oregon, and the last one was that day at Post. Still unridden, the Post saddle hangs up at Alice's house.

Pake ropin' left handed at Post, Texas, on Jed.
1972, First Average—Ferrell Photo

The next year, we went back down to Post. The steers were big, weighing 775 pounds, and I was riding Jed, who weighed 1,050 pounds, soakin' wet! Before the roping started, we lined up horseback in the arena for the introduction. Jed and I were in the middle of the lineup, and when I looked across the other ropers on their huge horses, it felt like I was standing on the ground. I asked myself, "What in the hell am I doing here? Ain't no way I can tie these big steers on this little horse." I learned that day that ole Jed had a heart as big as the hood on my pickup truck.

I had no expectations of winning anything—just didn't want to be embarrassed. Somehow, Jed and I managed to tie down the first three head and went in seeded number two behind the current world champion, Olin Young, going into the final steer. They took the top fifteen back, so we were last to rope. I remember riding into the box, and Daddy was standing out in front by the score line, when I asked him, "What do I do now?"

He said, "Just do what you did on the other three."

Pake ropin' on Ole Jed at Post, Texas. (You wouldn't believe how much fun this is.) 1972—Ferrell Photo

That's exactly what we did. Jed and I just tied the last steer down, won the short go-round and the average (total time on four head). When I stood in front of the huge camera for pictures, I was shaking like a leaf. I had never won a roping against my heroes! They gave me a Gary Gist–made belt buckle; even after winning many more since, I still wear the first Post buckle because my childhood heroes were there. It felt really good when steer ropers like Bud Upton walked down the arena to first congratulate me; then Olin Young, the present world champion steer roper did the same. Before the short go, I was nervous as a dog shittin' peach seeds. I rode up to Olin and asked him if he wanted to save entry fees. This meant if one of us went out and the other didn't, then the one that won would pay the other's entry fees. In this case it was $350. Olin necked his last one and went out. When I got home, I mailed Olin a check for $350. The next week, I saw Olin at San Angelo Roping Fiesta, and he handed me my check back. He said, "You asked me if I wanted to save one hundred dollars, not entry fees." I wrote him a check for one hundred dollars and learned what real steer ropers are all about. This is the reason I wear that buckle today: the honesty and integrity of not only Olin but other ropers just like him. What a great bunch of guys—lots of class.

Olin Young, 1966 NFSR, Vinita, Oklahoma, on Jim
Prather's horse Pete. 1966—Ferrell Photo

That day Jed and I won over four thousand dollars, and Clark kept it all because he was entering me everywhere else. This all sounds so easy, but there were thirty-five professional ropers trying to do the same thing, and I was just a kid, dumb enough not to be intimidated.

The next year in 1973, 1969 world champion steer roper, Walter Arnold, won it. In 1974, manager and steer roper Jim Prather got all of us ropers together to discuss the rules for the day. I wish he had sent these rules out to us prior to entering, but he chose to tell us minutes before it started. It really didn't matter to me; I was just glad to be there. Jim said, "This year the trip has to be between the hock and the hip of the steer when the rope gets tight in order to get a qualified time. If you don't get it between the hock and the hip, a ten-second penalty will be assessed, or you can get the steer back up and trip him correctly without the penalty. Monroe Tumlinson will judge the trip from the side of the arena. Are there any questions?" Eldon Dudley was the only one who spoke up and said, "Jim, do you think this rule is necessary?" Jim said, "Yes, I do."

This rule was not to my advantage because I was not an artist of handling cattle like the veteran ropers were. My specialty was get them roped and tied, any way I could and not very fast. To everyone's surprise, as it turned out, me and Sonny Worrell handled the new rule better than all the other ropers entered and won first and second. As in all ropings, the winners liked it, and the others didn't. If this rule had been kept in effect in every roping since then, there would be a lot less cattle crippled in steer roping. Even after agreeing to the rule before this roping, some were a little upset later. I'd like to see a rule that one cannot enter a steer roping until he has furnished cattle or put one on. This would end a lot of complaints.

Clark and I won over twelve thousand dollars in three years there at Post. In those days, that was good money. They had the event for a total of ten years, and the McEntires have some very fond memories of that roping. Thanks to all involved for the hard work it takes to have a roping of that multitude.

A roper must win the roping three years before retiring the beautiful trophy below. Guy Allen retained it after winning it three times in ten years.

Saddle maker Bill Price
presenting saddle to Pake
—Ferrell Photo

Pake receiving trophy that
was kept for one year
—Ferrell Photo

Chapter 41

SUMMER OF '74

The couple of months before the 1974 Post roping, I loaded up with James Allen from Santa Anna, Texas, to split expenses for a long summer rodeo trip. I first met James back in 1968 when he heard that I liked to heel steers in the team roping. He and Clark knew each other from roping steers.

Early one morning, Clark got up to feed his horses at Pendleton, when he saw an Umatilla Indian lying across the hood of James's pickup, dead from a knife stuck in his back. James was sleeping in the camper and never heard a thing but came out of the camper just as Clark walked up.

Reba wasn't doing much that summer of '74, so she went along with us on this adventure, and let me tell ya, we had a blast. We met James at Yukon, Oklahoma, and took his rig, a one-seater pickup. He had made a four-horse stock trailer into a gooseneck. The backend of the three-quarter pickup was loaded down with suitcases and one guitar. James and I roped calves, tied down steers, and team roped together.

James Allen winning First Average 1971 NFSR at Pawhuska, Oklahoma, on Randy Burchett's horse Chicken—Ferrell Photo

We roped at Greely, Colorado, one night and were up at Lander, Wyoming, the next morning, an all-night drive. I told James I was gonna sleep in the back of the truck in a sleeping bag, so when he got sleepy, just to wake me up, and I'd drive. I felt the truck slowing down and coming to a stop. I looked up over the side of the truck, and the sun was coming up, and we were in Lander. That was the best night's sleep I think I'd ever had!

James had gotten sleepy in the night and asked Reba if she wanted to drive, so she did. He lay down in the seat, falling off to sleep immediately, and soon felt the truck shaking. He raised up, and Reba was going eighty-five miles an hour down this big, long hill! He asked her if she thought she might be going a tad fast, and she agreed.

That morning was the first time I ever tied a steer in twelve seconds, and there weren't many twelve second ties in those days.

Never underestimate a good night's sleep.
— Cowboy in a sleeping bag
in the back of a pickup

After the slack, it began to warm up, and some cowboys were hanging around this water trough. Reba and I walked over there and saw two big, rough-looking guys selling iced-down beer out of the trough. Movie star Allen Keller from Olathe, Colorado, was there. Allen was the steer roping world champion in 1972 and steer roping and all-around winner at Pendleton. He made the national finals in the steer wrestling in 1969 and 1970. Allen was a gutsy steer roper, full of confidence, and wrestled in college. Although he didn't grow up on a cattle ranch, he learned from mentors, Don McLaughlin and Tuffy Thompson. Allen seemed to like to bar fight. The beer sales weren't going very well that day for the guys, so Allen made a deal with them. He said, "Tell ya what: I'll fight ya for the beer. If either of you guys can whip me, I'll buy all the beer. But if you don't, then I get all the beer free!"

They looked at each other and said, "That's a deal."

One of those big ole boys rolled up his sleeves and squared off and took a swing at Allen but never connected. Allen hit that guy about six or seven times. When the big guy saw this deal wuddin' working out as planned, he turned to his pardner and said, "Your turn!"

The pardner looked at Allen and said, "The beer's all yours!"

They walked off and the drankin' began. Allen was a real likeable guy if he liked you, so we got acquainted and became friends that day and have been ever since.

Allen Keller—Ferrell Photo

After several of those free beers, I got matched up in a horse race on someone's horse around this mile-long racetrack and got outrun by a woman. Her horse threw dirt clods in my face the whole way.

Later I met up with Jim Ward, from Heppner, Oregon, and got to running foot races.

Jim Ward "puttin' it behind him"—Family Photo

It's a plastic world, poly ropes and credit cards!
— ROY BURK

Chapter 42

PENDLETON ROUND-UP

In the fall of 1971, I was going to college at Easten State College, at Wilburton, when Clark, Jim Clark, and I all loaded up and went to Pendleton. I had gotten several gifts from graduating high school, and one was a wristwatch. This was the first watch I had ever owned, and I was real proud of it. So randomly, out of the clear blue sky, I would tell the guys the time. They got a kick out of that and told the other cowboys at Pendleton how on the way up there I kept us all on time.

They have an Indian relay race during the rodeo where three Indians, each on horseback, make a lap around the track, stop, and jump off the horse, jump on another horse, make a lap, stop, and jump on another horse, and then around to the finish line; first one across the line wins. Simple enough, right? One day, one horse got loose from the Indians and went the wrong way and ran head-on into the other two riders. All were on the ground, horses and Indians, all at the same time! It gets worse.

One horse jumped up in a panic, took off running, and before anyone could catch him, he lapped the track and ran through a gate at the foot of the grandstand. Then he ran over a big, fat lady wearing a red dress with white flowers on it, went down an alley, and ran into a ten-foot fence and broke his neck! Let 'er buck!

In the steer roping, I made it to the short go in second place that year, but my rope fell over my last steer's nose for a no time. Big disappointment, but I'll never forget my first Round-Up.

In 1997 Mark Sandman and I went to the Round-Up together, and he liked to bullshit people by walking up to them, sticking out his hand, saying, "Howdy, what's your name?"

They would tell him and then ask him, "What's your name?"

He would say, "Luke Warmwater."

Some would not get it and say, "Where are you from, Luke?"

Mark would say, "Coldwater, Texas."

One time he did this to a guy whose elevator didn't go all the way to the top. He said, "I'm Ty Murray. I'm in three events here at the Round-Up, expecting to win the all-around this year!"

Seems Mark had met his match in bullshittin'.

Ike Rude and Clark went to Pendleton together in Ike's truck when Ike was in his seventies. Clark was back in the camper, and he felt the truck making a strange noise. He looked up through the window, and Ike was going seventy miles an hour in third gear!

Later that night, he felt a bump in the road, and Ike pulled over and got out. Clark said, "What's a matter, Ike?"

Ike said, "I think I ran over a cow!"

Clark said, "Was she runnin' or standing still?"

Ike said, "Somebody had already hit her and left her in the middle of the road!"

The next morning Ike pulled into a car wash to wash the hair, blood, and guts off the side of his truck.

I've never in my life known of Clark to buy a newspaper, but when they went to breakfast, Clark picked one up, and Ike asked, "What are you looking for?"

Clark said, "I'm seeing if there was a hit-and-run back down the road last night!"

Clark McEntire riding Heel Fly at Pendleton
Round-Up. 1961—Howdyshell Photo

Grand Pap and Everett Shaw first started going to Pendleton in 1931. Years later, when they put Shaw in the hall of fame, his wife (and my second mother), Nell Shaw (whom Reba got her middle name from), accepted the award for Everett and said that night, "The first year Everett came with John McEntire. When they were getting ready to rope, Everett looked in their rope bag, and a rope was missing. He hollered at John and said, 'John, we had two ropes. Where's the other one?'

"John pointed and said, 'I gave it to that feller over there.'

"Everett said, 'But, John, we only had two ropes!'

"John said, 'Yeah, but, Shaw, he didn't have one!'"

Everett and Nell Shaw—Family Photo

I was a young man among old men, who was used to roping big steers in big pens over long scores (this means the designated head start for the steer) and made the Professional Rodeo Cowboys Association National Finals twice. Sounds important, don't it! Well, it ain't shit till you win the world championship. The best week of my life happened in September, 1984, at the Pendleton Round-Up. We were going up there anyway to rope, and about six months before, they called Clark and Jac and told them they wanted to induct Clark into the Round-Up Hall of Fame! Clark is famous up there.

Clark holding his 1947 Pendleton All-Around Saddle in front of the Limestone Gap School. 1947—Family Photo

Reba, Round-Up Queen Judy Lazinka, Mama,
Daddy, and Pake, Clark Pendleton Round-Up Steer
Roping Champion 1958. 1958—Family Photo

Clark won the all-around title at Pendleton in 1947, at the age of nineteen! This title means the most money won at the rodeo in two or more events. He went on to win the steer roping twice there and was honored to be put in the hall of fame. We arrived early because the banquet was on Monday night, and the slack for all the timed events started on Tuesday. Local wheat farmer and helicopter pilot, Stan Timmerman, volunteered to be our host, and he took us around all week. We had the best time because of Stan. We came to know Stan real well, and a nicer guy I've never met. Every year since then, I try to eat supper with Stan at least one night while I'm there.

Pake, Stan Timmerman, and Clark at
Pendleton Round-Up. 1984—Family Photo

Pake getting ready to rope at the 1984 Pendleton
Round-Up. 1984—Family Photo

Since 1963, they have given a practice-roping dummy steer head to the winner of the steer roping. Bill Severe, just a genius when it comes to leather and rawhide work, made the trophy for the winner. They called Bill a couple of months before the 1984 Round-Up and told him they wanted an action shot of someone roping a steer at Pendleton, with the Round-Up logo in the background of the picture. He found a 1961 picture of Clark roping on old Heel Fly, a chestnut sorrel, owned by Earl Corbin from Delaware, Oklahoma, when Clark won second in the average that year. Bill had the trophy finished, and then he found out they were gonna put Clark in the hall of fame that year! What a coincidence, right? It gets better. They take the twelve fastest times on two and let them rope one more head, called "the finals," on the last day of the rodeo. I caught my first two steers and went into the short go-round in second place behind Reece Jackson. So after Dave Brock (who went in third) roped, I had to be 15.7 to take the lead. I was 15.3. Reece had trouble and went out, so that let me win the Round-Up the same year Clark was inducted, and out of ninety-nine ropers, ole Black and I won the trophy with Clark's picture on it! As always, they stopped the rodeo, presented ole Black and me the trophy, along with a real nice trophy saddle, boots, belt buckle, and a hat.

Susan Corey presenting a Bill Severe handmade trophy to Pake, with Clark's picture on the front top. 1984—Howdyshell Photo

Pake accepting trophy boots from Round-Up queens. 1984—Family Photo

Clark on Heel Fly, Pendleton. 1961—Howdyshell Photo

Justin Merritt (Frankie Merritt's son) presenting Pake with trophy spurs. A great guy and friend, Frankie Merritt, was killed in the seventies in a steer roping accident, and I was proud to have these spurs in his memory. 1984—Howdyshell Photo

When someone wins the event (the fastest total time on three head), they stop the rodeo and present all the trophies in front of the south grandstand to the winner; then he gets to take a lap around the arena of seventeen thousand screaming, standing, and applauding fans. If I win it again, it would be more than great, but I don't think it could ever top that year.

Pake riding steer horse Black, leading Round-Up horse with Hamley Trophy Saddle. 1984—Family Photo

On the way home that evening, Clark and Jac rode back with us to Boise, Idaho, to catch a plane home to Oklahoma. On the way to Boise, at about ten o'clock, the starter went out on my Chevy truck, and I had to pay $250 (normally $80) to get a new one put in. After we got back on the road, Clark said, "Duddin' take long before reality kicks back in, does it?"

I look forward to Pendleton every year. I think I've had more fun at that rodeo than most of them put together.

Chapter 43

LET 'ER BUCK ROOM

At the Round-Up, they have the ever-popular Let'er Buck Room in back of the grandstand, a place that spectators and some of the contestants (myself included) frequent after the slack on Tuesday evening. No beer or girlie drinks. If you ask for something like that, they say, "The Dairy Queen's just down the street."

And when you ask for a name-brand whiskey, they say, "Sure." Then turn around and get the cheapest, sorriest, worst-tasting rotgut whiskey ever made and fill a five-ounce plastic cup, leaving about a half inch on top to put whatever else you want with it. I've accidentally drank fly spray that tasted better, but it sure is good! I like to drink mine with water. For an extra chip, you can get the famous Canadian-made Pendleton Whiskey, but after three of the bad stuff, you cain't tell the difference anyway.

One day in there, I had about three of these and noticed my steer roping friend's wife at the bar talking to another roper's wife. I walked up, all in fun, and asked her, "Why did you pick your husband when you could have had me?"

She looked straight into my bloodshot eyes and said, "You never asked!"

This was not the answer I was expecting, so with a half way grin I stumbled away from that conversation.

I soon noticed that when I first started going to the Buck Room, some of the girls with just enough hooch in 'em would get up the nerve to climb up on some guy's shoulders and pull off their blouses and show off their bouncy boobies. The bartenders then rang a cowbell and gave the girls a free "Let 'er Buck" T-shirt. Guess the city of Pendleton failed to see the humor in all of this, so they put up posters all over the place, saying, "Keep your clothes on! Indecent exposure will not be tolerated. Anyone involved will be banned from the premises! Pendleton Round-Up 2008."

I confiscated about a dozen of these posters, laminated them, and gave them to the kinfolks for Christmas. As a matter of fact, I do all my Christmas shopping at Pendleton and have not had one complaint yet. Don't expect to get one, either.

One day at the Buck Room, some cowboys were talking to these girls about tattoos. One of the girls said she had one, and she raised up her shorts and showed a flamingo on the inside of her thigh, way up high, just below her crotch! Bud Tillard said, "To hell with the bird, I wanna see the nest!"

That horse couldn't pull a sick whore off a piss pot!
— CLARK MCENTIRE

Fun can also be had outside the Buck Room. The Buck Room closes at 7:30 p.m. (thank God), so many like to sit on the big steps outside the exit of the room and see how drunk some of the patrons are when they come out.

Some of the cowboys like to tie their horses up along the racetrack inside the arena, still saddled, and go to the Buck Room. One year, Stephanie and I left the Buck Room early to go turn the saddles around backward on their horses. We hung around to watch the expressions when they found out something was wrong with their horse. J. P. "Stickett" Wickett came out and looked down the fence and said, " Ha, ha, ha… Look at what they did to C. A.'s horse."

Then he looked down the fence and said, "Motherfucker—they got mine too!"

We kept hanging around, laughing at the incident, and looked up to see Tyler Mayes had C. A.'s roan horse and was riding him backward over to the bucking chute; he put him in it and pretended to nod like the rough-stock cowboys do. That rotgut whiskey makes folks do some strange things.

One time I didn't go to the Buck Room and stayed to visit in the grass baseball parking lot. I looked up, and here came Rod Hartness, Jim Davis, and Mark Sandman. They were all pretty well oiled up, walking like waltzing pissants, and they wanted me to take them downtown to get some beer. (Beer on whiskey? Mighty risky!) Paul Rice lived at Pendleton, and Jim had rode into town with someone else, so he borrowed Paul's feed truck to get around town for the week. This truck had no taillights, but we all loaded up in it anyway and headed for downtown. We hadn't gotten out of the parking lot, when Sandman reached over and stepped on my foot on the gas pedal, and the old truck just sat there spinning on top of the ground. (I knew this was gonna be a memorable trip.) We got downtown and stopped at a red light. The Tapadera was across the street, so Davis jumped out and said, "I'm going to the Tap."

Rod jumped out; so did Sandman. I just put it in park and followed them to the Tap, with Paul's truck sitting at the red light (now turned green) with half a dozen cars behind it! We went inside and ordered drinks, and Davis said, "Sandman, go move that truck!"

Sandman said, "Ain't my truck."

Davis said, "Hartness, go move that truck!"

Hartness said, "Ain't my truck!"

Davis looked at me, and I said, "Ain't my truck, neither!"

Davis looked at us and said, "Fuck you guys!"

By the time he got to the truck, someone had moved it around the corner and was just getting out of it. Davis walked up to the truck. This guy said, real pissed off, "You ain't gonna believe it, but somebody left this truck parked at this light in front of a bunch of cars!"

Davis pointed and said, "You mean that truck?"

The guy said, "Yeah!"

Davis jumped in the truck and drove off, leaving the guy standing there staring as he went down the road.

One year, Ike Good and Ricky Canton wanted to go downtown, and they rode Buster Records's steer horse and somebody's steer horse they found tied up outside the Buck Room. They stopped along the way and bought themselves a six-pack of beer. The law stopped them and told them they could ride their horses downtown, but he had to take their beer 'cause they couldn't drink and ride. They gave it up but decided later that that damned cop took their beer home and drank every damned bit of it!

They tried to ride these horses downstairs into Crabby's Bar, but the horses would have none of it. Instead, they tied them up to a light pole outside. Guess the horses had better judgment that night.

A blind man was with two men looking at a horse.
One man said, "That sure is a pretty horse."

The blind man said, "Yeah, fat ain't he!"
— LEON MCCLENDON

Chapter 44

THE BIG CHANGE

In about the early eighties, steer roping changed. Steers began to cost more, and they started roping in smaller pens to get steer roping at more rodeos. This meant shorter scores and lighter cattle and ropers tying them much faster. This put us four left-handed steer ropers at a bigger disadvantage than before because most arenas were set up for right-handed ropers. After I got off the road with RCA, from playing music all over the United States and parts of Canada (and that's another story), I decided to make my move to right handed, not wrong handed. I built a new roping pen in front of the house near Pittsburg. It was 36 feet wide by 150 feet long, breakaway only. This means the hondo is fixed to only catch the steer, and when the horse stops, the rope will come off the steer's head quickly. My right arm and wrist were amazingly weak. After about three runs, I couldn't get the rope past the horse's head! My wife, Katy, looked at me real serious and said, "Are you sure you can do this?"

I said, "No, but I'm sure gonna give it a good try!"

Roping the practice dummy was a big help to build up the strength in my arm and wrist. The one thing I had not expected was the need to learn how to ride a horse all over again. The balance was all different. I found myself up to the front of the swells of the saddle, ready to rope, and then back to the cantle, not ready. Then I had to learn how to ride the left stirrup instead of the right.

Several of the cowboys asked me how long it took me to learn to rope right handed. I said, "I'm still learning!"

I would get a bunch of suggestions, from "get a bigger loop" to "get a smaller loop," and everything in between. Probably the biggest help was the Osage Steer Roping Club in Pawhuska, Oklahoma. They had, and still have, A, B, and C divisions. They let me in the B roping as long as I roped right handed. I also entered the A roping since I was there anyway. During the week, I was at home practicing. This was in 1989, and in each division, they roped two, and the top twelve would get to rope another in the short go-round. It was several ropings before I made the short go, and it felt like a call to heaven. After more and more ropings, I started placing in the average. By 1990, I started winning one and placing in the average in the other.

Pake riding Robin, winning short go and average, 1990 Ben Johnson Memorial, Pawhuska, Oklahoma. 1990—KW Photo

The Ben Johnson Memorial Steer Roping had been held at Pawhuska fairgrounds for over forty years, and we had been roping most all of the Osage Club ropings there also. I entered the Ben Johnson roping left handed for sixteen years and never came close to placing in the average.

That morning we left Pittsburg, Oklahoma, headed for the Ben Johnson. We had gotten about twenty-five yards from the house when I heard something just not right with the trailer. I jumped out to find the saddle compartment door had come open, and my saddle was draggin' underneath the trailer!

I had to jack it up to get it out. I went back to the tack room and got a backup saddle that fit another horse, not Robin (the horse I was taking), but sometimes you just gotta pick up the ball and run with it.

Grand Pap won a steer roping at Pawhuska in 1923. Clark started roping there in 1953 when they began the Ben Johnson Memorial and won it in 1958. We won the short go and the average that day—$6500 and a new saddle. Clark and I became the first father and son to win the roping in over forty years. In 2008, Brady Garten won it, and he and his dad Shorty became the second.

> *Courage is being scared to death and still saddling up.*
> —JOHN WAYNE

This was the second-best day of my life. This roping is always held on Father's Day, and Clark was there to see it. That was important to me. Clark is superstitious, thinking that if he's there, I won't do any good. My girls gave me a Father's Day shirt, and I wore it that day. It was hotter than nine kinds of hell that day, so Autumn and Calamity found a motorhome where somebody had the air conditioner on. When they saw the crowd starting to break up, they stepped out, and a roper walked by and said, "Hey, girls, your dad just won the roping!" I had been struggling for so long, so one of the girls said, "Huh-uh!" (That's slang for "bullshit!")

Autumn, Chism, Pake, Katy, and Calamity at 1990 Ben Johnson Steer Roping (a good Father's Day present for me and Clark). 1990—ReReal Photo

I went to Monahans, Texas, the next week to a steer roping, and Rod Hartness, Nickolas Stone, and I were horseback, talking. Nick said, "Who won the Ben Johnson?"

Rod said, "Pake did."

Nick looked over at me and then pointed to my horse and said, "On that horse?"

Stephenville 1997 was one of the "come together" days. Flip Miller and Chester Knight and I went down there for a PRCA two and a short, where all the steer ropers rope two, and the top twelve ropers rope a third. The roping order is from slowest time to fastest.

That day I rode a horse we called "Houdini." He got his name when a hired hand accidentally rode him off into a spring bog hole in the hills just north of our corral. Houdini was buried up to his belly when the hired hand stepped off and saw Houdini couldn't get out, so he walked back to the corrals. We looked up and saw the hired hand coming, and Houdini was right behind him with mud all over, beating the hired hand to the corral.

That day at Stephenville, Houdini and I were 9.4 on the first one, splitting first and second with J. P. "Stickett" Wickett; we came back on the second one and were 10.3, placing third and so had to be 12.0 on the third steer to win the average. The steer ran harder than the other two and strained on the tie some, but we were 11.7, to win the average for a total payday of $3,400. Once in a blue moon, when things come together like that, you feel really good—for a while. Clark was a roper who would never get too high on a win or too low on a loss, so when I called him and Jac to tell them the good news, he said, "Does old Whit Kenny still live down there?"

I had just had one of the best days of my roping career, and he wanted to know about Whit Kenny! I thought that was really funny!

Think nobody cares? Be two payments late!
—J. P. "Stickett" Wickett

Pake on Houdini, Stephenville, Texas. 1997
First Average—Jennings Photo

Chapter 45

RAY BINGHAM

In the late seventies, I had been playing music shows—like dances, festivals, rodeos, private parties, celebrations of all kinds—and, off and on, working to get a recording contract with a major record label. One day the phone rang at Chockie, and it was Ray Bingham, asking for Reba. Ray is a booking agent from Claremore, Oklahoma, and has been around the block and back again. I took the message, but before I hung up, I said, "If you run across anything I can work around your area, I'd be glad to do it."

Pake, Katy, and Ray Bingham. 1981—Family Photo

I really didn't expect to hear from him again. A couple of days later, he called and said he had a gig in Tulsa with the house band, and I was to do two forty-five-minute shows for $250! My current pay at that time was from free to about $100 for four hours of work. I drove my feed truck up there and did the show. I remember Ray and I were in the restroom at the club when he really did hand me $250 bucks in cash and insisted on not taking any commission! I found out Ray was just a level-headed, good-ole country boy like me. We visited all the way to the feed truck and discovered I had a flat on the outside duel. He jumped down and helped me fix it right then and there.

Later he got me hooked up with a bunch of great kids called "The Country Cousins"—three sets of cousins, all kin to each other, with one of the sets' dad, Al Talbot, managing the band. With his wife, Margie, he went with them, chaperoned them, and worked with Ray, while Ray did the booking. The Cousins even did seven songs on my *Rodeo Man* album, their first recording.

Donnie Talbot, Pake, Brent Self, Darlene Passmore, Red Steagal, Mike Self, Dale Talbot. The Country Cousins, Red, and Pake. 1981—Darlene Passmore Photo

Ray booked us several dates at Norm's Ballroom in Newkirk, Oklahoma. We became good friends with the owner, Norman Brown.

Our show was getting a little "ho-hum" because we had been there so many times. I knew we needed a gag to liven up the show some. I had recently seen the movie *Tootsie*, with Dustin Hoffman, and came up with an idea to spice up the dance/show.

Katy and I went into a shoe store in McAlester to buy me a pair of women's shoes. I was trying on a pair when a guy that worked there rounded the corner and said, "May I help you?" He looked at me, trying on a woman's shoe, and then said, "I can't help you!" We bought the shoes, went to Wal-Mart, bought a purple dress, pantyhose, a white purse with a long strap, and a red wig. I looked just like my sister Alice.

The idea was to dress up like Tootsie in the movie. Country cousin, Mike Self, introduced me like this: "Folks, we have a special treat for you here tonight. I want all you people to come up to the front of the bandstand. Yeah, come on up; you ain't gonna believe who you are fixin' to see. All the way from Los Angeles, California, make welcome to the stage, Tootsie!"

Brent Self, Tootsie (alias "Pake"), Darlene Passmore, at Norm's Ballroom, Newkirk, Oklahoma. (Get me up to your room; find out I got one too!) 1981—Darlene Passmore Photo

I came out struttin' and prissin' like Tootsie with the purse strap hung over my shoulder. Because of laughing so hard, the band liked to have never kicked off the song, "Sweet Thang," which Ernest Tubb and Loretta Lynn had a cut on back in the sixties. Brent Self and I did the duet, and the crowd just loved it!

We continued doing this act every time we were there, until the crowd got tired of it. One night at the end of the dance, I talked Brent Self into switching with me and dressing up like Tootsie. I would sing the male part, and he would do the female part. This task was not easy to do. He was not for it, some. When Katy got through putting on the garb, we discovered Brent was a little bit bigger boned and taller than I was, so the dress fit tighter, the makeup fit his complexion to a T, and if you didn't know he was a guy, you'd say, "Damn, that gal's hot!"

When I introduced Tootsie, Brent came out, and I noticed sweat beads on his upper lip. After we did the song, I said, "Let's hear it for Tootsie!" I didn't see it coming, but he had hold of the end of that long purse strap. We had the purse filled with paper, and he swung it around and hit me right upside the head!

That was the end of Tootsie; we couldn't get Brent back into the garb again.

We did a show together, opening for my hero, John Anderson, at the Woodward Elks Rodeo at Woodward, Oklahoma. We set up about three hours before the show and met Leonard, the caretaker of the building. Regardless of the fact that Leonard's light wuddin' always on, we went out of our way to be nice to him, so in turn he bent over backward to get us anything we wanted. However, when John's crew showed up, for some reason or other, Leonard didn't like them some. Later on that night, we did our show; John did his first show, we came back and did our second show, and John was gonna close out the night. Leonard was told by the fire marshals that the show *must* be over at 1:00 a.m. John was in the middle of his biggest hit, "Swingin'," when Leonard looked down at his watch and it was straight-up 1:00 a.m. He calmly walked over to the breaker on the wall and pulled all the electricity from the bandstand, leaving it pitch black! (Show over!)

Labor Day weekend 2008, I ran into Ray at Clinton, Arkansas, at Dan and Peggy Eoff's Chuck Wagon Race. Ray invited me to the Country Cousin's (later called Stone Horse) reunion in Claremore, so I accepted. Backstage, Ray told me this story.

"I was at a show that I had nothing to do with. I even bought a ticket to get in. I wanted to get backstage to mingle but had no connections for getting past the security guard. After standing in line, I approached the guard and said, 'See that couple in line here behind me; they are to have access to all areas backstage, and I'd appreciate it if they were treated with respect and hassle free!' This guard looked at them and then at me and said 'OK.' I walked in like I owned the place."

When my patience got thin, I started my own independent label in 1981, O Cross Records, where distribution was limited, to say the least. My first album was named after the song Robin Lacy wrote called "Rodeo Man." He wrote it while he was letting me work for the WH Corral Band at Sulphur, back in the late seventies. I would sell these at shows and rodeos, usually after I'd rope, walking through the stands like a hotdog salesman.

Chapter 46

RCA

Reba had had a recording contract since 1976, and she was busy with her career and had no time for mine. In the fall of 1984, Reba and her husband, Charlie Battles, had Bill Carter as their career music manager. Bill's background was the attorney business, and Charlie got me an audition with Bill and RCA producer Mark Wright. Reba's band was in Nashville, practicing at a warehouse turned rehearsal studio, so Charlie got me in there to practice three songs over and over for two days, a total of seven hours. At the end of the second day, Bill and Mark showed up, and on our way home, we got the call—we were in! Charlie, you got the ball rolling, got my foot in the door, and to you I am forever grateful. Thanks, Charlie.

Charlie Battles, Reba, and Cindy Owen at Fan Fair in Nashville. Around 1984—Reba Photo

You show me a person that works as hard as the McEntires, and I'll show you a successful person!

— GARY RAIBURN

Mark called me into his office at RCA and played me a demo from Lang Martine, Jr., called "Every Night." Coincidentally, Lang also wrote Reba's first single, "I Don't Wanna Be A One Night Stand" on Mercury Records in 1976. A demo is short for "demonstration tape recording," and it is just to show the foundation of the song. The demo does not have to have been recorded in any studio; in fact, this one sounded like Lang had sat down with his hollow-body guitar, turned on a five-dollar tape recorder, and let 'er fly—Nelly Bly! When Mark played it for me, I couldn't visualize our version, so I asked, "We're gonna record that?"

He said, "It won't sound anything like that when we get through with it."

Now, unless Lang cowrote it with someone else and doesn't sell it or give it away, he owns the song and will receive royalties from sales or each time the song is played on radio, jukeboxes, movies, or anyplace compensation is involved.

Mark also found the songs "Bad Love," "Savin' my Love for You," "Heart vs. Heart," and "Too Old to Grow up Now." We recorded these songs in April of 1984. When we got into the studio, there was the "A Team," a group of pickers setting up in clothes they would wear around the house. One of them was legendary steel player Buddy Emmons. I had heard about him all my life. Mark told me to sing along with the band, but we weren't gonna record me, just the band. We would come back later and lay down my vocal. The producer, Mark Wright, in my case, decides how the song is structured as far as tempo, what instruments to use, the feel, the atmosphere, and so forth. You may be wondering, "Atmosphere?" Yeah, I've seen them turn down the lights to almost pitch black on a slow, sad ballad like "Heart vs. Heart." He instructs everyone in the session, including the A&R man (arrangement and recording), on how he wants it and what to do. The record company pays the producer and everyone else.

They had everything charted out. This means the producer usually sits down before the session with one of the pickers, usually the guitar player or piano man, and writes down in picker's language the order or direction of the song. This way the picker doesn't have to memorize it, only read it from the chart as he plays it. They discussed it before cutting it in terms I was totally unfamiliar with and had no idea what they were taking about.

Each picker has their own direct line or separate track going into the studio in another room that runs through this huge sound control board that the A&R man operates. Some run direct, and some have an amplifier with a microphone in front of the amp for their own personal tone settings. Everybody has their own headset, with a box, setting their own preferred volume. These guys jumped on it like a chicken after a June bug, but they usually don't keep the first cut. I've seen them stop at the beginning, middle, or near the end and start over. Remember, they are human. They played like they had played together for years. You may think, "They all probably have played for years together." Well, not necessarily, for ya see, there are hundreds of pickers in Nashville, and most are real good but are constantly looking for work. They are all part of the pickers' union that is under strict rules and guidelines and scale compensation.

After they did it, commonly called "cutting it," sometimes one would ask the A&R man to go back and fix a mistake the particular picker had made, without having everyone else redo theirs, saving time and money. The A&R man will play a few bars before the boo-boo, and the picker will play along before it, and the A&R man will punch in the new version, erasing the mistake all at the same time.

You would think these guys would be stone-cold serious from years of doing this, but quite the contrary. They were doing everything short of playing grab ass! Poking fun at each other, I heard one call the other "Ass Face," for a reason unknown to me, and they all laughed! It's a lot of work in the studio but a lot of fun too.

> *There are people in this town who couldn't*
> *hear two freight trains run together!*
> —NASHVILLE SESSION BASS PLAYER

Reba told me that when they were cutting "I'm a Woman," there was a line in the song that said, "I'll give you the shiverin' fits." She accidentally got it turned around and said, "I'll give you the fiverin' shits!" She said they all got a big kick outta that.

Just after I was signed, two very good friends—singers and songwriters, Keith Whitley and Vince Gill—were also on RCA. Vince wasn't having much success with RCA, so Vince would sing harmony on other artists' cuts, and I am very proud to have had him on some of mine, like "Every Night," "Savin' My Love for You," and more. They knew he was gonna be a superstar someday but just couldn't launch him, so they just put him on hold.

The strategy was to release a single on Keith one month and then mine on the next. Keith had a drinking problem and would disappear for weeks, without even his manager knowing his whereabouts. When Keith was gone, they were gonna release mine next; then Keith would show up, and Keith was next. This went on for eight months, when finally between Christmas and New Year's, they released, "Every Night."

I was feeding for Clark one day over at Cairo when I saw this car coming up the road in a cloud of dust. I saw it was my car, and I knew it was Katy and suspected something was bad wrong. She jumped out of the car and told me that RCA had been trying to get hold of me all day—the record was going crazy! I drove to a phone booth in Coalgate, called RCA, and began the ride of my life.

The location for my first photo shoot (see above) was at a rock quarry somewhere near Nashville. It was January and about thirty-eight degrees. They hired a model to be in the picture with me, and she was a knockout! I felt kinda sorry for her on account of the circumstances because they had her in a real tight, skimpy white dress showing plenty of cleavage, and I couldn't help but notice goose bumps there. Like all of us, she was more than ready to be done with this shoot—the rest of us were freezing our tits off, although she never did.

Pake's first promo picture with **RCA**. **1985**—**RCA P**hoto

Chapter 47

ON THE ROAD

The first RCA road band consisted of Kent Johnson on drums, "Ranger" Rick Johnston on lead guitar, Joey Giovannetti on bass, and Dave Gant on fiddle and keyboards. Concessions were run by Mike Pierce, and sound was Andy Dearth.

"Ranger" Rick Johnston, Pake, Joey Giovanetti, Kent Johnson, Dave Gant. 1985—Mike Pierce Photo

Kent Johnson, Dave Gant, Joey Giovanetti, Pake, "Ranger" Rick Johnston, Mike Pierce. 1985—Kent Johnson Photo

Dave Gant. 1985—Family Photo

Dave, from Ada, Oklahoma, was the most talented musician that helped us on the road. His mom taught him fiddle, and Dave played great keyboards also. Traveling in an overcrowded pickup and camper, Dave finally had enough of the Pake McEntire Show. One day Dave said, "Pake, you treat us like cattle; you may as well rope and brand us! I'm not going out on the road unless the artist has a bus. I quit!"

Averaging fourteen shows a month, we were all tired, and life on the road is hard, at its best, with a bus, let alone a pickup and camper. The others followed suit: so one man's trash, another man's treasure. Dave has been with Garth Brooks all this time, and they still do shows on occasion.

Following these guys, Don Crider on fiddle and steel, Randy Altenbaumer on keyboards and steel, Boogie Tidmore on piano, Dink Terrell on bass, Robert Lankford on fiddle, and Shawn Tuil on guitar. We called Shawn "Tombstone" because he got drunk one night, and we found him in the cemetery talking to a headstone. Road managers (at different times, of course) were Hovie Walker and "Flossie" Rick Crabtree. These guys were great road managers.

Andy Dearth, Paul Jeffreys, Pake, Mike Pierce, Randy Altenbaumer,
Al Weir, Shawn "Tombstone" Tuil. 1986—Mike Pierce Photo

All the guys that were with me out on the road were just plain good-ole boys. We all had more fun than should have been allowed. But one ole boy stood out above the rest. Everybody especially liked Randy "The Rat" Altenbaumer. Multitalented, Randy played steel guitar and keyboards. He had been in a car accident, hit from behind, and suffered a lot of back pain, but he was never in a bad mood, always cheerful; he had a dry sense of humor but was downright funny. This Ashdown, Arkansas, native was very dependable, always on time, the kinda guy everyone wishes they had grown up with.

When we were practicing at Bob Woods's music store in Del City, at night I would go over to Midwest City and watch the playoffs of the state high school basketball tournament. They were playing "Every Night" on the radio a lot, so some folks began to know who I was from the record. I was sitting in the ball gym one night when here came about five grade school girls wanting my autograph. The first four were tickled to get my signature, but the fifth one looked at it and said, "Who are you anyway?"

I said, "Oh, honey, no one important!"

One day we were at the Holiday Inn lounge in McAlester, rehearsing, when we took a break. I saw Shawn at the back of the lounge, looking at a picture of Will Rogers. I walked up to him and said, "Shawn, do you know who that is?"

He looked at it and said, "Tex Ritter?"
I said, "Hell no, Tombstone, that's Will Rogers!"
He said, "Oh, I knew it was one of those guys!"

> *You can't have everything 'cause where in the hell would you put it?*
> —Shawn "Tombstone" Tuil

I learned a card game in college called "Stew," or "Two Card Guts." I introduced it to the band boys, and it seemed like we played it going down the road 80 percent of the time! It was easy to play, so the driver could even play and drive. Stew was a fast-paced game: you could easily lose your britches or win the next two weeks' wages from some of your friends. We kept score of who owed whom on the ceiling of old Snowball. On one trip, we were on our way to Florida and were playing in the truck when we stopped at a motel and continued playing. Alan Haggie, the sound man, got a little drunk and started playing wild, and it worked. He cashed in at the expense of Mikey and Gant to the tune of $640 a piece! Mikey and Gant roomed together and were lying in their beds after their losses, licking their wounds, naming things that $640 would have bought, and they were so low that Mikey told Dave, "Gantster, I only have an electric razor, so we cain't slit our throats. We are on the bottom floor of this hotel, so it wouldn't do any good to jump out the window. We don't carry pistols, so I guess we'll just have to live with it!"

While we were at that motel that night, the movie *Silverado* was on TV. There was a scene where a herd of Corriente steers were stampeding. I told the guys, "Y'all see those steers? I've roped some of those steers before."

They looked at me like I had just told them the biggest whopper ever told. They laughed and said, "Yeah right!"

I said, "No shit. Kenny Call, a steer roper who's in the movie, told me that those steers, owned by Bill Montin from Fitztown, Oklahoma, and Ed Gaylord from Guthrie, were the ones we roped all summer at ropings before they took them out to California for the movie."

They would have believed I saw a forty-foot monster before they would buy any of that. Later on, when I'd tell them something, they'd say, "Yeah right, and you roped them steers on *Silverado* too!"

You can lead a horse to water, but you cain't make him drink!
—A Clever Cowboy

Robert Langford and Pake. 1986—Family Photo

We were back east somewhere, maybe Ohio, and about a week before, we had played a show for the National Football League's Trainers Athletic Association. They gave us a five-thousand-dollar check on the Denver Broncos. I was running low on cash, so I told Mike Pierce to pull into the first bank we came to and cash this check. "Mikey," we called him, was about five foot seven, weighed about 225 pounds, and his head sat right down on top of his shoulders. He said he refused to grow a neck as a child. He and I went into this bank, and he walked up to the first teller window we came to, showed the check, and they pointed to a lady sitting at a desk. We walked over to her, and Mikey said, "Howdy, ma'am, my name is Mike Pierce, and this is Pake McEntire. I'm the manager for the Pake McEntire Country Music roadshow, and we recently did a show for the Denver Broncos, and we would like to cash this check."

She looked at it and asked, "Do you have an account here with us at our bank?"

Mikey said, "No, ma'am."

She said, "Well, I can't cash it."

I said, "How much does it take to open an account?"

She said, "A hundred dollars."

So I said, "OK, we'll open a checking account, and then will you cash the check?"

She said, "No! The only way is for someone who has a checking or savings account here that we know to cash it for you."

Now, Mikey loves a challenge, and she had just thrown a big one on him. Mikey jumped up from that chair and walked over to the first lady he came to standing in the back of the teller line waiting to do her morning banking. He put the spill on her, and before we knew it, he was leading her over to where the loan officer and I were sitting. The loan officer said to the lady, "I can't believe you're considering doing this!"

The lady said, "Well, it is on the Denver Broncos, and he does look a little like Reba, so I think it will be all right." She cosigned the check, and we got our cash; we gave her our address, phone numbers, and RCA's phone numbers. We then led her out to the truck and loaded her up with cassettes, pictures, bandannas, jam shorts, and anything she wanted while the whole time, she kept saying, "Boys, please don't screw me!"

Mikey stuck his chest out for weeks after that.

If ifs and buts were candy and nuts, we'd all have a merry Christmas.
— ANONYMOUS

We were headed for Kimberly, Wisconsin, for a Sunday afternoon show at a bar. We were traveling in old Snowball when the transmission went out in Champagne, Illinois. We rented a van from a limousine service and got to the gig forty-five minutes before we were to start. We jumped on stage, did the first set, and went to the concession autograph table. This lady came up and said, "You boys were just great. I mean, that was really a great show. You were even better than Faron Young, who was here last month! But come to think of it, Faron was so drunk he couldn't even do his second set!"

Mama, Minnie Pearl, and Pake. About 1990—Family Photo

We opened for Moe Bandy somewhere in Minnesota one night, and I had some time before we went on, so I went on Moe's bus, and we had a great visit. Moe said, "Pake, have you met Faron Young yet?"

I said, "No, I haven't."

He said, "I opened for Faron one time, and he said, 'Moe, if you ever get a heckler in the crowd and it's a man, tell him this. "Folks, when I was a kid, my daddy gave me some hogs. I wasn't very good at taking care of them. I wouldn't water or feed them like I should have, so my dad said, 'Son, one of these days, those hogs are gonna come back and haunt you.'" Then point to the heckler and say, "And I'll be danged—one of them hogs showed up right here tonight!" Now, if it's a woman heckler, say, "Ma'am, I don't know why you're giving me such a hard time. I don't jerk the mattress out from under you while you're making your living!'"

I can pick up more girls at a funeral than most guys can at a teen hop!
— CHOCK MAXEY

Being a country music entertainer between the years of 1935 to about 1965 was pretty tough. They traveled in cars, all sitting and sleeping up right next to each other, sometimes with a big bass fiddle in the laps of those in the backseat or strapped to the top of the car when weather permitted. They played small venues in smaller country towns, so this meant smaller motels with little or no accommodations. All-night drives, with no paid driver, and everyone driving their part, pulling into venues just in time to set up and play, hot, tired, exhausted, and then jumping on stage with a newfound excitement they didn't know they had left. The fans have been waiting for months to see them, are sitting on the edge of their seats full of energy from getting night after night of restful sleep in their home beds. These entertainers were just plain-ole country boys and girls hoping to live their dream.

Hank Williams Sr., Judy Garrett, George Morgan
(Lori Morgan's father), Dorothy Garrison, and
Ernest Tubb – Photo Source Unknown

This was before the days of road managers that tell everyone on the tour what to do and when to do it. Road management is very important. It was before million-dollar Silver Eagle Buses with a bunk for everyone so you can close the curtain and sleep to the humming of these quiet diesel engines. Where you can stand up, walk around, watch anything from CNN to *Gone with the Wind*, go to the restroom, and get something to eat or drink, with iceboxes and microwave ovens. Cell phones and GPS systems—all you have to do is put in the address, and the GPS will tell you where your next turn is and then pull into a big city with nice high-rise hotels, with every convenience from room service to spas and swimming pools. At big venues, you can put on the contract rider from hot meals to the finest whiskey to almost any wine you prefer. The pay gets so good that some entertainers lease huge auditoriums and skip the middleman for larger profits.

The artist has to repeatedly tell himself, "This is the business I've chosen, so do your job." There is a constant reminder to the artist that he or she is here for a short time, shorter for some than others, and one has to make hay while the sun shines. After the show is over, the fans go home talking about what a good show the artist put on and then snuggle up in their warm beds, while the artist loads back up and heads down the road five hundred miles for another all-night drive to another show. I've heard more than one artist say, "Those booking agents must have a United States map on their wall, blindfold themselves, and throw darts at it to determine where we play, because the routing stinks!"

He stopped lovin' her today; who'd buy that morbid son of a bitch?
— GEORGE JONES

Actually the agents book gigs as close together as they can. A new-and-struggling or has-been artist is hard to book and has to take what he can get. You may ask, "Then why doesn't the artist refuse to go those hard routes?" It's because the artist needs the work, and when the artist is struggling to make ends meet financially, he'll take almost anything.

Now, if the artist is out of sorts, grumpy, hung over, mad, or aggravated about something that went wrong with the sound check or on the trip to get there, and the fans notice it, they don't understand why the artist is not having fun like they are. Some artists get so burned out, they pull no-shows. It gets so bad that some get a name called "No-Show Jones."

Hank Williams, Jr., drank a little too much wine and chased it with whiskey in Kansas City with a pro football player the day of a show, got on stage, and began cussing out the crowd with bad, bad obscenities, saying in so many words that if the crowd duddin' like his or his family's music, they can kiss his fuckin' ass. Also expressing what a very popular country music superstar at the time could do to his upfront, down-yonder private part! The fans got so unruly, they began throwing things and setting their T-shirts on fire! Mike Pierce, a friend and former concession vendor on the road with me for over two years, was selling concessions that night and was in the lobby, hearing the uproar of the crowd. I asked him what he did when he saw the fans in an all-but-riot manner. He said, "Oooooh, I boxed up all that merchandise. I knew then and there we wuddin' gonna sell shit that night. I hid my access-to-all-areas ID tag inside my shirt and headed for the bus, hollerin' like everybody else, 'Fuck Hank! Fuck Hank!' I didn't want them mad sons a bitches knowin' I was part of this show till I got on the bus!"

The fans threw rocks at the bus as they drove away! Hank's manager shouldn't have let him on stage and should have just cancelled due to sickness. When Hank sobered up, they played the tape back to him, and he couldn't believe what he heard.

When these artists get to a certain level of playing huge auditoriums, soon after the show, it is very common for them to get sued by one or more fans. Something like, "I fell on the steps," or, "I tripped over a cord on the floor," or anything they can think of to sue them over. Then the artist begins to get death threats and stalkers, and like anybody would, he gets paranoid.

Elvis got so scared someone was going to kill him that RCA had to bring the recording studio to his home at Graceland to record. Artists inform the FBI of the threats, but about all the FBI tells them is to be nice to them. This is just some of the bleak side of the business, and it gets worse.

However, on the brighter side, it is very rewarding to stand up behind a microphone and sing or play a God-given talent to folks—put them up on a pedestal and call them "heroes." Hard-working people spend their hard-earned dollars and travel what they think are many miles to come and see them and only them. They rush up to an autograph table just to get their autograph and shake their hand. They give them the respect they don't get with their job. The entertainment business is a good life as long as the artist can keep control of himself and the ones around him.

We loved Elvis to death, and we nearly did the same thing to Johnny Cash!

—MERLE HAGGARD

Ralph Emery, Reba, E. P. Lucchese, Susie, Pake, and Chism—Family Photo

I was fortunate to have been on about six Nashville Now shows with Ralph Emery. I got to know him pretty well and loved listening to his country music stories. If you haven't already read his book that Tom Carter helped with, I suggest you read it. It is one of a few that I have ever read that I really liked.

The picture above was shot just after airing Nashville Now. This show was with Susie and Reba and me and was rated in the top five shows Nashville Now did over a long span. After the show, they wanted to do a promo for the next night's show. Reba had previously taught Chism to stick out her tongue and blow when asking her a question and pulling the pacifier out of her mouth. Didn't matter what you asked her; just ask her anything and then pull the plug, and she'd do it every time. After the promo, I was talking to the director while holding Chism, and I said, "Wanna see something cute?"

He said, "Sure."

I said, "Hey, Chism, what do you think about ole Ralph?"

I pulled the pacifier out of her mouth, and she did it on cue. He laughed and asked, "Will she do it every time?"

I said, "Yeah."

He looked across the room and hollered out, "Hey, Ralph, we need to do the promo over again."

Ralph said, "How come? What's wrong with the last one?"

The director said, "We just need to do it over."

We did the promo over again, except at the end this time, I said, "Oh, by the way, Chism, what do you think about ole Ralph here?" I pulled the pacifier, and she stuck her tongue out and blew a big wad of slobbers out!

Chism doing her thing. 1986—Family Photo

We were invited over to Ralph's office after the show, when Ralph asked us, "Does she do that to everyone or just me?" Reba said, "Just you, Ralph!"

RCA was on me to buy a bus, for image reasons and fearing old Snowball would break down, causing us to miss a show. I had bought a van from a family in Kiowa, so I took the van and Snowball on some shows, giving the band boys extra room. After about a dozen shows, the van broke down, so I had to pull it home with Old Snowball.

RCA kept on at me about purchasing a tour bus and quitting old Snowball. They wanted me to buy Charlie and Reba's bus for a hundred thousand dollars and balloon the note. Against my better judgment, instead, I bought an old worn-out bus we called "Black Bart" and fixed it up. I put hard-earned money (and it loved money) in it to make it road worthy. We traded off driving Black Bart but later hired a great guy from around Poteau, Oklahoma, Scotty Scott.

On one tour, I left the boys in the Northeast to fly to Nashville to do some TV shows and sent the bus to meet me at another show. I got a call from Joey, the road manager, who said, "Pake, we got a problem; we got pulled over by the highway patrol!"

I thought they were speeding, so I said, "Just pay the ticket and go on."

He said, "It wasn't for speeding. Old Black Bart is smokin' so bad that the people behind us cain't see to pass, so the highway patrol made us park it!"

They had it towed to a garage, where they overhauled the engine for five thousand dollars! I'd love to keep your beliefs alive and tell you that all it takes to make money on the road is to have a couple of hit records on the radio and be on several TV shows, but lie to you I will not! A bunch of mistakes in management were made, like touring all over the United States instead of building a following regionally, like Strait did in Texas. Another mistake was having too many band members. I should have stuck with guitar, bass, and drums to cut costs. I was in the hole financially most of the time.

Booking was done by Bobby Roberts Talent, and Bob Younts was the guy that did most of our booking. He played drums for Mel Tillis for eight years when Mel was named entertainer of the year by the Country Music Association. He used to tell us stories about their road days. Like the year after Mel won the CMA Entertainer of the year award, he told the booking agents to book him anywhere and everywhere, not to turn down any offer if they could get there. He said they played 109 straight days or nights; they had twelve bunks on the bus with seventeen people! They didn't carry sound, so sometimes the sound would be old megaphone-shaped speakers. Once there was only one electrical outlet on stage, and it was right above where Mel stood, so the cord hung right in front of Mel's face.

Mel had a brother nicknamed "Bread Man" because he previously ran a bread route for a bread company. He went over twenty years without a single accident, but on the way to his retirement party, the truck stalled on a railroad track and demolished the bread truck.

He sold concessions for the Tillis show, and at one show, two ladies came up to the concessions table where Bread Man was and said, "Do you have a record with the song 'Who's Julie?'?"

Bread Man said, "Yes, ma'am, we have it on a two-album set for ten dollars."

One of the girls said, "I don't want the whole two albums; I just want the song 'Who's Julie?'!"

Bread Man said, "Ma'am, would you give seven dollars for an album with 'Who's Julie?' on it?"

She said, "I sure will!"

Bread Man picked up the two-album set, took the plastic off of it, unfolded the two albums, pulled out his pocket knife, and cut the two albums apart and handed her the album with "Who's Julie?" on it. He collected the seven dollars from the lady and then turned to the other lady and said, "Ma'am, would you like to buy a Mel Tillis album for three dollars?"

She said, "I sure would!"

He took her three dollars and handed her the other album.

One trip, we left Orange, Texas, at 4:00 a.m. after a show, and headed for Chatham, New Brunswick, Canada, 1,659 miles away, with seven of us in the pickup truck and camper. Halfway we were all but worn out. We stopped late one evening at Bangor, Maine, at a motel, just to clean up and go again, when the motel man said, "Boys, ya 'bout got it whipped out; you only lack five hundred miles of all-night driving on a two-lane road!"

At the Canadian border, the customs agents were determined to find drugs on us, so they took everything out of the truck, camper, and trailer and had it all spread out on the ground behind the trailer. They opened every suitcase, duffel bag, road case, and did everything but have us bend over, spread our cheeks, and butt search us! They made us stand inside the office building, looking out through a big, glass window, when they opened a suitcase and pulled out a ziplock bag of white powder.

I said, "Whose bag is that? "

Our bass player from Minnesota said, "It's mine, but it's laundry detergent!"

I said, "It better be, or I'm gonna leave you up here with these Canadians!"

They looked at us through this window, and into the office they went, proud of what they'd found. Shore 'nuff it was laundry detergent, and eight hours later we were on our way.

We were gonna make several shows on the way back, but while in Canada, I got food poisoning! We ate that evening at a fish place that was really good, but when we got back to the hotel, I got real dizzy in the shower. I sat down on the bed and knew something was bad wrong. I made it to the camper and puked out the backdoor, all the evening supper. I remember the band boys backed the truck up, so they could load up the camper. I attempted to sing but couldn't hold the fiddle because it felt like it weighed fifty pounds. I sang about four songs, when it hit me again. In this club, the restrooms were up this long staircase, so I climbed them and continued to shit and puke all at the same time. I went back downstairs and tried to sing some more, resorting to the long staircase again. This process went on until I could do no more. I could only do thirteen songs, so the club owner docked me thirteen hundred dollars. I had to go to the hospital and stay the rest of the night.

I never would let the band boys smoke in the truck for two reasons. One was that I hate cigarette smoke, and the other was we had a hundred-gallon propane tank just behind the backseat, underneath the lower camper bed. On the way back from Canada, we were running on gasoline, and we were all dog tired. The boys had bought some long and skinny stogies called "Player cigarettes" they were all just dying to try. They kept on after me wanting to smoke in the truck. I listened to them go on at me until I said, "OK, under one condition: I get to smoke too!"

They liked to have broken their arms getting out their cigs and lighters. We all fired up, and I noticed they were staring at me! Randy Altenbaumer said (they liked to call me "Pakester"), "Pakester, watching you smoke makes me wanna quit!"

Out on the road, the days and nights all run together. It's hard to remember where you are at the time, let alone where you were last week or even last night! We would talk about that, and some could remember what others couldn't. We had more fun in those almost two years than most folks have in a lifetime! The things you see out on the road are amazing—like the fair we played at where a man had a goat that would blow up balloons! He'd blow up as many as you would hold to his mouth!

On one tour, we had about ten dates with Reba, heading north into Wyoming, to Montana, up into Canada, and back to the Northwest, to Washington State, Oregon, and down to California. We were up in Montana when our bus, Black Bart, wouldn't stay in fourth gear. We did everything we could to get it into fourth, but to no avail. We would always leave for the next one right after we played, not staying to see Reba's show, to make up for things like this. We had to travel 430 miles in third gear, going only thirty-eight miles per hour, and barely got there in time! When we left that show, we tried it again, and it went into fourth gear with no problems. We never did know what was wrong with it before.

During all of this, we opened for popular entertainers like Garth Brooks, Reba, George Strait, Alabama, The Judds, Eddie Raven, Ed Bruce, John Anderson, Keith Whitley, Ronnie Millsap, Marie Osmond,

Moe Bandy, The Belamy Brothers, David Ball, Shenandoah, Asleep at the Wheel, The Everly Brothers, Restless Heart, Eddie Rabbit, Vince Gill, Sawyer Brown, Exile, Earl Thomas Conley, Glen Campbell, and many more. Fans think these people are like God and are above or different than the working-class people, but I found these folks are working-class people that work at a different job, only theirs is of free enterprise. All were down-to-earth and not above their raising at all. Some acted a little inferior, for unknown reasons to me.

RCA released our first record "Every Night," and it went as high as twenty on the Billboard charts; then "Savin' My Love for You" went to number three and was followed by number twelve, "Bad Love." After that, things went downhill, with "Too Old to Grow up Now" somewhere in the forties and then "Heart vs. Heart" in the sixties—all off of the *Too Old to Grow up Now* album. Then we went back into the studio and recorded an album called *My Whole World*, which released "Good God I Had It Good" and "Life in the City." After very little success with those, RCA released me and sent me home.

Reba suggested I pursue MCA records, the label that Vince and Reba were on, but I declined. The girls were still little, and I realized all the things I was missing out on that they were doing, so I decided to come home and help Katy raise them. My ins and outs at home were not fun for them because while I was gone, they had their routine, but when I came home, I changed all of that, and I would hear them ask me, "Dad, when are you going back out on the road again?"

Other band guys said their families said the same thing. Life on the road is not for the family man.

A fan walked up to me in excitement and said, "Are you Pake McEntire?"

I said, "No, ma'am, not anymore."

So far my CDs or albums include, from first to last:

- *Rodeo Man*
- *Back to Back*

- *Too Old to Grow up Now*
- *My Whole World*
- *And They Danced*
- *Your Favorites and Mine*
- *Singin' Fiddlin' Cowboy*
- *The Other Side of Me*

Most of these can be purchased at our website: pakemcentireshow.com.

Chapter 48

TERRY INSCHO

Terry Inscho lived at Chockie and was a big, stout kid, about six foot three, and he had the back of an ox! When Terry was young, he and Kevin McCormick used to walk over to the lots and sit on the fence and watch us work cattle. When they got older, we put them to work. When Terry was about twenty-four, I had one more music show to do before getting off the road, and it was in Dallas, Pennsylvania. I didn't have a band, so the promoter said he'd have one there for the show. I asked Clark if I could borrow Terry to help me drive, so away we went. We stopped in Muskogee to get gas, and when we got back in the truck, I said, "Terry, have you ever been to Pennsylvania?"

Terry said, "I haven't ever been to Muskogee before!"

Chapter 49

GARY COFFEE

Gary Coffe and Clark McEntire. 2012—Sherry Loudermilk Photo

The next story comes from my best friend, Gary Coffee. I first met Gary around 1981 when I had just recorded the *Rodeo Man* album. Back then we had albums, eight tracks, and cassettes. Gary came up to me at Sandman's Drive Inn at Coalgate and asked me if he could take some and try and sell them for me. I gave him a box and completely forgot about it until about two months later when I ran into him again. He walked up and gave me a handful of money and a box with a few unsold cassettes. I tried to give him some of the money, but he refused. Since then, we know so much on each other, we have to be friends!

One day Gary called me up, laughing, and said, "Gotta tell ya something funny!"

I said, "Let 'er hap 'em, Cap'em!"

He said, "A friend over here at Coalgate recently got a divorce, and he told me, 'You know, Gary, I think she still loves me.'

'I said, "What makes you think so?"

'He said, "The other day, she calls me up and said, 'I hope you die the most horrible death of cancer anyone has ever experienced!'"

'I said, "Damn, with an attitude like that, what makes you think she still loves you?"

'He said, "If she didn't still love me, she wouldn't have called me or even thought about me!"'"

*I've been through so many divorces that next time, I think
I'll just find some girl I hate and buy her a house!*
— MICHAEL GILLIAM

Gary is a real people person: he likes to talk with them and is interested in what folks have to say. He was county commissioner here in Coal County and was elected to the Oklahoma State House of Representatives. We even had the pleasure of doing two shows at two different rallies in Davis, Oklahoma, with over one thousand people there, and I like to think we helped a little bit toward the victory.

He loves political rallies and was at one in Stonewall, Oklahoma, at the back of the crowd, talking briefly to a farmer in bib overalls, who was picking his teeth with a toothpick. At the podium, running for associate district judge, was Jess Green, from Ada, talking about "family values." His wife was sitting in the front row, with their little, young daughter standing between her legs. Jess raised his hands and then pointed to his wife and said, "I want you folks to know right here and now: the most important thing in my life is right there between my wife's legs!"

At that moment, everybody looked at his wife, but their little girl had moved over and was sitting in a chair beside her mom! The farmer in overalls standing next to Gary pulled out that toothpick and said, "He's an honest sumbitch, ain't he?"

I called Jess up and asked him if it was all right to include this story, and he said, "Oh yeah, if it will help your book, go ahead. Right after I said that, and the crowd began to get a kick out of it, a local county commissioner stood up and yelled out, 'That's one honest judicial candidate, and I'm gonna vote for him!'"

Gary told me, "When I was in the House of Representatives, one day at the capital, I was visiting with Clem McSpadden and State Senator John Dahl. Clem said, 'I shore do wish I had some of that southeastern Oklahoma moonshine; every now and then, those guys from New York ask me for some.' John said, 'I do, too; been a long time since I had a pull.' They both looked at me and asked if I could get them each a gallon. I told them I'd try. I knew a friend from Tupelo, so I asked him, and he told me he had a contact from Antlers. I picked up two gallons, put them in a brown paper bag, and walked right by the security guard there at the capital, took it up to the top fifth floor to Clem and John. I had my excuse already planned out if I got caught. Hell yes, I did it. In southeastern Oklahoma, we call it economic development!"

I gotta tell ya, I hate politics—period. Arguing about politics is like arguing about religion or abortion. You can spend days talking about the subjects and not solve a friggin' thing! A few folks have suggested I run for a political office, and the first thing I think is, "What did I ever do to make you insult me this way? I thought I was your friend!"

Government takes from the needy and gives to the greedy.
—RONALD REAGAN

Grand Pap was in McAlester when he heard that Will Rogers was coming through on the train and stopping briefly. There was a huge crowd gathered to see the local and national hero. Pap said they introduced Will, and he walked out to the end of the train car; the crowd cheered, and he finally said, "Folks, I'm not running for any political office!" The crowd laughed and cheered, and Will went back inside the car, and the train left.

Chapter 50

GENE STIPE

You can like Gene Stipe, or you can hate him. I choose to like him. On occasion, someone would come up to Gene and say, "Senator, I'm running for a political office, and I need your help."

Gene would say, "OK, you want me to be for you or against you?"

Gene is a yellow-dog Democrat. This saying may have been invented by Gene, meaning, "I'd vote for a yellow dog if he was a Democrat before I'd vote Republican!"

He was in politics and served southeast Oklahoma in either the House of Representatives or the State Senate for over fifty years. A very powerful and influential man in the state and particularly southeastern Oklahoma was Gene. The people he helped could fill a book four inches thick.

This story was told to me after he was out of office, at a Gene Stipe toast-and-roast banquet. An undertaker was at the podium and said, "I was at the office one morning, working on a corpse, when I heard the front doorbell ring. I went up front, and it was Gene. I said, 'Gene, come on back here; I wanna show you something.' On the table was a man who was well endowed in the private sector, if you know what I mean. I pulled the sheet back on the corpse, and we both looked at it, and I said, 'Gene, have you ever in your whole life seen anything like that?'

"Gene said, 'Well, yeah!'

"I said, 'Really? On who?'

"Gene said, 'On me!'

"I said, 'You got one that big?'

"Gene said, 'No, but I got one that dead!'"

The story I got was that one day on the house floor, Gene was speaking against a bill strong and hard, when one of his constituents, Senator Capps, from western Oklahoma, came up and whispered, "Senator, you are supposed to be in favor of this bill; in fact, you're the coauthor!"

Gene turned to the crowd and said, "And now that I've told you all the bad things about this bill, I'm gonna tell you all the good things about it!" Gene turned it all around, and the bill passed!

While running for U.S. Senate against David Boren and an unknown independent, all three were at a political rally, hoping to gain support. They let the independent have a go at the podium first. He said, "Folks, I wanna give you two reasons why you should vote for me instead of my two opponents. One is a crook, and the other is a queer!"

Gene launched up out of his chair, turned around to the crowd, and yelled out, "I'm the crook!"

Gene was a fighter when it came to legalities and could courageously stand up to the IRS, the federal government, or anyone, but when his brother Francis died, being tenderhearted like he is and for the love of his brother, he showed his emotions, just like all of us.

Any man who thinks he can be happy and prosperous by letting the government take care of him better take a closer look at the American Indian.

—HENRY FORD

Chapter 51

LITTLE KIDS

Little kids: As of present, I do not have any grandkids, but if any of you grandkids from the future get ahold of this book, you better not let your mama hear you talk like your Grand Pappy Pake, or I guarantee she will whip yore little ass! I don't know you yet, but I know her well!

Autumn, Reba, Pake, Calamity. About 1985—Family Photo

I do like kids. What, Pake, you don't love kids? Well, hell yeah, I love my own kids! But there is a difference between liking and loving. Haven't you ever seen *Shenandoah* with James Stewart? If not, better get it, boy! You can love someone but not like them. I always loved my kids, but when they were little, at any point when I didn't like them, I simply changed them. I wrote in a bio one time when asked about my pet peeves—things I cain't stand are parents of misbehaving children. I was watching one of those TV shows the other night about a nanny coming into this younger couple's house and advising them on what to do with their misbehaving children. This couple was living proof that some people should not have children. These kids would throw the damnedest fits for hours upon hours, and they tried everything but the right thing. Seems people are afraid to give them what they need. Spare the rod and spoil the child. They are afraid the government will step in and take their kids for cutting a switch and using it on them. I never had it happen, but if one a my kids had ever threatened to call DHS for a much-needed thrashing, then I would simply dial the number for them, and see how they like living with the government!

I asked Clark one time what he would do if Mama ever locked him out of the house, when he said, "I'd set the house on fire and wait'll she came out!"

Now what in the hell has that got to do with raising kids? Only this. Sometimes one has to be stubborn. Bear in mind that no one (myself included) is a perfect parent. It's an imperfect job and full of mistakes. I think that if a parent does these things, they will get along better than usual.

Number one is never lie to the child. Time and time again, I've heard parents say, "If you don't quit that, I'm gonna jerk your arm off and beat you to death with it!"

That's bullshit. Everyone including the kid knows that's a lie.

The other big mistake is to say, "Don't do that, don't do that, don't do that, don't do that, don't do that!" Get the picture? When you put a jerk line on a steer horse, and it's dragging behind him and tied to the shank of the bits, and you get off of him, and he takes off running, you holler, "Whoa!"—*once*. Then you hook the jerk line over your hip and *stop him*! Same way with kids.

Katy used to tell me, "The kids do what you say the first time you tell them, and I have to tell them over and over!" The secret to this is to tell them once at an early age and then back it up. Too many times I just shake my head when I hear a mother say, "Oh, he's only three; he's too young to discipline." What a crock of unadulterated horseshit! If you tell the children twice, then you're lying to them. This means the first time was a lie. That's right; I'm sayin' it: too many parents are liars! Why? Because their parents were liars, too, and lied to them the first time when they didn't back it up, and they think that is the way to do it! When they get into society, they think they can get by with it until they are told three or four times. Then the law steps in and sends them to jail or prison. If you don't lie to them, then they are respecting you and will listen to you when you try to teach them other things.

The second thing is teach them how to work!

Feed a man fish, and you feed him for a day. Teach a man to fish, and you feed him for life.
—A WISE PERSON

Give them responsibilities at an early age, and teach them to be responsible! I'm not saying put them on a backhoe at age five, but simple little chores of responsibility, like "hand me this" or "hand me that." Try to do things with them; don't send them to do things all the time; go with them, and do it with them.

At Pittsburg, I used to shoe the roping and ranch horses, and the girls would hand me the tools. I'd say, "I'll do the tall stuff, and you do the short stuff."

Take them with you whenever you can, and never, never, never pass up a chance to teach them something or build integrity. Don't let things go by, saying, "Oh, the teacher at school will straighten her out!"

People that use the teacher excuse shouldn't have kids. There are many other things you have to do to be a good parent, but these few are the golden rules. I have found that most (not all) teachers are bad parents because for some reason they use the time-out bullshit or the I'm-gonna-ground-you bullshit or the "you can't do sports if your grades ain't up to par." I say, don't punish them in a way that keeps them from learning and succeeding at what they are good at. For example, if their grades are failing, and they love to play fiddle, don't take the fiddle away from them until they are passing at school. Tell them one time that if they don't get their grades up by a deadline, that you are gonna cut a switch—now get your ass in there and play that fiddle! Most important, remember to back it up. It ain't gonna work if you lie to them and don't back it up.

Sometimes one has to appear mad-dog mean to get a point across to a hardheaded child. I would not teach in a school that did not permit paddling. The first time a boy or girl (high school, for example) seriously got out of line, I would bend them over a desk in front of all the class and use the board on them. This stops any further bullshit from that kid or any other.

I liked Kiowa High School, but too many times, I've seen a spoiled high school boy start picking and picking at a man teacher, and he would warn him and warn him, taking up time; students wanting to learn had to sit through this bullshit until finally the teacher, after a half dozen threats, would go bend him over the desk and whip the piss out of the dumb bastard, and the kid would cry like a little baby.

That advice is worth just what it cost ya!
— ROBIN LACY

Now on the funnier side. One day, Alice needed a babysitter for little Trevor, who then was about four or five, so she called Reba up. Reba and Charlie lived east of Stringtown, so after Alice dropped him off, Reba went through the house, showing little Trevor what not to touch. A little later that morning, Reba and Trevor got into it crossways about something, so little Trevor throws him a little cowboy fit and starts running all through the house, knocking everything over and off tables, the very things Reba had told him not to touch. Reba ran to the phone and called Alice and said, "You come and get this little bastard!"

I'd a whipped his little ass, made him put back the things he knocked over, and then been his best friend. I thought it was funny that Alice had to leave work and go get him.

Another time, little Trevor was sitting in the front row at church, getting a little rowdy with some other little boys. His dad, Robert, came down the aisle and picked Trevor up and headed up the aisle to the backdoor. Trevor looked over his dad's shoulder and said to the congregation, "Y'all pray for me!"

Any time I got the chance to have fun with the girls, I'd take it. One morning Katy was in the kitchen cooking breakfast when the girls and I were wrestling in our bed. Calamity did something, and I told her playfully that I was gonna call the sheriff and haul her off to jail. We had two phones: one in the bedroom and one in the kitchen. Instead of the sheriff, I called Katy in the kitchen and said, "Sheriff, I have a girl that needs to go to jail; just keep her there until she straightens up. When you get here, come to the back bedroom and knock on the door. Thanks, Sheriff."

Calamity didn't believe the prank, so she ran over to the door and backed up against it and put her arms out to the side and said, "I'm not gonna let that sheriff get through this door!" In about five seconds, Katy knocked real hard on that door, and Calamity's eyes got bigger than a silver dollar, and she ran, jumped in bed, and grabbed me around the neck and looked at the door! We all had a big laugh out of that!

He's as happy as a dead pig in the sunshine!
—Jac McEntire

Katy's mom and dad, Betty and Chief, babysat Autumn some when she was little. I loved teaching her things like counting to ten in English and Mexican before she was two. Chief had read the "Brer Rabbit" story on a big-page storybook so many times, that one day we were all up there, and Chief showed us how Autumn could read the book by memorizing the words by looking at the pictures. Pretty remarkable to see her do that.

One night, she came home from Chief and Betty's, and I was on my last leg, worn smooth out. Here came little Autie with a storybook. I said, "Autumn, didn't Paw and Granny read enough to you today?"

She said, "No, Dad, they're old!

I told Chief and Betty what she said, and we all had a good laugh—that they were too old to read.

When Chism was about four or five, the Thanksgiving and Christmas holidays were approaching. Katy and I were discussing with the kids what we all wanted to do over the up-and-coming holidays. When it came Chism's turn, she said, "I wanna go see *Home Alone 2*, at theaters everywhere!"

Harold Toaz told me one time to hold our kids back a year, beginning first grade to purposely have them be older than the rest of the class, and that we would never regret it. Chism was born July 15, 1985, and when she had just turned five, we reluctantly sent her to Linda Casey, the Kiowa Head Start teacher. Linda was in the same grade with Alice at Kiowa and was a great person and teacher. Katy, Linda, and I, all made a pact that at the end of Chism's kindergarten year, if she showed any signs of immaturity, regardless of grades, we would hold her back another year. When I visited her class at Easter, I noticed Chism was very quiet and reserved, not outgoing like at home. So at the end of the year, she had good grades but on her achievement test showed obvious signs of immaturity. Only one choice, right? Keep her in kindergarten another year, plain and simple—no problem, right? Wrong!

Chism told Katy that she wanted to go on with her classmates and not be held back. I completely understood how she felt. Now my choices were to go with a five-year-old's wishes or stand my ground and do the right thing. Here came Katy, suggesting we let her go on. Here came Clark, scolding me for being cruel, saying I ought to be ashamed of myself for holding her back and not letting her be with her friends.

Katy told Chism that she needed to go to me and convince me to let her go. (Yeah, thanks a lot.) I'll never forget that day. I was sitting at the kitchen table when she walked up to me. I could tell by the look in her eyes: it took a lot of courage to say what was coming. Big ole tears came to her eyes, as she said, "Daddy, I want to move on to the first grade and be with all my friends."

Part of me wanted to cave in, but I just couldn't make myself do the wrong thing. I reached down, picked her up, held her in my arms, and said,

"Chis, you will make new friends in kindergarten, and your old friends will be just next door, and you can still play with them on the playground at recess."

This decision was one of the hardest ones I ever had to make as a father, but somehow I was able to hold my ground. She came home from school the first day and said, "Daddy, all those kids say I'm so smart!" I knew then she had stopped being a follower and became a leader. Thanks, Mr. Toaz.

Chism McEntire. 2000—Family Photo

When Chism was about ten or eleven, I taught her how to drive a pickup. Now, she had been sitting in my lap and steering the truck since she was about five or six, but now it was time to learn how to drive a four speed with a clutch. At the time, I had a three-quarter-ton, black, four-wheel-drive Chevy I'd bought off of Greg Sexton, and she was going to learn on that one. We had a pretty steep hill that led to the house from the county road, so I told her to get a run at it and don't let it die going up it, which was exactly what happened.

When it died, it started rolling backward, so she pushed in on the clutch and brake, got it stopped, looked over at me a little nervous, and said, "Now what?"

I said, "Keep your clutch in with your left foot, put your right heel on the brake, and put your right toe on the accelerator; turn the key on, and start the engine. Let out on the clutch slowly with your left foot, while letting off the brake slowly with your right heel, and giving it a little gas with your right toe all at the same time. Don't pop the clutch with your left foot because if you do, it will just spin the rear wheels since we are on this steep hill."

She looked at me and said, "You gotta be kiddin'!"

I noticed sweat beads beginning to pop out on her face, when she took a death grip on the steering wheel, revved up the engine to the sound of a jet airplane, let off the brake, popped the clutch, and the tires went to spinning, and the back end was bouncing up and down, slinging gravel down the hill for at least twenty feet, when it finally took hold and made it up the hill.

The next time she drove up that hill, she got a run at it like she was at the Daytona 500! I said, "Chism, you don't have to go so fast!"

She said, "I don't want to let it die like it did the last time!"

Pake, Shelby Blackstock, and Clark. About 1992—Family Photo

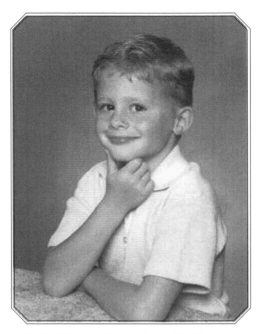

Shelby Blackstock, age five—Family Photo

When Shelby was in kindergarten, the teacher took the class to El Chico's for a class outing. Shelby told the waitress, "I'll have a strawberry daiquiri made by virgins."

Randy Dobbs and Buddy Boy Bryant were in Hunts Department Store in McAlester, just before Christmas. They slipped off from their moms and found Santa Claus. Randy got up on Santa's lap, and Santa asked, "Well, have you been a good little boy?"

Randy said, "Oh yeah, Santa, I've been a good little boy."

Santa said, "What about your little friend there. Has he been a good little boy?"

Randy said, "Oh no, Santa, he hit me on the nose yesterday."

Buddy suddenly went to screamin' and crying, running up and down the aisles of the store until he found his mom and said, "Mama, that son of a bitch told Santa I've been a bad boy, and I won't get a goddamned thang for Christmas!"

Chapter 52

BUTT HOLE BUTTONS

I hate most Shetlands for kids, but Uncle Slim (Leslie Thompson) had a Shetland named Buttons that was pretty good. Most of his grandkids rode him until they outgrew him and then passed him on to the next kid. When Autumn was real little, after she went to bed on Christmas Eve, I drove to Atoka and picked up old Buttons and brought him home. That Christmas morning, I got up early and tied old Buttons up to the back porch and told Autumn Santa Claus had brought her a horse. She asked, "How did he get him here?"

I said, "In his sleigh."

She asked, "How he did he do that with all the other presents?" (I knew this answer and used it when I would get hemmed up with kids.)

I said, "With magic!"

She said, "Oh."

Now, old Buttons was starting to get some age on him and could be a little ornery, so we nicknamed him "Butt Hole" Buttons.

A couple of years later, Calamity would ride him and help pen sick cattle or help me practice roping. When I would saddle all the horses, I'd saddle old Buttons first, and she liked to ride him around the house. She repeatedly loped him and turned him at a certain spot, and he would drop his shoulder and go back to the tack room. I told her to quit letting him do that and lope him past that point. She was expecting to go past that point when he dropped his shoulder wheeling back to the tack room, sending her flying off the other side. She jumped up and looked straight at me and said, "He bucked me off!"

I kinda laughed and said, "No, he didn't; you just fell off!"

One day at the roping pen when she was about five, Calamity and ole Buttons were in the crowding pen, turning out the steers, so I could practice tying them down. I kept the front gate open and put several tires in the chute, so it would slow the steers down and they couldn't get such a running start on me. I told her to bring one at a time, and she could do it. We were getting along real well, when I roped this one steer, went to the end of it to trip the steer, and for some reason the rope came off. I was over in the stirrup, and the last thing I remember was the ground coming at me. I woke up lying on the ground with a splitting headache, and the horse standing over at the fence with the rope tied to the saddle horn. I caught him and rode back to the pens where Calamity was still on the Shetland, and I asked her, "How long was I down there?"

She simply said, "Long time."

Shoot low, Sheriff; he's ridin'a Shetland!
—UNKNOWN

Chapter 53

THE BREMMER

We used to get steers in by the loads from Mississippi, and one time a Bremmer (this is cowboy slang for "Brahma") steer came up to the feed truck and started being real friendly. I knew he had been somebody's pet. You could pet and rub around on him, and he liked it. We put a halter on him and found out he would lead. Calamity wanted me to take him to school for show-and-tell. She asked the principal, Mr. Casey, and he told her that if he messed in the classroom, she had to clean it up, so she asked me if I would meet them all at the playground during recess. I was dreading this ordeal a little because I didn't really know how this Bremmer was gonna react to all of this. I could just see him head butting, kicking, or stepping on one of the children. I sure as hell didn't want any kid hurt!

Calamity Jo McEntire, eight years old—Family Photo

I unloaded him at the playground that day and waited a few minutes. When the bell rang, all of a sudden out of nowhere, I looked up and here comes a thundering herd of kids out of that school like a bunch of wild Comanches! I thought, "Oh shit! Now what?" Those kids ran up to that steer, just a-grabbing and a-rubbing him everywhere imaginable, and that steer didn't even untrack. That steer seemed to like all the attention they were giving him.

One evening Greg Sexton came over to the house to practice roping, and he stayed for supper; then we got on the beer. We went outside to the lots and caught this steer with a halter and led him to the tack room, saddled him up, and led him into the house! The kids thought this was really neat, but thought I would get in trouble with Katy, especially when we put him on the hearth in front of the fireplace and took pictures. During that whole ordeal, even after leading him though the kitchen, he never pissed or shit on anything. Hell, I've seen kids that didn't act as good as that steer!

Chapter 54

CBS SPECIAL

Alice, Susie, and I helped Narvel and Reba do a CBS special one time. The camera crew came to Stringtown and Chockie and filmed us riding horses, doing interviews, and so forth.

Clark, Susie, Reba, Jac, Alice, and Pake at
Chockie. 1999—Family Photo

They wanted to see Reba, Alice, and Susie run barrels and for me to rope and tie down some steers. We met Butch Mellor up at Melvin Hall's house south of McAlester, and Rocky Garnett brought some of his roping steers over there. I had two horses, called "Woodrow" and "Houdini," and they ran barrels on Houdini, and he took to it like a duck to water, even though it was his first time.

The next ten pictures were taken at Melvin Hall's house just south of McAlester.

Susie and Houdini—Family Photo

Reba and Houdini—Family Photo

When I backed into the box for the first time, preparing to tie down this steer, I looked down the arena, and the camera crew was right in the middle of the roping pen.

I said, "Hey, y'all, you better back up a little bit, maybe all the way to the back fence." After I ran a couple and they saw what we were doing, they said, "We're sure glad you told us to back up."

Pake and Houdini roping steer—Family Photo

Pake tying steer at Melvin's for CBS Special—Family Photo

I remember backing in the box, and the filming crew wanted to shoot Alice, Reba, and Susie putting the steers in the chute to turn them out for me to rope. I was feeling a little cocky and told Alice to step it up a little and quit drag assin' around, when she point blank told me to kiss her ass! Felt just like old times.

Pake, Houdini, Alice, Susie, and Reba—Family Photo

Reba shutting the front gate.
(Making a hand!)—Family Photo

Susie and Mama visitin'—Family Photo

There's just something about being in a roping pen that brings back memories and smiles.

Back row: Narvel, Mama, Reba, Autumn Calamity,
Sandi Spika, Susie—Family Photo

Pake, Calamity, Mama, Butch Mellor, Autumn, Daddy,
Max Kinyon, and Wayne Blankenship—Family Photo

Max Kinyon, Alice, Reba, Daddy, and Shelby—Family Photo

Chism and Luchesse—Family Photo

For us helping with the TV special, Narvel and Reba took us all on an Alaskan Cruise. Plans were that I was to rope at the Ben Johnson

Memorial Steer Roping at Pawhuska, on a Sunday afternoon, and meet up with them at the Tulsie Airport. Mark Sandman went with us to bring the horse and rig back home.

After the roping, we stopped and ate supper at Wynona, my favorite place to eat. When we got on the private plane, things were more than a little bit tense. Turns out they hadn't eaten yet, and when a McEntire gets hungry, they get cranky, in this case downright bitchy—and then mean as a rattlesnake. (Notice I said "they.")

Reba said directly to me in a less than pleasant tone of voice, "Where in the hell have y'all been, and what took ya so long?"

I said, "The steer roping took longer because of the wild cow milking."

They began to hand out Styrofoam plates of food, and I turned it down, saying we had already eaten. At that moment she turned from Reba McEntire, the country music superstar everybody loves, to Little Miss Hateful!

She said, "You mean, you stopped and ate?"

I said "Yeah, you didn't tell us y'all had something here and that we were all gonna eat on the plane!"

I noticed then I was falling into the Mr. Hateful syndrome in my tone of voice too.

She began to light in on me, saying, "We have been sitting here for over two hours waiting on you…" Blah, blah, blah! (You get the drift.)

At the time, Little Miss Hateful was used to pushing people around because she paid everyone's bills, and they just took her bullshit, but she forgot she duddin' pay my bills, so before I thought about what I should have said, right in front of Clark and Jac, I stopped her in the middle of all of this and said, "Now, you just hold it right there. I didn't wanna go on this fuckin' trip in the first place. I'm getting off, and you can go straight to hell!"

I was settin' in the inside next to the window, had my feet up in the seat, stepping over Katy on my way out the door when Reba said, "All right, hold it! We've gotten all that out of the way; now, let's just put this behind us, and let's go have some fun."

I looked at her and got back in my seat, feeling like an immature kid for the way I'd acted. I reached up and turned on the air vent, pointed it right at my face, and asked if anybody had any whiskey. I looked at them, and no one answered, avoiding more of the storm I guess.

We first flew to Vancouver, BC, and met up with the rest of the family, twenty-three in all. We toured the city for a couple of days, going through this beautiful flower garden. (This duddin' sound very cowboy, does it?) I remember all the Chinese tourists there, and when you met them, walking toward them, I noticed they wouldn't try to move over, like they expected us to walk around them. I thought I was the only one experiencing this when Narvel said, "I'm through dodging Chinese people; they can move over a little too; from now on they can just get shoulder bumped!"

We then boarded the ship headed for the Alaska coastline and continued on with the best vacation I was ever on. We ported, went on a rubber raft ride down a glacier-fed stream, went on a train ride up in the mountains, where the old timers prospected for gold. Garrett tried to back out of the train ride because of celebrating too much the night before with the younger bunch, but Reba insisted on her going since they paid a hundred dollars a ticket. She went but kept her head on the side of the passenger car, the whole way sufferin' death.

After we got back on the ship, we ate so much we decided to join the exercise class, so we could eat more, when we discovered the hot-looking lady giving the class was from Tulsie! The ship ported in Ketchikan, Skagway, and Juneau.

At one port, we were standing on the balcony of the ship and heard someone playing country music downtown. I suggested to Katy that we go down there and listen to them play up close. Turns out it was two of them, a guitar and sax player, singing on the street for tips. When they took a break, I asked, "Where are you boys from?"

One of them said, "I'm from Oklahoma City, Oklahoma."

I said, "What places have you played there?"

He named the Continental Club, so I asked him, "Do you know Joey Giovannetti, Kent Johnson, and Rick Johnston?"

He said, "Who are you?"

I told him, and he said, "I was working with them at the Continental Club when you hired them all to go on the road with you, and they asked me if I wanted to go too, but I decided to stay home."

Like they say: it's a small world!

— Gus McCrae

At one port, we went into the Red Dog Saloon that Johnny Horton sang about in his song "North to Alaska." Some of us had the legendary drink called "The Duck Fart."

If you haven't been on an Alaskan cruise, do yourself a favor and go. I didn't wanna go in the beginning, but they had to pry my hands off the railing of that ship, sayin', "Sir, you don't have to go home; you just cain't stay here!" Thanks, Narvel and Reba, for a more-than-memorable time.

Chapter 55

CANCUN

Narvel and Reba have a vacation home in Cancun, Mexico, and invited me to come down there on a family visit. About a couple of weeks before leaving, Clark said, "Are you goin' down nare?"

I said, "Oh yeah!"

He said, "You won't like it!"

I said "Why not?"

He said, "That ole ocean just goes *aaahhhhmmm…aahhhmmm…*over and over, and just aggravates the hell outta me."

I told him, "That thang's been doing that for a long time."

I said to myself that I was gonna prove him wrong but found out the real reason he didn't like it after we got there.

Debbie Crawley and I were dating, so she went with me. We ate dinner and had some drinks at the bar in the DFW airport waiting on our plane. We got on the beer big-time, and I began buying drinks for folks around us I didn't even know. By the time we got to Cancun, I had sobered up a little, when Debbie asked me, "Where are we going when we get to the airport?"

I said, "I don't know."

Then she said, "Who is meeting us at the airport to pick us up?"

I said, "I don't know."

I really didn't know all of these questions. At home there are responsibilities times ten, and when I go on a vacation, I like to be totally irresponsible. On all our show tours, Debbie took care of all the road management down to the last detail. She obviously thought I had taken care of all the details on this trip. Debbie, with a quiet, laid-back personality, was beginning to get this concerned look. When we got our luggage at the baggage claim, she turned to me and said, "What do we do now?"

I looked around and saw a man stationed at this counter. I said, "Go up to that man and ask him where we go to find a taxi or someone to take us where we need to go."

She came back with look of panic and said, "He told me that we are to go through that door, but when we do, we can't come back in because that is Mexico!"

I said, "Well, Mexico is where they all are, so let's go!"

We walked outside, and there was a big crowd of people with signs held up in front of them. I said, "You go this way, and I'll go that way, and if you find someone with our names on their sign, holler out."

Pretty soon I heard her: she'd found a man with a "McEntire" sign. He loaded us up in a new van, and we got a seat right behind him. I noticed the man didn't speak much English, when Debbie asked me, "Where are we going?" I said, "Hell, I don't know; for all I know, he's gonna take us out in the woods and rob us!" The driver started laughing at us, so I knew we were safe.

He took us to Jimmy Buffet's Margaritaville, and it was about one thirty in the afternoon, where all the family were all havin' a high-bobbin' good time! They were all laughin', tellin' funny stories; the food was good, and I told Debbie this was gonna be a fun three days! Jac and Luchesse were singing and laughing and holding up this big wall as we were all walking back to the house.

From that day on, it all went downhill because the next day they were all so hung over they wouldn't drink anymore. I had my back brace on most of the time from the back surgery earlier that year but could take it off to go snorkeling. I had my head down looking at the purty fishes and coral reefs, and we were all in this roped-off section. I bumped into someone, looking up to find my face stuck right up this big, fat lady's ass!

The next day, Paul, Robert, Alice, and a few more were gonna go deep-sea fishing. They wanted me and Debbie to go, but I was afraid it would be too rough for my back, so we declined. They came back saying we'd better be glad we didn't go because it was like a buckin' bronc the whole time, and they got sicker'n shit!

They decided to go bowling, and I had to watch because I was not to pick up anything over ten pounds, and the twisting didn't sound good either. Debbie had some sandals on and forgot to bring socks for the bowling shoes. If you've ever seen me dress, you know that my give-a-shitter broke a long time ago when it comes to what folks think about my wardrobe, and on this day I had on unmatching socks, a red top and a blue top. I had another pair just like 'em at home. Debbie needed socks, so I took mine off and gave them to her, when she said, "You'd think that one day out of the year you would have socks that matched!"

She didn't decline from having a good time, so she put them on, and I admired her for it.

Now, before we left home, everyone not kin had told me what a great time we were gonna have down there because they had. Ya see, people that ain't in the public business can go down there, stay at modest places, go to places where they meet new people from the States, party with a crowd of people, get a little drunk, let loose kinda speak. Now don't get me wrong: I appreciate Narvel and Reba for inviting us and showing us a good time, but you cain't have much fun around them because they have to avoid the public. They like to go to real expensive places where the food is half as much, not tasty, and three times the price. You cain't stand up and holler, "Yee haw!" or you might get thrown out! You look around, and there's a rich-looking old man with two beautiful long-legged big-titted hookers at his table, looking bored stiff out of their minds, or a family with a bunch of little children.

Alice ordered something that was still on fire on some coals on top of the table, which smelled like it had rotted for a couple of days. Now, I can eat almost anything, but that made me a little woozy just smellin' it.

Reba likes to play sit-down games of all kinds, to fill her competitive needs, or sit and relax and read a book. I wanted to go have a rip-roaring good time. You cain't very well go on your own way 'cause they want you to stay around them. On this trip Debbie and I reminisced that the best time we had was at Jimmy Buffet's and the Dallas–Fort Worth Airport.

Chapter 56

BASKETBALL

When we moved from McAlester to Pittsburg in 1978, Katy's girl Becky was about eight, and Autumn was just born. Later of course Calamity and Chism came along. The kids eventually went to Kiowa School because that's where I went. They all three fell in love with basketball from the third grade and played until they were in high school, with Chism playing college ball for four years. Ever since they were old enough to learn, I've had them doing things from singing to digging postholes. Katy and I always kept them busy doing something constructive and positive. I was never one to interfere with the school's business of running the school except for one time, and here's the story.

When Autumn and Calamity entered high school, local boy Wade Daniels was the high school girls basketball coach. Wade was a good guy, came from a good family. His dad, Robert, used to come to our place and help fight fires. The two girls would come in and tell us about Wade's coaching, and most of it didn't make sense. Finally I told them one day to either make the best of it and take it as it was, or we could go before the school board and suggest Wade be removed and a new coach put in. That was my mistake. I should have picked a third option and taken them to another school, like we did in the long run.

We went to the school board meeting, where about four hundred people showed up, with about 95 percent for Wade. But when the vote among the board members came, it was a narrow 4–3 for keeping him. We then loaded up the three kids and took them to Canadian school forty miles away. Basketball was the first-hour class, and they had to be on the floor ready to play at 7:00 a.m. The coach there was Jim Jensen, who just hated to loose. You are probably thinking we had lost our ever-lovin' minds, since there were nine schools closer, but we wanted them to be with a good coach and a good team. The way it turned out, my only regret on this whole deal was we should have gone two years sooner. Autumn's senior year made it to state but was beaten in the semifinals. Calamity's junior year won the state tournament championship, out scoring their opponents the last three games by a total of seventy-three points.

One of the highlights of that year happened in January. I was in Odessa at the rodeo, when they were invited to the Tournament of Champions at Wilburton, Oklahoma. This tournament consisted of some of the best teams in the state, no matter what class. Canadian, a 1A school, matched up with Sapulpa, a 5A school. Calamity's shot just at the buzzer tied them up and put them into overtime. When the dust finally settled, Canadian beat the huge Sapulpa school by three points and went on to win the tournament. Sapulpa went on to win the Class 5A State Championship, and their loss to Canadian that night was their only defeat for the whole year!

Another highlight that happened that year was bittersweet. We were scheduled to play Kiowa, at Kiowa—my hometown and my home school. Kiowa had five starting seniors compared to Canadian's two. Kiowa had the best team they had had in several years. Before the game that night, I was visiting with some of the parents I had gone to school with, really trying to be nice (since most of them were mad at us for leaving), and one parent told me they were going to play us real close because they had a good team this year. I commented that I hoped so, and that it would be a good game. When the dust settled, Canadian beat Kiowa, 52–9. Jensen was big on defense, and that was one of his strong points. He used to say, "Offense wins games, but defense wins championships."

I don't think I could have won even a dog catchers election race at Kiowa after that game.

Canadian came back the next year to win runner-up Calamity's senior year. When I attended these tournaments, I learned a lot about kids. I found out that other schools who didn't make the state playoffs and got put out either in the district, regional, or area tournaments would bring their basketball teams to Oklahoma City and watch other teams that did. This was to bring up their belief level. To show them there really are teams making it to the state tournament, and there really is a state champion at the very last game.

I also saw that about 90 percent of the time, the same schools made it to the state tournament year after year. I also noticed schools that rarely made it to the big tournament were ecstatically, deliriously happy just to get into the first game of the tournament. I saw that we were that way when Autumn made it the first year as a senior. But after they were there, the second time is different. They wanted more.

For example, when Calamity's team won runner-up after winning the state championship the year before, after it was all over that night and the kids got dressed and loaded up on the bus, Jenson noticed the second-place trophy was not on the bus. He asked, "Where's the trophy?"

No one seemed to know or care. They had not achieved what they set out to do, and that was to win state. Second place was totally unacceptable to all of them. He had to go back into the dressing room and get the real nice trophy himself because the kids didn't want to be reminded of the loss or failure they had just experienced. I love this about athletes and competition. Ya see, this is what makes winners. Expectations go up as achievements go up. Some parents would be disappointed at them not wanting to accept anything but the gold-ball championship trophy, but I thought it was a neat way of thinking big and was proud as hell of all of them.

You show me a good loser, and I'll show you a real loser!
— PAKE MCENTIRE

When Chism was a freshman, there was a change in the coaching staff at Canadian. Jim Jenson left to retire, when they hired another coach, and Chism got behind her freshman and sophomore year. During Chism's junior year, Jensen then came out of retirement and got a coaching job at Alva, way out in the western panhandle of Oklahoma. Katy and I had recently divorced, so she and Chism moved to Alva. They won the state tournament in Class 3A basketball, and went on to win runner-up Chism's senior year. Chism got a full scholarship to play ball at Miami, Oklahoma, Junior College, where one night she hit nine three-pointer shots and set the record for the most three-pointer shots made at home. She went on to play at Rolla, Missouri, for two years, also on a paid scholarship.

Looking back on all of this, I feel mixed emotions about all the moving we did while the kids were still in high school. I feel bad toward leaving Kiowa and hurting their basketball program. But my responsibility was to my kids, not the school. The school is there for the kids and the kids only, not just so someone can keep their job. I feel lucky that our kids didn't have a car wreck, driving that far, eighty miles a day. Was it more expensive compared to a local school? Hell yeah! But it was cheaper in the long run because of the jobs Calamity got from it. Had she not gone to Canadian and been on a team that won state, she may not have gotten jobs recruiting and assisting coaches at colleges. Had Chism not been on a team that won state, she may not have gotten the scholarships to play college ball. If John McEntire taught me anything, he taught me to be all you can be. Go for it. Hit 'em a lick! As you may know, it ain't easy making all the right decisions as a parent, and I ain't saying I made all right ones, but I did the best I could do. After the dust settled, a few parents came up to me and said that they wished they had moved their kids and gave them the same opportunity Katy and I gave ours.

Chapter 57

THE GHOST

In 1977 the famous Hunt brothers, Bunker in particular, got deeper in the ranching business and bought more than one hundred thousand acres in southeastern Oklahoma. These people trying to ranch would be like me attempting to be an astronaut. In five years they made about every mistake there was to ranching. They bought a place called Pine Tree and Pine Top, twelve thousand acres of hill country near Daisy, Oklahoma. One of their mistakes was chaining (that's tying an anchor chain between two D-nine dozers and dragging down the timber) the timber and burning it instead of logging it. Some say they chained and burned over a million dollars' worth of timber. To them a million bucks was chicken feed. They hired over thirty so-called cowboys to run it all for them, when some of the help started stealing T-posts, barbed wire, feed, seed, and diesel—anything they could get their hands on. They tried to sell us feed, but we told them we weren't in the habit of keeping thieves in business, so they didn't ask us again. I will admit, they dug many ponds for water and did a lot of fencing. After one profitable year out of five, they decided to get out of the ranching business and lease out some of the ranches. Clark told me Pine Tree and Pine Top was for lease, so I leased it. This was a magnificent ranch, and I really loved operating it. The first year—I think, 1983—was not good because I got into a drought. Clark, Charlie Battles, and I kept the lease for over ten years, all having it in different years. When the place sold, Clark wound up with the southern half of the place, called "Pine Tree," of about sixty-five hundred acres. All of us except Clark fell in love with the place, but he bought it to trade on. Every time he'd set a price, the real-estate brokers would bid under what he wanted; then the price of land would go up, so he'd go up. We all but begged him not to sell it, but the thrill of this magnitude was just too irresistible.

One year at Pine Tree, Glenn Hyde was living in the first house near the pens and was helping me work the cattle. We dry lotted about fifty bulls (so they wouldn't bleed so much after castration) one evening and were gonna cut them the next morning. Glenn said he may have a guy come and help us. The next morning, I picked Glen up at the house, and we went to the barn, loaded up some hay, and went to the hay meadow and fed some steers. As we were coming back to the barn, some cattle across the fence to our right were walking toward the feed truck. It was a little bit foggy that morning, but as I looked at those cattle, plain as day, walking along with them was a man dressed in a 1940s brown hat, pointed in the front like Indiana Jones; khaki britches; and a short brown light jacket, with a stick in his hand, looking down dabbling at the ground as he walked. I noticed the cattle weren't paying any attention to him. I looked over at Glenn and pointed at the man and said, "Is that the guy who's gonna help us?"

We both looked in the direction of the man, and he was gone! Glenn looked at me and said, "He's at the house."

We went directly to the house and picked up a fat kid in a T-shirt. Before this happened, I couldn't say that I believed in ghosts, but then again I couldn't say that I didn't. Was this a ghost? Was it a figment of my feeble imagination? Was I suddenly under some kind of hypnosis, schizophrenia, bipolar, manic depression, hallucinations, an out-of-body experience, or was this really a ghost? Now this didn't scare, upset, or spook me in any way; it was more like a calming feeling.

Glenn moved out of the house that fall and worked for us off and on. About two years later, I got a call from Flip (Philip Miller), and he said, "You remember that story you told me about the ghost at Pine Tree? Two game wardens came into the restaurant last night and told me they were out at Pine Tree the other day, patrolling, and said they drove by the house Glen used to live in, and someone was standing at the window of one of the rooms looking at them. They stopped and went inside, but no one was there. Also Joe Ward was at Pine Tree one day, riding his four-wheeler, and passed by the house and went around the bend just before the little creek past the pens, when someone jumped on behind him on his four-wheeler! When he stopped, no one was there! He said it was the most eerie feeling he ever felt!"

I didn't believe in ghosts before because I'd never seen one, but I think that was one I saw that day at Pine Tree. I hadn't seen one before that day, nor have I seen one since.

This guy was attending college at night and was sitting in the back of the room when the instructor was lecturing about supernatural beings and such; he asked, "Has anyone here tonight had any contact with a ghost?"

A few in the crowd, including the guy in the back, raised their hands. The instructor asked another question, "Has anyone had any physical contact with one?"

All lowered their hands except the guy in the back. The instructor said, "Sir, what kind of physical contact have you had?"

The guy said, "I've had sex with one."

The instructor said, "You've had sex with a ghost?"

The guy said, "Oh no! I thought you said a goat!"

Chapter 58

FIDDLE

In 1984, one night I asked Katy to guess what my next project was. She said, "There ain't no tellin'."

I said, "I'm gonna learn how to play the fiddle." At the time there were only two songs I was interested in learning how to play, "Faded Love" and "Orange Blossom Special," but I later got so sick of those two that I ventured out and learned a lot more.

I called up Clark Rhyne and told him of my intentions, and he said, "Call Phil Milner from Allen, Oklahoma, and buy from him a reasonably low-priced fiddle; that way after a few months, if you don't want to play, you won't be out much money."

If many a mother or dad had gotten this advice, there wouldn't be expensive electric guitars and amplifiers in kids' closets all across the country. I bought a fiddle, case, bow, rosin, and tuner for forty dollars. On the way back from Allen, I could whack out "Faded Love." (That is, if you were real familiar with the song.) One day I played it for Charlie Battles, and he said, "I didn't realize that song was so long."

We were at San Angelo, Texas, for the Roping Feista, and the night before, we were all getting ready to go to bed. Katy was making the bed for the kids, and I was standing up in the back of the camper going back and forth with my little finger on the E string, working on the vibrato. Katy turned around and said, "Can't you play something else—that's getting on my nerves!"

Calamity was about seven or eight, and she said, "Dad, why don't you just throw it away!"

It's hard to be around someone just beginning to play fiddle. Vassar Clements told Garner Boyd that when he was young, he was playing his fiddle in the house, and his mom said, "Take that thing outside, in the smokehouse—just anywhere. Get it out of here; I cain't stand anymore!"

It'll make you take back things you didn't even steal!
— BUTCH MELLOR

When Katy and I divorced, I went to Coeur d'Alene, Idaho, and dated a sweet lady, Mary Munger. I play fiddle left handed, and always before, I would just restring right-handed fiddles, which affected the tones and made them harder to play because of the key pegs, and most players don't know that the finger board slopes toward the hand. Mary bought me a fiddle for my birthday that Lundin Violins in Spokane, Washington, completely dismantled and converted over to a left-handed fiddle. Back then I would play every chance I got, especially when I was waiting on something or somebody. If someone asked me to play a song, I'd do it. Usually they wanted "Devil Went down to Georgia," "Faded Love," or "Orange Blossom Special." I kept it with me most all the time in a real convenient road case that hung on my shoulder. Those places were airport terminals, motel rooms, doctor offices, waiting rooms, gas stations, auto repair shops, and many other places if I was waiting or had down time.

Pake (with Mary's fiddle), Benny Kubiak at
Studio 7, Oklahoma City. 2009—Family Photo

I first met Benny Kubiak in about 1968 when he first started playing fiddle at the WH Corral. Benny has played for over sixty years, thrown his whole life into it. A former band member of Bob Will's Texas Playboys, he told me that Bob and all the boys treated him really good. Benny loves to play harmony to a lead fiddle and has encouraged me, making me want to practice more. Nowadays Benny plays from five to six nights a week.

One day at an airport terminal, I was playing and had my hat off, placed with the top down. A lady came by and dropped five dollars in it. I looked up and said, "Ma'am, I ain't playing for money."

She said, "I enjoyed your playing and just wanted to."

One day I was coming home from Idaho when we changed planes in Denver. The flight attendant said, "If you hurry, you can get on standby [at gate so-and-so]."

I ran to the gate only to find the plane pulling away from the terminal before I could get on. I asked her if she had a seat on that one, and she did. As soon as that plane got up in the sky, they grounded all the planes because of icy conditions. The whole airport was real crowded, so for the next seven hours, I went from terminal to terminal playing my fiddle. I would move on to the next one when they began to get a look of murder on their faces. I looked up one time and saw a camera on an iPod videoing the passengers. I got back home late that night, and the next day I got a call from Jim Ward, from Heppner, Oregon. He said, "Were you in the Denver airport yesterday?"

I said, "Yeah, how'd you know?"

He said, "I saw you playing your fiddle on the ten o'clock news. They were showing the airport delays."

Sometimes I would ask the people around me if they minded me playing, and most would say no. One lady one time said, "It depends on how good you play."

One time at DFW, legendary fiddle player Johnny Gimble walked up while I was playing. I got really nervous playing in front of him, but like the professional he is, he complimented my playing.

I only had one bad experience of playing in public like that. One night in Oklahoma City, at the Will Rogers World Airport, I was playing, and this guy in a business suit walked up and said, "You need to stop playing."

I said, "Excuse me?"

He said, "Nobody wants to hear you play, and it is annoying all the passengers in the terminal."

I said, "Well, sir, that's your opinion, but from the looks of folks, it duddin' seem to bother them."

He said, "Then I'll go get airport security!"

He stormed off, and I never saw him again. Another guy saw the whole thing and came up and said, "That guy must be having a bad day."

I rarely give advice about anything anymore because I used to be in the persuading business. I've sold singles, albums, eight tracks, cassettes, CDs, health, life, and disability insurance, annuities, motor club, cattle, and over twenty multilevel network marketing opportunities. I am dog tired of talking about concepts or giving advice on what other people should do. I think that I may have mentioned that I wish I could take about three of the things that I'm partially good at and combined them into one thing to make that one thing better and be really good at that one and only thing. My problem is I've fallen in love with all three things and cain't drop two. It ain't impossible to be great at two or three things, but next to it.

Here's the advice: for example, let's pick an extremely hard instrument, and you wanna play fiddle. Play that thing until you cain't play it anymore, rest, and then go at it again. I mean, play it until it becomes a growth under your chin. Eat, drink, sleep, think, talk, and breathe fiddle. Watch other fiddle players, get tips from them, don't be afraid to ask for pointers, but 99 percent of it is playing it.

I've heard asinine ropers say, "I don't need to practice; I just watch videos of other ropers roping."

Bullshit! Cain't learn how to swim by sittin' on the bank! I've also seen ropers in such a fever for it that they would cheat, rob, steal, or anything to get to the next rodeo, but you don't have to do that. Make it more than a habit or just something you like to do; make it an addiction, a sickness with a fever, something that you go to bed thinking about, the thing that wakes you up in the middle of the night thinking about a better way to do it, and the first thing you think about when you wake up in the morning. Make people around you so sick of hearing you talk about fiddle or hearing you play, they make you take it somewhere else. Play it so much that folks ask, "Is there anything else you ever talk about or do?" If the answer is no, then you are on the right track, and if you have any talent at all, then you will get better and better at it.

Chapter 59

THE ZONE

You will come to a point that will take you into what musicians, entertainers, or athletes call "the zone." Now I've not had the hard-drug experiences like some of my friends talk about, being in the spirit world and out-of-body experiences, full of hallucinations, which ain't nothin' but poison in their veins puttin' them outta their weak fuckin' minds, but this zone thing is something above and beyond normal everyday life, without drugs. I've only been there a couple of times, but I've talked with other people that have and can describe it like this. During everyday practice or performing, you gradually get better, sometimes without noticing much improvement, but in reality you are. At the start of the day, you are recouping or attempting to regain what you worked on or learned yesterday, losing some of it in your sleep. On this same day, when you get past the point of recouping, you start improving, adding layers upon layers, sometimes hours upon hours, of improvement, when you slip into another world of playing called "the zone." Things suddenly become easier and automatic by simply falling into place. You start playing remarkably unplanned, unexplained things that come out of nowhere that amaze even you. You begin to start thinking, "Now I get it!"

It's like your body takes over with muscle memory, rebelling from listening to your mind or thoughts. You get real excited with adrenaline, and your heart starts pounding, and you don't wanna stop, so you don't stop; you keep going, riding the rush of the "zone," until you give out, falling over in exhaustion, lying on your back, recapping what in the hell just happened!

The next day when you start all over, you cain't wait to begin from where you left off from yesterday, only to find your memory has to kick in to remember what you did in the zone. This part is very frustrating and doesn't come easy but certainly gives you something to work on. Guy Allen doesn't have a boastful bone in his body, and I've seen him in the zone before—like twice winning all four go-rounds and the average at four head steer ropings with over thirty ropers entered. I've heard him say after roping a near perfect roping, "I hate going back to the practice pen tomorrow when there's nothing to work on."

Above all of this, he is still going to practice! No one I've ever seen rope can realistically say that. I'm not talking mediocrity here; I'm talking perfection. I've heard professional basketball players talk about the zone and how the basket looked bigger than a Hula-Hoop!

Practice doesn't make perfect. Perfect practice makes perfect.
— Roy Cooper

Shada and Trevor Brazile and Roy Cooper – Internet Photo

Imagine working on your fiddle the day after being in the zone and working long enough to get into the zone again. If you do this day after day, you could soon be a professional.

On a lighter subject, one day we were insecticide ear tagging cattle, and I showed a boy from Coalgate how to put the tags in. He did about fifty, when he said, "You know what, Pake? If I keep this up, I'll be a professional!" All of this can apply to your passion whether its fiddle, roping, or mumble peg!

Keep your dreams alive, live them to the fullest; the moderately composed know nothing so lovely as the divinely inspired.
—CLARK RHYNE, SEPTEMBER 29, 2005

Clark and Sue Rhyne. 1969—Family Photo

Now, most of us steer ropers would call our roping career a success if we won only one world championship, but Guy Allen is an eighteen-time world champion steer roper. Yes, you heard me right—eighteen times! He has dedicated his life to roping steers. Rarely do we see someone who throws his life into one and only one thing. While we were playing basketball, playing music, or running steers, Guy was roping steers. His dad, James, had over one hundred roping steers and fifteen head of steer horses, and he has seen Guy rope, trip, and tie as many as sixty to one hundred steers down a day.

No tellin' how many times Guy has experienced the zone. James said that when Guy got off the school bus, instead of going in the house and changing clothes, he'd come out to the arena, lay his books on the ground, and say, "Daddy, which horse do you want me to ride first?"

Guy Allen is an example of what someone can do if they dedicate 100 percent to something and throw their whole life into it. He is the most dedicated person toward his profession that I've ever been around.

Guy Allen – Internet Photo

No doubt there are others—like Mark O. Connor, Johnny Gimble, Vassar Clements—in the fiddle world that was that dedicated, but I wasn't around them. Guy did it for fun and for a profession. Now I know a few ropers that if they ever won a title, then they would be real hard to be around from being too boastful, and we would never hear the last of it, but not Guy. I've known him since the late sixties, and I'll say it again, there is not a boastful bone in his body, just ain't there.

I just try to do the best I can and hope it's good enough to win something.
— GUY ALLEN

At first thought, one thinks, "Why, hell yeah, everybody tries to do the best they can and hopes it's good enough to win."

But if you think about Guy's statement and know what he meant was if you draw a nine-second steer, then be nine; but if you draw a thirteen-second steer, don't try to be nine, just be all you can be and hope it's fast enough to win something; and if it's not, then you've done all you can do. Anyone who's ever roped, tripped, and tied steers know that the steers are all different, and you only do what they let you do.

Success does not mean practice until you get it right;
instead, practice until you cain't get it wrong!

—UNKNOWN

Chapter 60

TEN BY TWELVE

Mary Munger is a very pretty lady inside and out and has a wonderful family consisting of a son named Cory and a daughter named Kerry, with several beautiful grandkids. Mary owns a very successful electrical surge protection business. Mary liked to take vacations, and we would go to Las Vegas, to the PRCA National Finals Rodeo; then she would come to Limestone Gap and find out how ranching was. She enjoyed riding horses and looking at the cattle and looking at the scenery and the history of the land. One time she invited me to go on one of her business trips to Jamaica. Everything we did was fun. She couldn't stay here because of her business, and I couldn't live in Idaho because of my roots in southeastern Oklahoma and my Western way of life, so our long-distance romance dissolved, but we keep in contact and are extremely good friends to this day.

Pake and Mary Munger. 2001—Family Photo

I came home and needed a place to live. Katy and I had made a $576-a-month house payment near Pittsburg for twenty-three years and then sold it. I was not gonna do that again. Clark half-jokingly reminded me of the ten-by-twelve cake house over at Pine Tree that had a tongue-and-grove floor. It had a sheet-iron roof that didn't leak. I told Jac I was going to move up to Limestone Gap, and she said, "They'll kill you up there."

I understood this statement well because of the drug dealers. Limestone Gap was a haven for drug trafficking. I often wondered if it was because of the hideout feeling it gave crooks and gangsters. There are caves in the big limestone hill, where the outlaws of the late 1800s and early 1900s used to hideout in. Pap once told me, "Bob [his younger brother] came to the house here at the Gap one evening and told me that he went cave huntin' that morning and went through seven rooms and squeezed out through a small hole on the other side of the big hill. He was just a shakin' because of the huge rattlers he saw."

Nowadays it is mostly marijuana and methamphetamine, more commonly called "crank," and it is common for them to trade their goods for cold, hard cash there. A highway patrolman stopped me one day going in and asked, "What are you doing here?"

I said, "We own this place and run cattle up here; why do you ask?"

He said, "Limestone Gap is where the drug dealers come to do their business."

One of the guys that works for us has done that shit and said, "One time me and your dad and another guy was riding horses up at the Gap, looking for cattle, when we rode up on this big weed patch [marijuana]. Clark didn't recognize it, but I turned around to the other guy and quietly pointed the patch to him as we went on through. We were gonna go back later and harvest it, but by the time we got back, someone had beaten us to it."

Another time we were at the McAlester Airport, to pick up Narvel and Reba, when these national guardsmen were landing in helicopters. They were carrying big bundles of marijuana plants, when Clark stopped and asked, "Where did y'all get that?"

The guardsman said, "On your place at Limestone Gap."

I was gonna lease Limestone Gap from Clark to graze yearlings, so he and I loaded the cake house up on the back of a feed truck and hauled it up to where Keno used to live, between the Gap and Blue Hole. When we went through the tunnel under the railroad at the Gap, the top screeched and scraped all the way through! If it had been two inches taller, it wouldn't have made it through. I had to trim trees out all the way up the holler. We unloaded it where the A-frame house Keno used to live in before it burned down was. I tied the house onto a tree and drove out from under it. When I called the electric company, they wanted one thousand dollars to run the line because of the distance from the existing line. I then loaded it back up and took it down to the lots near the line and saved a grand. I told Clark that if we went broke in cattle, we could get in the house moving business!

Alice and Susie in front of the ten by twelve. 2001—Family Photo

Joe Mike Smith and I got it level, put some cement blocks under it, called Leroy Jarvis to come and put a new door on it, insulate it, install electricity, and put up particle-board paneling, and then I called the "Hey Culligan Man" to set up a water system. Now this was the handiest cattle outfit bunkhouse ya ever seen. You could heat up or cool down this house instantly. I had Jim Bob Winslett install a small air conditioner in the wall. I said, "Jim Bob, do you think it's big enough?"

He said, "It'll freeze ya' nut sack off!"

For heating I only had an electrical floor heater that would be cool to the touch and would kick off if kicked over but would run you out on even the coldest day. I had satellite TV, satellite internet, running water, landline phone, cell phone, and front porch. This little cottage of ten by twelve was living proof that most everyone has wasted space in their house.

Picture this: Beginning in the northwest corner was a dresser cabinet that a real nice lady from Holdenville, Lee Jean Stafford, gave me that I kept my underclothes in and also my computer. There was a nightstand between it and the double bed that was in the southwest corner, and on the south wall was a full-length mirror. In the southeast corner heading back north was a stand-up shower. Next to it was the roost, throne, can, crapper, shitter, or whatever you wanna call it. Now if there was company and someone wanted to take a dump, pinch off a loaf, taking the browns to the Super Bowl, drop a load of mud, take a crap, puttin' out wolf bait, gotta go see a man about a dog, go pay my respects to Castro, doo-doo, shoo shoo, dukey, stool, lay one, or lay a big one, cut a caper, (have I named what you call it?) then the other person would merely go outside. I kept matches on the back of the commode for the unpleasant odor. Never underestimate the pleasure of a foot-long floater! (It's OK to look.)

Just north of the can was a sink, and joining the sink to the north was a countertop with a convectional microwave oven Mary bought me for the housewarming. Above the sink and countertop were shelves for various things like canned goods and so forth. On the north wall in the center was the ice box I bought from Betty Jo, my ex–mother-in-law, and on top was the TV. Next to the ice box was the door. I had Billy Weir, a truck driver who needed to get off the road for a while, build a ten-by-twenty storage house for the washer, dryer, freezer, water system, saddles, and other storage needs. I had Hell Bob Robinson help me build a porch and a bandstand to the east toward the lots. Clark and Sam Rhyne nailed up a sign above the front door with red letters and four stars that read: "McEntire Hilton."

The only hard part of this whole operation was getting the cattle in there. A pot truck of 140 head couldn't get under the railroad track, let alone get up through the creek crossings to unload at the lots, so with having Junior Edge's place leased too, we unloaded them at his house and drove them over the steep hill between us. This took some extra fencing but was possible. It took at least three good cowboys to get this done, and Jr.'s had to be clear (no cattle) on the north end of his place to make this work; so with up to a dozen hands, we built a two-sided lane from the tunnel at Limestone Gap, on the top of the big hill, so one man could get in behind 140 head, sometimes two loads totaling 280, and drive them to the lots at the house. Now this was a cat's ass! I lived there for four years and loved the place.

Corrals at Limestone Gap house. 2001—Family Photo

Back when Clark and I brought the cake house to Limestone Gap, I was dating a real nice lady from Atoka named Pethy Hayes. She later became a lawyer—and a good one at that. Gary Coffee was dating a girl I had known for about thirty-two or thirty-three years, and her name was Debbie Hall. Her brother Gary and I graduated from Kiowa in 1971 together. We had a class reunion a couple of years back and noticed that out of twenty-eight students in our graduating class, everyone had their own biological mom and dad alive and living at home! (Not many if any classes can say that today!) Anyway, one night Flip Miller invited me and Gary Coffee down to his house to watch a football game. I took Pethy, and Gary took Debbie. I guess because she and I had gone to Kiowa School, I found myself talking to Debbie and reminiscing old times at Kiowa more than I was talking to the rest of the crowd there. After Pethy and I broke up, I couldn't get my mind off Debbie Hall. She and Gary had broken up, so I called her and asked her out, and surprisingly she accepted. Debbie is a great country gal, raised up at Harpers Valley, about five miles west of Kiowa, who rarely thinks of herself and is especially kind and considerate to everyone around her.

Pake and Debbie Hall. 2002—Family Photo

On my forty-ninth birthday, I decided to have a birthday party at the house at Limestone Gap. Debbie helped with the invitations and everything. We prepared cream can cooking that consisted of taking a normal-size metal cream can, sandblasting the inside rust out, then greasing it down, so the food wouldn't stick, and then placing tinfoil on the bottom to prevent the corn from burning. Then we stood the ears of corn up, placing new potatoes on top of the corn; then we put celery, carrots, and cabbage all mixed on top of the potatoes. Then we put Italian sausage on the very top, poured in a quart of water, and put the lid on the can, so it could let out the steam. If you put the lid on tight, it will pressurize and eventually blow the lid into the next county. Hungry yet?

Cream cans used to cook with. Note the grates on hot coals we sat them on to the left. 2002—Family Photo

Debbie made me this great birthday cake. 2002—Family Photo

We invited over four hundred, and three hundred fifty showed up! Each cream can fed about fifty people, so we cooked about seven cans and had a few left over. We invited musicians to come and play and counted twenty people that got up and sang or played. A few of these guys and gals were Clark, Kelly, Sam, and Todd Rhyne, Gary Raiburn, Royce Sparks, Benny Kubiak, Sid Manuel, Dusty and Kris Rhodes, Lloyd Rush, Gala Hargrave, and many more.

Debbie also made a cake for her dad, David, who has the same birthday as me. I announced to the crowd, "Folks, today is also David Hall's birthday, and he and I are thirty years in age difference to the day." About three cowboys yelled out, "Who's the oldest?" 2002—Family Photo

Two of my favorite people, Debbie's parents: Lois and David Hall, from Harpers Valley, Oklahoma. 2002—Family Photo

Debbie and Pake, with musicians, forty-ninth
birthday bash. 2002—Family Photo

Lloyd Rush, Royce Sparks,
Clark Rhyne. 2002—Family Photo

Lloyd Rush, Royce Sparks, Gary Raiburn, and
David Jones. 2002—Family Photo

Pake, Lloyd, Royce, Kelly Rhyne, and David. 2002—Family Photo

I was not doing any shows at that time, concentrating only on the cattle business at Limestone Gap, when one day Ernest Hay, of Haystack Productions, from Duncan, Oklahoma, called. He said, "Pate, people are asking about you and want you to come back and do some shows. Would you like to come to Duncan and do a show for me?"

I said, "Well, yeah!"

I got a band together, and Debbie went with me. We kept doing other shows, and Debbie got to selling concessions, like CDs, pictures, and so forth. The dreaded revolving door of musicians began to turn with a constant effort of finding one to replace the one that had just quit.

Chapter 61

SOUND TRACKS

Later on we were doing a recording session at OKC with my band and having more hell than a man on a wrong train. Brad Binge was producing the effort, and he kept telling me, "I know professional musicians that can cut this easier and cheaper in the long run."

I finally threw in the towel and met up again with Terry Scarberry and Steve Short, guys I'd played with years ago.

Steve was with Reba for about three years. One year Reba let me go on the road with her and open for her using her band. We were in Éau Claire, Wisconsin, in the wintertime, and we stayed at a Holiday Inn. Steve and I shared a room on the top floor, facing the cold north wind. We had the heater turned up on high but were still freezing our Southern asses off! We put our clothes back on, still freezing. We then decided we were gonna have to sleep together or freeze to death! We did, when I heard Steve say, "Pake, you tell anybody about this, and I'll kill ya!"

Steve Short. January 28, 2012—Sherry Loudermilk Photo

In the studio, the A-team consisted of Steve on drums, Terry on guitar, Dennis Borycki on piano, and Dave Copenhaver on bass. These guys were really good, but I couldn't afford them out on the road. Susie suggested I do my shows with sound tracks, as she and Paul had been doing for years. This idea did not hit well with me at first, but I was not happy with the guys I was able to hire to play, so I did it. The timing was right, for nowadays, the listening public had gotten used to the idea of tracks, unlike crowds of yesteryear.

I contacted chamber of commerce offices in local towns, and they sent me booklets with calendars of events. This listed the event, date, contact name, number, and even whether they had entertainment. I entered all of the potential prospects in my computer and began calling them. They asked me for a packet with a CD, picture, bio, and references of where I had played in the past. After about a year of calling and booking, I looked up one day, and I had over three thousand prospects in the computer. One August, I looked on my phone bill, and I had made over thirty-five hundred calls. I have given this advice to up-and-coming, newcomer singers when they ask me what they should do at the beginning of their careers, and they want none of this advice. They don't want to sit down at a computer and put in three thousand prospects, call them up, and book themselves; they want me to introduce them to Joe Galante of RCA records and sign them up on the spot. It just wears my country ass out when I talk to these people because they want advice, but only the advice they want to hear.

I asked the Friday night band boys at the local Kiowa Community Center if I could play while they took a break, and they agreed. It was a little bit lonesome and weak compared to a band. I got up with the band later on that night, and it felt great. Debbie agreed that it sounded better than our tracks, but we knew a band for us was a dead-end road. Gotta tell ya, it was the best suggestion anyone had ever given me regarding the music business. The sound tracks were never late, drunk, drugged up, outta tune, moody, full of nonsense egos, quit unexpectedly after a show, quit unexpectedly before a show, and I didn't have to travel fifty miles to Ada once a week to rehearse with a band that would not practice their parts. To give you a better picture, this was like pulling a foot-long hemorrhoid out of my ass!

The music shows had become fun again! Debbie went with me to the shows and eventually set up, ran sound, did road management, and often booked. She'd worked at the district attorney's office for over twenty-five years and had some leave time built up, so we went over a ten-state area, doing from twenty-five to fifty shows a year! One Labor Day weekend, we did eight shows in nine days! This let me work on my talents instead of working with pickers to help them learn theirs.

At one point in the show, Debbie would stop the music, and I'd tell a story that kinda went like this: "Friends, I wanna tell ya a story that happened to me back when I was in high school at Kiowa, Oklahoma. Instead of having a brass marching band for the school, we had a country music band class. Our class was one hour long, four days a week, and we even got a grade for it on our report card. We were to play for anything the school needed a band for, like football games, pep rallies, country music concerts, country Christmas concerts, and I suppose if they'd had a hangin' downtown Kiowa, we'da probably played for that too! Fortunately there were no hangin's.

"There were nine of us in the class, and all but three are still playing country music today. There was one student in the class I wanna tell ya about. His name was Roger Wills! [I'd raise my hand expecting a huge applause but nary a peep from the crowd.] Humm...no standing ovation there! Oh well, Roger was a tall, stand-up, lanky kinda kid, one that was always outgrowing his britches with high-water ankle tops—you know the type. Anyway, Roger came to school the first day a-strummin' on this old, beat-up electric guitar. Now, he knew about three cords on that thang, played no leads, didn't sing, and was so bashful he would hardly even talk to ya. Now, we needed a bass player in the band because our teacher, Mr. Clark Rhyne, played bass, which didn't make sense because it was an all-kid class. One day before Roger got his guitar out, Mr. Rhyne walked up to him with the bass guitar and hung it on his neck, saying, 'Roger, play this thing.'

"He showed him a few notes and away we went, and, folks, I'm here to tell ya, for a couple a weeks, it was a little bit rough! No, actually it was a lot rough, and it got a lot of strange looks and raised eyebrows from the rest of us 'cause we thought we were professionals and that Nashville was gonna come callin' on us any day—not!

"Well, Roger stayed with it, and to my knowledge, to this very day he has made his entire living playing bass guitar. And who does he play for today, and has been for the past twenty years? Alan Jackson! Now let's hear it for Roger Wills! [The crowd at this point would ooh and aah and give an enthusiastic round of applause.]

"Now, there were two other students in that class I wanna tell ya about. One girl was about yay big, dishwater blond hair, with a sprinkle of freckles on her nose. Now, she wouldn't come anywhere near the front of the bandstand, wouldn't sing any lead parts, and was so shy she made ole Roger Wills look like a blabbermouth! What she liked to do was sing beautiful harmony for any lead singer and would sing with ya all day long. She went on to become a superstar in the gospel music industry, touring all over the United States and parts of Canada, with over fifteen CDs to her credit. Are there any Susie McEntire fans in the house tonight? [And the crowd goes wild!] If you haven't seen Susie's show, do yourself a favor and go see her when she's near ya.

"Now, there was another girl in the class, and let me tell ya she was anything but shy. Bright redheaded and a *bunch* of freckles. She loved to take center stage and sing Dolly Parton songs like 'Joshua' and 'Gypsy Joe and Me.' She went on to become a superstar in country music, winning every award possible, like Single of the Year, Video of the Year, Album of the Year, Female Vocalist of the Year, and even Entertainer of the Year. She even has her own sitcom on TV that I think is really funny. My only disappointment with the show is that I wave at her all the time, and she never waves back! Are there any Reba McEntire fans with us here tonight? [And the crowd goes wild again.] Well, friends, have I got a treat for you; recently we were all home for a family reunion, so make welcome to the stage my two sisters, Reba and Susie McEntire! [And the crowd goes ape shit! So I hold out my arm, pointing to the side of the stage, and Debbie hits a sound track of a four- or five-second rendition of excitement music.

The crowd stops cheering. I look back at the crowd in big-time disappointment and say...] Wouldn't that be great? Sisters—after fifty-five shows, they stood me up one more time!"

The first time I pulled this, I wasn't sure of the response, but I found they laughed and got a kick outta being set up like that. It's funny how far you can lead an audience with a microphone. Clark and Jac didn't like the gag and said I shouldn't do the people that way by lying to them like that. I look at it as a form of entertainment and fun. I think that people like to know about the history of our childhood days and how we got started playing and singing. Look at you reading this book—kinda proves my point, don't it?

The first time we pulled this gag was at Oklahoma City, for Ernest Hay, of Haystack Productions, at a music showcase for fair buyers. This was about the second time I'd done tracks, and Ernest was not for the tracks idea at all—not even some. Ernest has a little trouble sayin' his *r*'s, so when the show was over, he walked up to me and said, "Pate, I 'bout had a hot attack when you said that about Weba!"

A little while later, one night we opened for the Belamy Brothers at the Poncan Theatre in Ponca City, Oklahoma, and there was house sound provided with two men running sound and the CD player. Debbie repeatedly told them of the gag we were gonna do with Reba and Susie and explained over and over that they weren't really going to be there, so when I introduced them, the guys were to hit the dramatic sound track. She said that when I gave the signal by introducing them, the two guys looked over to stage left, with their eyes glued wide open, looking for Reba and Susie, forgetting to hit play on the player. Debbie began hollering, "Hit play; hit play!" But they were in such a trance looking for the girls that Debbie had to literally climb over them to hit the play button, making it late, but still effective.

We kept this gag in the show for a long time and were amazed at some of the reactions we'd get from the crowd. Some people that saw it before at our previous show still liked it. One night at Enid, Oklahoma, one girl stood up screaming, pulling at her hair like a demon had possessed her! Steph and I recently did a show at Coalgate, Oklahoma, when a lady came up and asked, "Where have you got Reba hid tonight?"

CHAPTER 62

BACK SURGERY

During his younger years, Grand Pap roped calves, roped steers, bulldogged steers, rode bulls, rode saddle broncs, or anything that had hair on it. (Don't get off course on me now!) He broke his ankle and didn't have it fixed, so it grew back crooked. Not to mention all of the ranching years that took a toll on his body. All of these years of fun probably led to the back surgery in the early fifties. He went to the McBride Hospital in Oklahoma City for the surgery, and they told him to give it time to let it heal. They put a body cast on him, and Clark said that he lost so much weight that near the end, he could turn the cast 360 degrees. He stayed down at one of the houses near the subprison at Stringtown, with Dub Wheeler, for literally months, giving this operation time to heal. The surgery turned out to be a great success; nine men from the Atoka area heard of Pap's back ordeal, so they all headed to McBride's, eager to have their back pain stopped. Instead of letting it heal, they came home and went back to work immediately and had nothing but more trouble. One of them had to go back and have another surgery.

As long as I can remember, Clark has had back trouble, and why he didn't go get his operated on I cain't say, but he liked to frequent chiropractors a lot. One in particular was Doc Barnes from McAlester. A big guy, Clark would coach him, saying, "You gotta hit me hard, or it won't go back in place!"

Pap told me repeatedly that if I ever have to have back surgery, the secret was to let it have plenty of time to heal.

When I was eleven years old, I helped Louie Sandman pick up the end of a cattle sprayer that we used to spray the cattle. The chemicals kept the flies off before the insecticide ear tags came along. You guessed it: I hurt my lower back for the first time. Many more times followed, like getting bucked off horses, flanking too many calves, falling off haystacks—you name it; I made countless trips to numerous chiropractors until the year 2000 when I told my favorite chiropractor, Shane Mills, "Fix this damn thing!"

He looked at me and said, "I don't think I can."

I was losing strength in my right leg, with some paralysis, so I went to Durant for an MRI, and the problem was obvious: several degenerating lower discs in the L4-L5 and the sacrum.

Bob Debord at Kiowa had neck surgery at the Oklahoma Spine and Brain Clinic in Tulsie, so I called them for his doctor; but he was booked up, so they gave me Dr. Kyle Mangles. On January 2, 2004, they did a fusion on the lower vertebrae, and Debbie Crawley took off work to sit up with me, sleeping on the couch at the hospital for three nights. When we left the hospital, she invited me to stay at her house in McAlester and took care of me during the first month of recuperation. I went home to Limestone Gap and started booking shows on the phone, listing all the three thousand prospects I had gotten out of the calendars of events from chambers of commerce within a four state area, in my brand-new computer. Debbie and I continued dating and doing shows until 2006. Breaking up with Debbie was the hardest thing to do because we were so close. She had a family and job to tend to, and I needed someone here with me full-time, so it was inevitable for our courtship to end.

CHAPTER 63

CAIRO

Kenneth and Kay McEntire house, where
we live in now—Family Photo

I was also renting Clark's place at Cairo, 2,000 acres of good flat land with a few rolling hills. Cousin Kenneth and his wife, Kay, lived there on 140 acres. They decided to sell the house and land and move to town. Clark bought it at a land sale, auctioned off by Gary Coffee, and Clark needed someone to move into the nice house for insurance reasons. Actually he would have just burned it down, but Jac wanted to keep it, so I loaded up my stuff and moved in; been here for five years now. I wouldn't move all my junk over to Cairo at first. The first night was real lonely, maybe because it was so big. Remember, I just came out of the coziest place imaginable, one hundred twenty square feet, to two bedrooms, two bathrooms, a living room, dining room, kitchen, and an extra living room, somewhere around fifteen hundred square feet. You can even get exercise just walking around in the place lookin' for stuff. I would alternate back and forth until I gave into the fact that the Cairo place was more comfortable and handier. Since then we have put up new barbed-wire fence around 90 percent of the pastures, built new corrals, spent over $7,500 just to repaint three big barns that Uncle Peck built back in the sixties, spent over $50,000 in clearing brush, and the latest venture is aerating the pastures. This means dragging a round cylinder with eight inch cleats over the pastures that puncture the ground to let moisture in deeper. This makes more grass in the summer. This is a first for me, and I am anxious to see the outcome this summer. This place is handy, being only ten miles from Coalgate, and far enough in the country to be quiet. Can you tell I love this place?

Kenneth and Kay McEntire—Family Photo

Bonnie, Stacy, and Larry Cometti—Family Photo

Stacy is my fourth cousin; her great-grandmother Margaret was a sister to Grand Pap John McEntire. Born with muscular dystrophy, Stacy was helped through school and college by Larry and Bonnie, and she makes her own living teaching science at Cottonwood public school for the past fourteen years. I totally admire this family, working under extreme conditions I'm probably not even aware of. To see folks on government assistance, cripples with two good legs, waiting on mailbox money. Then there's Stacy, having "true grit," with many obstacles, making her own living. Think how strong America would be if we all were like the Comettis. My hats off to this family.

Chapter 64

STEPH

Around the first of December 2006, I went to my mailbox at Limestone Gap and found a letter and picture from a young lady named Stephanie Ann Shoemake. A college student from Ashland, Ohio, Steph had read Reba's book and was asking to come to Oklahoma for the summer and work as a ranch hand for room and board, taking a break from college life.

Steph—Family Photo

As I sat in my truck that day, many things were going through my mind. First of all, this is not the first fan mail I've ever gotten, but it was the first one that offered to come and work for room and board! Now at that time, I was single, not dating anyone, available, but this girl was younger than Autumn and Calamity and not much older than Chism. The thought of dating her was not my first intention, but then I sent her back a letter that said, "Dear Stephanie, got your letter; give me a call; let's talk. Pake."

I left my phone number and e-mail address. I expected to talk to a young, shallow-minded, unsettled girl that was all giggly, eager to stay up late nights, listening to loud rock music. Quite the contrary. When she called, I explained to her that I was not married, and I was looking for a girlfriend, and I wanted to know more about her. I asked if she wanted to come to Oklahoma and go with me to Odessa, Texas, to the rodeo in early January, and see how it goes. She agreed, and we had a blast. We got a lot of kiddin' from the cowboys, like, "Is that a color book and crayons in that backpack?" and "Hey, Pake, y'all get a double discount at restaurants! You eat off the senior menu, and she orders off the kiddie menu!" They didn't know it, but I thought this was all in fun, and I liked the wit of the humor.

A week later, we got back from Odessa, and she seemed to really like feeding cattle, even though I put her through some of the hardest parts. I asked her if she wanted to return to Ohio, load up her stuff, and come live with me. One day I saw her coming up the driveway in an old Ford pickup, pulling a U-haul trailer, with the tongue hitting gravel at the high spots in the road. She continued to help feed, doctor, brand, and rope steers and liked doing all of it. When roping, she would load the chute with steers, turn them out when I called for them, and then run down the pen and untie them for me, hand me my string, and then run back and load the chute again! What a gal! She loves spoiling me as much as I love being spoiled!

Steph's life in Arizona was quite different from our life now. For example, she worked for Maricopa County Forensic Science Center, also known as the medical examiner's office, in Phoenix, Arizona, and ended up doing autopsies for three years. Steph said the funniest reaction she gets from telling someone about her job is when they say, "Oh, that's so cool! I could never do that." I found out later that Steph's mom, Debbie, was scared to death about the safety of her kid (and I certainly don't blame her) and was saying things like, "What if this guy isn't really Pake McEntire, just some serial killer?"

Debbie Burris and Steph—Family Photo

When I finally got to meet Debbie, she thanked me for being good to Steph and not getting her too hurt on the ranch. Oh yeah, she has had her share of bumps and bruises. Some I could foresee, but some were unavoidable, just because of the occupational hazards of ranching and rodeoing.

Once we were at the roping pen, and she turned out a longhorn steer. He went to the middle of the pen and turned around and stopped. She shook the hot shot at him and turned around to bring the next steer into the chute when suddenly there he was. He ran over her, jamming her thumb back to her wrist. I try on a daily basis, whether it's a hired hand, friend, or a girlfriend, to not get anyone hurt. I've seen people put folks on horses they knew would buck or rare up and fall over backward, just to see them get bucked off or hurt, but I have never done—nor will I ever do—this. I'd try real hard to kick somebody's ass if they did me that way.

If you have spent any time at all on a cowboy outfit, you know there are 1,001 ways to get hurt on a working cattle ranch.

We had a tremendous amount of rain, and we were riding, checking a fence near Coal Creek, when she rode a black, bald-faced horse called "Eight Ball" too close to a deep ditch full of water. The horse slipped and fell over backward, sending Steph and Eight Ball into the water. I got off my horse but stayed on the bank, when she suddenly swam out. I had heard of people jumping in too soon and both drowning. She got upset when it looked like the horse was gonna drown, but she loosened the back cinch on the saddle, and he wallered out.

I bought a horse we called "Chockie" from Susie's boy E. P., and the horse was a little fresh and started crow hopping and pitched her off, bruising her shoulder.

Steph and Chockie—Family Photo

The worst one came one winter when it seemed to rain, sleet, snow, or be cloudy all winter long. David Ainsworth showed up seventy straight days in a row, helping us feed and doctor new incoming cattle. We were using horses to drag off dead cattle from sickness and small hay bales from the haystack to the pens. Instead of dallying the rope around the saddle horn, I had tied an eye in the rope that could easily be looped over the horn. David had gone home that evening, when I forgot to take a ten-foot panel around the east side of the barn. Steph was riding Rusty, so I tied the rope to the panel; she looped the rope over her saddle horn and turned to drag it around the barn. As she turned, Rusty stepped over the rope with his right hind foot. I saw it and hollered, "Stop!" She was not in a mood to listen that day, so she continued on, and when the rope got tight, it pulled up into Rusty's flank, and he took off like a bat out of hell! Lunging, pitching, half bucking, and running away, he came to a cross fence of hog and barbed wire and didn't stop. He ran through it, flipping over forward, sending Steph to the ground. I was right there and hollered for her to get up and run 'cause he was trying to get up, and I knew he was gonna pull that panel through the half-down fence. She jumped up, and sure enough he did too and ran off, pulling that panel, barely missing us. He headed toward the house, went to the end of the trap, broadsiding a steer and knocking him down, and headed back toward the barn, when I hollered, "Run for cover; he's gonna kill us all!" Luckily, he ran round the trailer we had backed up in the lane and hung the panel, nearly jerking him down. He stopped gasping for breath, when I looked and Steph almost had her britches torn off her. (Quite the wreck, huh?)

Sometimes I get hurt too. For example, a year ago last April 24, she was turning out roping steers for me to rope at the roping pen, when this horse named Green Briar stepped on a steer's hind foot, just as I was throwing, and stuck his and my head in the ground! I got up, and my shoulder was throbbing like a wedding dick! My arm was sorta weak and lifeless, and I couldn't coil up my rope. We went to the hospital in Ada, and my arm had a linear fracture on the humerus, extending down to my elbow.

Since we couldn't rope, I ordered seventeen hundred steers. One morning we got in four loads over at Chockie, 532 head, and Steph caught all of them in the Powder River chute (not the hydraulic kind, but manual) and branded while I gave them three shots, with my arm in a sling, and we had three hired hands ear tagging and three putting them in the chute, and we were done by noon!

Steph and Pake livin' in Cattleman's Paradise! (Notice the pore Mexican steers.)—Family Photo

Stephanie likes to buy CD music, and on occasion I heard her sing in unison with the CD and noticed how close she sang with it. I completed the lead vocals on the "The Other Side of Me" CD and was working on the harmony at home, when I said, "Steph, sing the harmony part for me." She said, "I don't know how to sing harmony!" So I said, "Just sing unison with me on the harmony, and I'll show you." She did, and I couldn't believe how well it blended. Not everyone's voices blend when it comes to lead and harmony. Bloodlines—like Alice, Susie, Reba, and me—have a real noticeably close blend, but far as I know, Steph and I ain't kin. (I sure as hell hope not!) So I asked her, "Would you like to record a couple of harmony parts on the CD?" She said, "I can't sing in front of anyone; it just scares me to death. Who is gonna watch?" I said "Just me and Dave, the A&R [arrangement and recording] man." She said, "Sure, I'll try it." I told her, "I ain't making any promises, so if it doesn't go well, we just scrap it, and I'll do the harmony." Dave and I were impressed, and we wound up putting her on eight songs. The next weekend we had three shows: one on Sunday afternoon in Clinton, Arkansas; one Saturday night in Versailles, Missouri; and the killer at Sand Springs, Oklahoma, on Friday night, which was four forty-five minute shows at a smoky ping-ping casino! I told her I needed help and asked if she could sing at least one of those forty-five-minute shows. She agreed, and the crowd just loved her! The next week we went back to OKC, and she recorded her first CD; we called it Stephanie Ann. Since then, she sings on all of my shows and has improved them tremendously. I suppose we have as good a life as anybody—get to rope steers, play music entertaining folks, and then go home and enjoy the Western way of life, running steers.

Steve Short, Dennis Borycki, Dave Coppenhaver, and Steph recording her CD—Family Photo

Terry Scarberry—Family Photo

Happiness is limited on this earth, so better grab ya some before it's too late! No outsiders can pick a pardner for someone else. Steph and I have had more fun than should be allowed, even though we have shocked my family and hers. If you had told me years ago that I would have a twenty-seven-year-old college student girlfriend from Ohio, I'd have thought you had lost you're ever-lovin' pea-pickin' mind! Seems the older girls think our relationship is sick; I got an anonymous letter from an old girlfriend that said, "Old man, you're nothing but a pedophile!" The guys, on the other hand, think it's cool! (Go figger.) When it comes to worrying about what people think, my give-a-shitter broke a long time ago. I got too much livin' to do to worry about what other folks think about me. Not that I think we've started a trend, but since we've been together, I've noticed older guys with much younger girls. I've found out by talking to them (not only Steph) why some prefer older over younger guys. Seems they are willing to give up younger guys with all their hair, muscle tone, no wrinkles or sags, for older guys who treat them with respect, courtesy, security, affection, and patience. I think the older Pake has these things compared to the younger Pake I remember of yesteryear.

Steph and Pake—Family Photo

I like older gals 'cause they don't tell, they don't swell, and they're grateful as hell!

— CHOCK MAXEY

Steph's first time in the Let 'er Buck Room at the Pendleton Round-Up was more than memorable. She doesn't like any liquor drinks, but when in Rome, do as the Romans do. She ordered the Pendleton whiskey with

Coke, when I said, "You might want to consider drinking that with water because the Coke may make you sick." She said, "I don't like the taste with water." I said, "After three drinks, you won't know the difference!" She stayed with the Coke, and in no time, the Buck Room was spinning like a top, so we went outside to get some fresh air. She decided that eating a corn dog would help stop the dizziness, but after that she began to puke it all up! There was a row of steer ropers on a bench watching the fun, when Steph walked over to a trashcan near them, put both hands on it, and stuck her head down to puke, without realizing this was a collapsible can. She rode it all the way to the ground! I then had to go see about her in the girl's restroom and found her stretched out on the floor! A great bull and bronc rider named Jesse Bail walked by us and saw her leaning over, puking in a trashcan, and hollered, "Hang in there, baby!" With head still in the trash can, without giving a shit who it was that was having fun at her expense, she raised the middle finger on her right hand to exchange pleasantries! The next day was less than pleasant for Steph, so she vowed to never do that again. I joked and said, "You're the first one to ever say that!" We went to the rodeo that day, and Jesse Bail was up in the bull riding, and this bull did a tap dance on his whole body right out of the gates. I said, "Steph, you should run over there and tell Jesse, 'Hang in there, baby!'"

> *There's two things an old man duddin' need:*
> *a green horse and a young woman!*
> —CLARK MCENTIRE

I always listened to Clark but didn't always take his advice: because in December 2011, I asked Steph if she would like to be my mate in marriage for the rest of my life. Good for me, she said yes. We had talked about just keeping it simple and quiet—her and me and the preacher—but I thought this was a good occasion to have a real wingding, on January 28, 2012.

Introducing Mr. and Mrs. Pake McEntire. 2012—Sherry Loudermilk Photos

Pake and Steph. 2012—Sherry Loudermilk Photos

I sat down and made up a spreadsheet on the computer, listing 528 families I wanted to invite. Now, if you didn't get yours, it was just a mistake. I overlooked some really good friends and even kinfolks—an embarrassing mistake. Wayne and Greg Sexton cooked the cream cans, and Carol Ervin and Cindy Wallis took care of everything else and did a fantastic job! The Ritter family let us use their real nice building at Limestone Gap, a real fittin' place for it, with over five hundred folks attending.

Our wedding cake, made by
Beth Ann Shirley and Ella Mae Ward.
2012— Sherry Loudermilk Photos

Our wedding planners and friends,
Cindy Wallis and Carol Ervin.
2012—Sherry Loudermilk Photos

Pake and Mama Jac have a dance.
2012—Sherry Loudermilk Photos

Steph and her daddy, Greg,
have a dance. 2012—Sherry
Loudermilk Photos

Robin Lacy married us, and I typed up this information, and he read it. Here it is:

Pake and Stephanie want to thank each of you for attending this very special event. There are folks here tonight from Oklahoma, Texas, Arkansas, Kansas, Ohio, Wyoming, Colorado, Arizona, and Iowa. If I didn't name your state, stand up now, and tell us where you're from.

Pake and Steph chose this site for this festive occasion for more than one reason. We all thank the Ritter family, from Atoka, for allowing us to use their beautiful facility. Their charitable hospitality reiterates the true meaning of "fine neighbors."

This exact site was once the home of Captain Charles M. Leflore, deputy US marshal, from 1883 to 1905. Captain LeFlore used to have parties just like we are having here tonight. Many of you remember the historical two-story home that was built in 1880, from before it was bulldozed to the ground about fifteen years ago by a previous owner. Captain Leflore and his lawmen captured outlaws and often took them to Judge Isaac Parker in Fort Smith, Arkansas, better known as "the hangin' judge." In his later years, his daughters, Chickie and Chockie, brought home from college a girl about their age named Lou. Later she and Captain Leflore were married. Even though no relation, everyone called her "Aunt Lou." Captain Leflore died at his home here at Limestone Gap on September 10, 1920, at the age of seventy-nine, and is buried just one half mile north of here. His record as a lawman ranks with the best of those who served on the Western frontier. Just a half mile east across the highway and railroad tracks was the Limestone Gap School, established by Captain Leflore and James Joseph Ward in 1907. Classes were held until 1961. I'd like for those here tonight who went to Limestone Gap School to stand up and be recognized.

The old Captain LeFlore House, the exact site of the Ritter Ranch Building where Pake and Steph married—Family Photo

About one hundred yards north of the school lived John and Alice McEntire and son, Clark, where steer roping practice resulted into four world championship titles. John repeated many times, "Clark, if you're in the practice pen, and you see the house is on fire, you just keep on ropin'—me and ya maw will put it out!" Clark married Jacqueline Smith on March 17, 1950, and moved from Bethel, near Wardville, to Chockie, Oklahoma, in 1960, about two miles south of here. The town was named after Captain LeFlore's daughter Chockie. There they raised Alice, Pake, Reba, and Susie and taught them ranching, rodeo, and singing.

In 2007, Pake was batching in a ten-by-twelve cake house, back up the holler, a mile north from John and Alice's house, and was running steers in the Limestone Gap hills east of here. This was near where his uncle Keno lived for more than forty years. One day he went to the mailbox only fifty yards from here and found an unusual letter addressed to him and his ex-wife Katy.

The letter went like this:

Dear Pake and Katy McEntire,

My name is Stephanie Ann Shoemake. I am a twenty-three-year-old college student attending school at Ashland University in Ashland, Ohio. My major is biology/premed, and I am working toward the goal of attending medical school to become a doctor. Some of the extracurricular activities I participate in include running Ashland University cross-country, attending Jelloway Methodist Church, and I often go to the music appreciation club on campus.

I was born and raised in Phoenix, Arizona, and I recently moved out to Ohio to finish my education and experience living in the country with a small-town connection. Even though I was born and raised in the city, I have always been a country girl at heart. I have a strong, long-lasting love for the country, riding horses, going to rodeos, and simply being free from city life. Although I have enjoyed my time in Ohio, I will be moving back to Arizona after I graduate to be closer to my family.

I have always been able to find comfort in a family story, song, examples of one's faith in God, outstanding morals, and the unmatchable work ethic your family has shown. My mama has always said to my brother and me that we need to chase our dreams and make them happen because no one else is going to do it for us! I have done my best to follow Mama's advice and make the most of the life I was given.

This approaching summer marks my last summer vacation before I graduate college. I can't think of anything I'd rather do than come work with your family on your cattle ranch for the summer. I know this is a big request from a young woman you've never met. I need you to know this has been on my mind for over a year. I have spent a great deal of time considering my request and spent time in prayer. All I can say is, I have only feelings of peace and excitement about spending the summer with your family. I ask you because you are the only people I feel I know enough about to feel comfortable for my own safety and well-being.

I am willing to work without pay in exchange for room, board, and meals. I would fully accept responsibility for myself in health and safety and would understandably sign any waivers at your request. My experience is limited, but I am an eager and fast learner. I spent a summer helping a good friend with guided horseback trail rides in Phoenix. I can ride horses. And I spent a couple months working at a dairy farm milking cows. My reasons for this request are to learn as much as I can about ranch life, rodeoing, and add to my existing work ethic, morals, and spiritual growth.

I believe with all my heart this experience can only add to my life and give me immeasurable memories and knowledge that I will carry throughout my life. Hopefully I am fortunate enough to pass what I learn on to my children and the patients I will help as a doctor.

I hope you will give my request careful consideration. All I can offer you is my word that if you consent, I will be there on your doorstep for a summer of hard work and memories. I've been taught that my word is everything...If given the chance, I will shake your hand on my promise.

Sincerely,
Stephanie A Shoemake

P.S. I have enclosed a copy of this letter to Mr. and Mrs. Clark McEntire as I was unsure who to send it to.

Pake sat at his mailbox that day, realizing this wasn't just an ordinary country music fan requesting an autograph on her guitar. Never before had *anyone* offered to come and work for free on this never-ending day-to-day grind, shoestring, balin'-wire cattle outfit. He responded by mail, giving his phone number and saying, "Let's talk."

Pake invited her to come to Oklahoma for a week to get a sample of feeding steers in the wintertime. He told her he didn't want a pardner that had a job, career, kids, or other things to do. He had enough going on for three lifetimes and wanted someone to enjoy them with him. Pake didn't pull any punches on the day-to-day chores of the cattle deal and let her wade off into creeks, waist-deep, fixing water gaps, building fence, building rock corners, digging postholes, driving steel posts, stretching barbed wire, doctoring sick cattle in the rain, mud, floods, snow, and ice storms, droughts, heat—the whole nine yards. Her favorite Okie sayin' is, "Don't worry 'bout the mule; just load the wagon!"

Steph building fence
—Family Photo

Steph feedin' Green Briar
an apple—Family Photo

She's been kicked and ran over by steers, bucked off, ran over, ran away with, ran through fences, almost drowned by horses, and every time getting back up and never quitting, never shirking a task.

Steph is so practical. Before she came to Oklahoma, she'd never driven a four-speed transmission and had difficulty learning to drive the show and rodeo truck and also the feed truck. She would tell Pake, "I can't believe here in 2008, when there are automatic transmissions everywhere, they still make standard transmissions." Pake used to tell her after missing a gear, "If you cain't find 'em, grind 'em!"

At a roping near Pawhuska, Oklahoma, Steph was telling Pake and Rod Hartness that in this day and time she couldn't believe they still put clutches in feed trucks. Rod said that boyfriends today are getting their girlfriends breast implants. Steph said, "I don't want a boob job. I just want an automatic transmission!"

Steph fell in love with the Western way of life, doing the everyday, hands-on work. After going and getting her things, she never returned to Ohio or Arizona, other than a few family visits, and is now a real-life Okie. Everyone that has taken the time to know her understands why Pake loves her so much.

Pake and Steph are tied at the hip, and safely saying they are with each other 90 percent of the time and have been together for five years now, enjoying ranching, rodeoing, and playing twenty-five to fifty music shows a year.

After realizing he had looked far enough for the right lady and found his match, a month ago Pake asked Steph to marry him.

The honeymoon will be after the yearlings are turned out to grass this spring and shipped this fall, but until then, it's back to feedin' in the mornin'.

Just in case anyone is wondering, they are not in a family way but plan to be, in the near future.

Well, the family way came along pretty soon: Steph and I are expecting our first of many children come around December 19, 2012, and we aim to name her Nora Ann, if a girl, and Pecos Pete, if a boy. Some folks think that is my name, but we've covered that already. Now, we really don't know the sex yet; we don't wanna know. She will deliver here at home with me being the doctor. What? Bullshit on that! We are using a midwife, Gail Brown, who has delivered over nine hundred babies in the last twenty-nine years. (Had ya going there for a minute, didn't I?) We are sick of doctors making the delivery date to fit their schedule or decidin' they don't wanna do it at two o'clock in the morning. We want it naturally, without the help of a knife-happy doctor. We have found the Cesarean rate in Oklahoma is 36 percent, which is unacceptable. Now, if Gail says a homebirth is not possible, and we need to have it at a hospital, and/or a C-section is necessary, then we will take her advice. But until then, it ends where it all began: here at Cairo.

Chapter 65

SONGWRITING

Old dogs care about you, even when you make mistakes. God bless little children, while they're still too young to hate.
— TOM T. HALL

On occasion somebody asks me if I write all the music I sing. I'd like to say, "Sure did, every hit you've heard me sing tonight is my very own, baby!"

But like Jason (Rook) Cooper says, "I know right, and that shit ain't right."

I'm not a songwriter simply because I don't like to write, but on occasion when the mood strikes me, I do write one. Kelly Rhyne wrote one called "I'll Sleep on the Wet Spot Tonight." Robin Lacy had several song titles that were never completed, like "You Ran over My Heart and Squashed That Sucker Flat!" Another one was "Who Spit Tobacco Juice on Molly's Wedding Dress?" And my favorite is "I Cain't Get over You Till You Get out from under Him!"

I'll be down to get'cha in a taxi honey!
— DAVID HALL, HARPERS VALLEY, OKLAHOMA

There used to be a motel at Stringtown named the Rocky Ridge Inn that had some girls who worked there—if you know what I mean. Clark

McEntire wanted me to write a song called "The Undercover Agents at the Rocky Ridge Inn."

On my first album, Robin Lacy wrote "The Rodeo Man," and I wrote "World's Champion." On my latest effort, *The Other Side of Me* CD, I wrote a song called "Bute 'em Till They Die." H. L. Todd actually came up with the idea and told it to Butch Mellor, and Butch told me about the part, "Ace 'em till they're twelve years old, and bute 'em till they die." The song also talks about Guy Allen.

Charlie, Reba, and I were in Nashville, and they were looking for songs to record when they invited the legendary songwriter Harlan Howard out to dinner and asked me to come along. We were waiting on our meal when Harlan said, "I remember back in the early sixties, my wife and I were really struggling just to make ends meet. We lived in a ratty apartment here in town. I had two songs on the charts: 'Pick Me up on Your Way Down' and 'Heartaches by the Number.' We were so poor we didn't even own a car. I went to the mailbox one day, and there was a check from song royalties with my name on it for $28,000! The first thing I did was go downtown and by a brand-new car for $1,600. The next day I went back to the mailbox and found another royalty check for $31,000. I felt like I had just stepped off into heaven, and it ain't been bad since."

Before Roger Miller got a record deal, he was a songwriter hanging out in Nashville, and he and Mel Tillis would write together. Mel had a record deal, so Roger went out on the road with Mel just for the fun of it. After some gigs, Mel and Roger would hang around the hotel and party for a couple of days after the bus went on to the next gig. Someway, Mel and Roger would catch up with them.

Roger suggested Mel hang around the hotel lobby in his nudie suit, looking prestigious, buying more time to party on the hotel's dime. After wearing out their welcome at this hotel from charging meals and drinks to the room, one morning the door flew open, and the hotel manager stormed in, yelling, "All right, you guys, get your asses up and out of this hotel. You haven't paid your bill, so I want you out immediately!"

Mel threw back the covers, jumped to his feet, and stuttered, "Who… in the hell do you think you are…king of the road?"

This incident gave Roger the idea to write the smash hit "King of the Road."

> *The best job in Nashville is to be a successful songwriter. The worst job in Nashville is to be an unsuccessful songwriter!*
> —WAYLON HOLYFEILD

Chapter 66
PARTY OF A LIFETIME

On March 17, 2000, about five hundred people and I attended the best party of our lives. It was Clark and Jac's fiftieth wedding anniversary. Here is the way some of it happened.

Around January of 1999, the four of us kids—Alice, Susie, Reba, and me—all got together to plan the anniversary. One of the first meetings was in a bedroom at Jac's house, secretly discussing the plans. The first thing that we agreed on was to make it a surprise for them, and from then on, that was about as far as the agreeing went! After that it was almost total disagreement. First of all, just about everything Reba suggested, the rest didn't want to do, and what I suggested, Reba sure as hell didn't wanna do. Reba wanted it first-class all the way, and she and Narvel to foot the bill, but in doing so, all would be done like she wanted. For example, she wanted to hire Ray Price for seventeen thousand dollars, have it at the Cowboy Hall of Fame in OKC, and invite five hundred people at forty-two bucks a plate. Pay Cindy Owen to do all the arrangements, and we were not to sing. I had to remind her that they were our parents too. We suggested having it somewhere close to home, having locals do the entertainment, pot luck dinner, split all the cost. Reba is used to having things her way and is almost as hardheaded as I am, so it was to an extent. We OK'd the Ray Price deal, the hall of fame location, the forty-two bucks a plate (if she wanted to spend that much), but we were gonna get up and sing some of Clark and Jac's favorite songs. This is where Reba balked.

Her reply was, "All we're gonna do is get up there half-cocked and look and sound stupid!"

We argued that it didn't matter: it was the thought that counted, and it was from our hearts for our parents.

She said, "Y'all can get up there and sing whatever you want, but I'm not gonna do it!"

I said, "OK, but you're gonna look mighty stupid sitting there in the audience, with everybody looking at you, thinking you're Little Miss Goody Two-Shoes, too important to sing with us!"

I think that's the one that did it. She finally agreed to sing with us, and we picked "Sioux City Sioux," "Sugar Moon," and "Heart over Mind."

Autumn wanted to do "I Wanna Be a Cowboy's Sweetheart," which was Mama's favorite when she and Clark was pitchin' woo, but Reba was totally against that.

She said, "Why are you going to let her sing that? All the other grandkids will hate her because she got to sing, and they didn't!"

I said, "Let one or all of the grandkids that want to sing, play, dance a jig, whistle Dixie, fart the national anthem, or whatever for Jac and Clark. Whatever they do, Clark and Jac will love it!"

As it turned out, Autumn was the only one that wanted to entertain. Michael Gilliam played round-hole rhythm guitar for us and came with me to Chockie on several different occasions to practice with Susie, Alice, and me. We then e-mailed Reba, discussed over the phone the songs, and she said she would have her part ready.

I would have to write another book to tell you all the detailed work that Cindy Owen did. Us four kids sent her a list of all the people we wanted to invite, and she called each one of them personally, sent them an invitation, made motel reservations, booked the hall of fame—the whole nine yards. This was a twelve-month effort on Cindy's part. The night of the party, Cindy had the cattle people seated at a section of tables, the music people at one section, the family at one section, the home local neighbors at another section—without a doubt the best-arranged party ever!

Alice was to bring Clark and Jac to Oklahoma City, with the excuse the DHS was giving Alice an honor presentation, and she wanted them to be there. About an hour before they were to arrive, Susie, Reba, Michael, and I were in a room going over the songs, and we found out that Reba hadn't learned the songs! She read the lyrics from a sheet of paper, had trouble remembering which line was Susie's and which was hers, and it soon became funny! When it came time for us to do our songs on stage, Reba put the cheat sheets on the floor, only to figure out into the song that she couldn't read them that far away. Susie would tell her during the song, "You're on my part," and it became comical purely by accident, to the point that the crowd simply loved it! I think I made a statement during all of this, "Can you believe we make our living making music?" I wondered after that if we all had missed our mark by doing comedy instead of music!

Reba, Alice, Susie, Pake, and Michael Gilliam. 2000—Family Photo

Mama and Ray Price. 2000—Family Photo

Cindy had slideshows of past years that were more than remarkable, showing interviews of us four kids and grandkids, with stories mainly about the Ken Lance popcorn! We all had a different version, but adding them all together it went like this.

We were playing at Ken Lance's dance one Saturday night when Jac, who on occasion likes a mixed drink, drank a little too much and then ate some popcorn on top of it. On the way home, she got sick and told Clark to pull over for her to puke! He did and she did! After she leaned out the open door and let 'er rip tater chip, she shut the car door and said, "Now, let that be a lesson to you kids—never eat that Ken Lance popcorn!"

Clark and Jac at Ken Lance dance the night of the dreaded "Popcorn Incident"—Family Photo

Of all the family events we have had in the past, this one has to be the tops. Thanks to the monetary effort of Narvel and Reba and all the hard work and dedication of Cindy, I will be forever grateful.

Pake, Clark, Jac, Calamity, Alice, Autumn, Reba, and Susie—Family Photo

Chapter 67

ORNERY FRIENDS

Clark McEntire tells about a boy that was about Grand Pap's age, named Dewitt Young. Before Dewitt went to school, his father told him that if he has any trouble with those teachers, just come home and tell Papa, and Papa will straighten everything out. Well, sure enough, Dewitt went to school and got crossways with a teacher. He hightailed it home, eager to tell Papa what had happened and watch him go give that there teacher the what for. When Dewitt explained to his dad the incident, Papa grabbed the plowlines and began to work Dewitt over big-time. Papa straightened things out all right, at Dewitt's expense.

Dewitt was a little bit ornery. One time Papa was digging a well and told Dewitt to guard the top of the well and keep their old blind mule from accidently walking off into the well on top of Papa. This mule had a bell tied around his neck, so after Papa got in the well, Dewitt tied the mule up to the fence, took the bell off of him, and rang it close to the bank of the well and occasionally kicked a little dirt off into it. Papa had this kind of a speech impediment and began hollering, "Devitt! Oh Devitt!"

About five years ago, Clark stopped by the fruit stand at Stringtown. There was a lady with great big knockers wearing a halter top, selling fruit. Clark noticed that she had a tattoo sticking out at the top of her shirt.

Clark pointed to it and asked, "What's that?"

She pulled her halter top waaaaay down, exposing most of the huge breast, showing him the tattoo!

He then asked, "Got one on Ole Wooley?"

She said, "No, I don't have one that far down!"

Steph and Rod Hartness at our wedding.
2012—Sherry Loudermilk Photo

J. Paul Williams, Rod Hartness, and I went to Elgin and Prineville, Oregon, to the rodeo back in 1996.

On the way back, Rod says, "Hey, Pake, didn't you have a song out called 'Rodeo Man'?"

I said, "Yeah."

He said, "Sing some for us."

I took off singing, "I'm a rodeo rider, a pickup truck driver—"

Rod cut in, "That's enough!" They both got a big kick outta that.

Adren Cunningham winning the Cheyenne
Frontier Days. 1980—Jan Spencer Photo

Adren Cunningham was a good steer roper who, at the time, lived at Sayre, Oklahoma. Adren is as happy-go-lucky as anyone, and I don't know anybody to this day that duddin' like him, but on occasion he got into scrapes when it came to fighting. One time he was in a café that sold beer in the dead of winter, and there was ice and snow on the ground outside. He was looking for a booth when this guy had his feet stuck out in the aisle in front of him. Adren stopped, and this guy left them in the aisle and didn't move for him to get by. Adren kicked them back under the table and went on to his booth. He sat there for a few minutes, when he noticed the man motioning for Adren to go outside with him, and Adren knew it wasn't to exchange pleasantries. The guy was walking in front of Adren and opened the door to go outside, when he stopped to turn around and hit Adren. Adren beat him to it and landed one right on the nose! When the guy hit the frozen ground, he began hollering, in agonizing pain.

Adren was on top of him pounding away, when this guy hollered, "Stop, stop—I think my ankle is broken!"

Adren said, "It better be broken, or I'll give you a lot worse."

Sure enough, when Adren helped him up, he had broken his ankle by slipping on the ice. Because it was so cold, there was no one there but the two of them, so Adren loaded him up in his pickup and hauled the guy to the hospital. When they got to the emergency room, they put the guy in a wheelchair and made them wait. Only the two of them were in the hallway when the guy said to Adren, "It's all your fault; if you hadn't kicked my feet at the café, this wouldn't have ever happened!"

Adren said, "If you had moved your feet, I wouldn't have kicked them!"

Right then, the guy wheeled the chair over to where Adren was standing and kicked Adren on the shin with his good foot!

Adren said, "To hell with ya—I'm leaving!" So he did.

I'll have to retain the identity of the character in the next story, and you'll soon see why. A steer-roping friend and I were talking, sitting on our horses, waiting to rope at a steer roping, when he said, "Pake, I gotta tell ya what has happened to me lately. I've had a girlfriend in my hometown that I thought my wife didn't know about. One day I came home, and she looked me straight in the eyes and told me that she knew about my extramarital affair. The deal was that I had to choose between the two. Since that was a no-brainer, I walked over to the phone, dialed up the girlfriend, and told her that my wife knew about us, and our affair was over and done.

"So for about three months, everything between the wife and me ran real smooth, until one day we were driving through town and stopped at a red light. Lo and behold, who walks right across the intersection in front of us, but my old girlfriend. I noticed she had put on a few extra pounds. When the light changed, we drove out of town about ten miles, nary speaking a word, when my wife said, 'I'll say this for ya, honey; at least ya did keep the fat fucked off of her!'"

The mid-eighties, former trick rider Faye Blackstone and her husband, Vick, from Bonifay, Florida, decided to come and visit Clark and Jac. They brought along three little grandkids that had never been on a horse before. They wanted a picture of all these kids on a horse at the same time. Alice went out to the barn and saddled up a gray horse of Charlie Battles she knew nothing about. She led him up to the house, where they were all ready for the Kodak moment. They loaded up all three grandkids, with Vick standing in front holding the horse. Just before they all said, "Cheese," ole gray broke in two (buckin'), and it began raining grandchildren left, right, and straight up! The horse ran over Vick, pile driving him into the gravel driveway, putting a kink in his left shoulder. When the dust settled, Alice ran and caught him and decided she'd get on him and straighten him out. She jerked and hung the spurs in him, and he bucked her ass off too!

No one was hurt, and that was all they could talk about for the next two days. They had more fun out of that than anything they did while they were here. Oh, by the way, they took ole gray back to the barn and got another horse for the picture and had to do a lot of persuading to get the three kids back on another horse!

Ornery Friends

Garner Boyd, Clark Rhyne, and Pake. None of the stories in this chapter pertain to these guys, but I wanted their picture in the "Ornery Friends" chapter because both are full of piss and vinegar.—Family Photo

A close friend showed up at my insurance office one morning and looked like he hadn't slept in many nights, when he said, "My new bride of six days is driving me nuts! She keeps me up all day and night, hounding me to buy or build her a new house in Ada, in the ritzy part of town, and rub elbows with the high society, and I don't wanna do it. As you know I'm just a plain ole country boy that enjoys county living and coon hunting. I need advice: what should I do?"

I was real busy but never too busy for my good friend, when I said, "Here's what I'd do. I'd go to her and say, 'Honey, we are going to build a modest little two-bedroom house: one room for us and one for our guests. A cute little kitchen with a cozy little fireplace, out in the woods on the 160 acres I own near Stonewall, Oklahoma. This will be close enough for you to go to Ada anytime you want and close enough for me to be in the country and go coon hunting when I want. Are you in or out?"

He looked at me, turned around, and out the door he went. The next day he came back with a look of freedom on his face.

He said, "Well I did it!"

I said, "You did what?"

He said, "I did exactly what you said. I told her about the little house in the woods near Stonewall, and is she in or out. She stared at me with a calm-before-the-storm look. Then she began calling me every obscene name she could think of, some I'd never heard before. Took the four-thousand-dollar wedding ring off her finger and threw it at me. Then she began running around the house, gathering up all my clothes and pictures off the walls, throwing them all on the front yard faster than I could load it all in my pickup truck. I drove away from there, and—man!—I feel better."

Bill Murray walked up to Ray Wharton at New York Rodeo and said, "Ray, can I ride your horse in the calf roping today?"

Ray said, "Shore, but I gotta tell ya about that horse. When you rope the calf, wave your slack, get over in the stirrup; you'll think he ain't gonna stop, and shore enough he won't!"

I was on *Hee Haw* one time and got to know Archie Campbell, who was more fun than a barrel of monkeys. Ralph and Archie were real good friends, and Ralph went to see Archie on his deathbed. Ralph said, "When I went into the room, Archie was lying on his deathbed with his eyes shut. I walked over closer, and Archie looked at me through a death-like haze. Archie said, 'Ralph, come here. I want to ask you something.' I walked closer to the bed, and Archie said, 'Come here a little closer.' So I bent down to where I could hear Archie's faint voice, when Archie said, 'Ralph, had any pussy lately?'"

Pake and Archie Campbell on *Hee Haw*. 1986—Hee Haw Photo

When I was about twenty, good friend Frank Ward from Athena, Oregon, called after the Pendleton Round-Up and asked if he could come down for the winter and rope calves with me.

I said, "Hell yeah, come on!"

He brought his friend, bull rider Bobby Albers, and we got a lot done, but roping was not one of them! It rained (seemed like) every day they were here! We did get a lot of practice, tying calves in the barn and roping the dummy. After a while, Bobby went back to Oregon, and Frank stayed till spring. Frank was tall and slim and had a narrow build from behind, so Reba and Susie nicknamed him "Lizard Ass"! Now, he wasn't particularly proud of this name, but like all of us with our nicknames, he put up with it. About a week before Christmas, Frank's rope-can lid came up missing. Santa Claus must'a brought it back because it showed up under the Christmas tree Christmas morning. Santa (a.k.a. Reba) had drawn a big lizard on it, with "Lizard Ass" written under it! Now, Frank didn't like it some and soon threw it away. He has told me time after time, he wished he had kept it for shits and giggles and old time's sake.

Susie McEntire and Frank Ward. 1973—Family Photo

Roy Cooper of Decatur, Texas, better known as "Super Looper," was hotter than a two-dollar pistol on the Fourth of July back in the late seventies and all of the eighties and won six world championships in calf roping. He flew to some of the rodeos he competed in.

In this story, he sent a horse with Marshal Bracket, better known as "Big Ticket," and Brad Gjermundson, four times world champion saddle bronc rider, to a rodeo in Florida. Roy told Big Ticket that this horse named Big John had some age on him, and Roy wanted him to have a roof over his head, like at a rodeo grounds or fairgrounds, every night, on the way down there and back. Big Ticket and Brad went through New Orleans, and the Mardi Gras was on. They wanted to party like everyone else but couldn't find anywhere to put Big John. They checked into the Howard Johnson motel and requested a room on the ground floor, but none was available, second floor only. They checked the elevator and found the weight limit was one thousand pounds, which was gonna be overloaded with the two guys and the horse, so they found a service elevator with a limit of two thousand pounds. They took Big John up the service elevator, along with some hay and feed for him, ran the bathtub full of water, locked the door, and left for the big party. (I didn't ask, but I wonder if they turned the TV on for him too!) They got purty drunk at a party and wound up somewhere else and didn't wake up until noon the next day. They remembered putting the horse in a motel but couldn't for the life of them remember where! After driving around and sobering up a little, they remembered the Howard Johnson. When they rounded the corner, there were sirens, lights flashing, fire trucks, police cars, sheriff cars—the whole nine yards. They realized then and there they were in deep shit! They knew in order to get Big John, they had to fess up to the sheriff and admit it was their horse, so they did, and this sheriff was pissed big-time. He told them to get that horse out of that room now! The cowboys replied, saying that the service elevator they took the horse up in was out of order. The sheriff told them he didn't give a big rat's ass how they got him out—just get him out! So they took him down in the regular elevator, and the sheriff escorted the two cowboys and Big John out of town, past the city-limits sign, and told them not to come back! As far as the damage to the room—and you can imagine what horse piss and shit smells like in carpet—well, the boys checked in the room and paid cash and didn't put it on a credit card, so the regular room rent was all they were charged for.

It's a thousand-dollar fine if a PRCA rodeo does not have an ambulance standing by during a performance or slack. Most cowboy's cain't even spell *sympathy*, let alone give it. During the steer roping slack at Bandera, Texas, one day Vance Vest stepped of his steer horse to run down and tie the steer, when he twisted his knee and broke it. He hit the ground in agonizing pain, stopping the slack, waiting on the ambulance to come from town. We were riding around in the arena, keeping our horses limbered up, realizing that all of us Okies were at least four hundred miles away and were all eager to get on back home. After about twenty minutes, two-time world champion steer roper Shawn Burchett from Pryor, Oklahoma, hollered at the crowd gathered around Vance, still on the ground in the middle of the arena, "Just drag him over to the fence, and let's get on with it!" Vance raised up on one elbow and hollered real loud through the gathered crowd, "Fuck you, Shawn!"

Ask anybody today who the best all-around cowboy with a rope ever was in history, and they'll tell you, hands down, it is Trevor Brazile. Trevor has loved to rope since he was real little because his dad, Jimmy, roped also. Trevor used to take his rope to school, even to bed with him. When he was about ten years old, one morning we were at San Angelo, Texas, Roping Fiesta, riding around the arena, getting ready to rope. I was riding a Hamley saddle from Pendleton, with a big cap saddle horn.

Trevor rode up to me and said, "Hey, Pake, I know why you have a big saddle horn."

I said, "Why's that, Trevor?"

He said, "So you can set Cokes on it."

Phil Lyne at 1971 National Finals Rodeo, Oklahoma City, Oklahoma. 1971—Ferrell Photo

The best all-around cowboy in all events that ever was is Phil Lyne. South Texas cowboy from down around George West, or Cotulla, could do it all and do it well! He rode bulls, bareback, saddle bronc, roped calves, bulldogged, team roped—yes, he did it all. One year he won the average at the National Finals Rodeo at Oklahoma City, in two events, the calf roping and bull riding. After he retired at an early age, sick of traveling, he decided to take up steer roping, so he went to Santa Anna, Texas, to James Allen, because James is a great steer roper and always had lots of horses and steers to rope. One day they were practicing at James's pen, when James got a bad case of the gaulded ass!

James said, "Phil, you keep some of that Chap Stick in your pocket, don't you?"

Phil said, "Yeah, you need some?"

James said, "Yeah!"

So Phil reached into his pocket without knowing what James was going to do and handed James the much-needed medication. James dropped his laundry, bent over, and spread' em; he pulled the cap off of the Chap Stick and began applying where needed in generous proportions. When he got through, he put the cap back on the Chap Stick and tried to hand it back to Phil, but Phil looked at him and said, "You keep it."

After that, every time you wanted to borrow Phil's Chap Stick, he would make you hold out your hand and smear some on your hand.

It ain't cheatin' if it's in the rulebook!
—MIKE "CHEATER" CHASE

Some of my favorite people live or were raised up in southeastern Oklahoma and east Texas. Steve Slack from Idabel was like me, a left-handed calf roper. A six-foot-four, 225-pound, stand-up kinda guy who would not back down from any fight. If you jumped on Steve, you'd better bring your lunch 'cause he had no quit in him!

One evening, Steve was mowing his mama's yard when the riding mower quit. He got some tools and attempted to get it running—to no avail. Dark was approaching, so he left it there, intending to come back in the morning to fix it and finish the yard. He returned the next day and discovered someone had stolen the mower. He went to Idabel to a rough all-black beer joint and asked who stole his mower. One guy spoke up and said, "Steve, I didn't get it, but I know who did—a friend of mine who works at the sawmill."

He gave Steve the name, so Steve went down there and looked him up. The guy said, "Mr. Steve, I didn't know that was your mower. I shore wouldn't have gotten it if I'd know it was yours!"

Steve said, "If that mower ain't in my mama's yard in the mornin', I'm gonna come back down here to see you, and you won't like it!"

The next morning Steve went to his mama's house, and sure enough there sat the mower. Steve got on it, hit the starter, and it fired right off! The guy had fixed it!

I was at Aspermont, Texas, at a steer roping, when Tom Gibson and an older gentleman came walking up, and Tom introduced him to me.

Tom said, "Old Pake here is ambidextrous!"

The older cowboy said, "Oh yeah, what does that mean?"

Tom said, "Means he cain't rope with either hand!"

If they ain't making fun at ya, they don't like ya.

We were staying at the Motel 6 in Cheyenne, next to Buster and Jane Record, and their two little girls were excited about me being Reba's brother, so they came over to our room one morning. They looked at my bald head without my hat on and ran back to their room and told Buster, "Dad, he's a cone head!"

One time Alice, Reba, and I went to Tucumcari, New Mexico, to a steer roping. On our way home, Alice pulled into a truck stop to go to the restroom, and Reba got out of the camper and went in too. I got under the wheel, Alice came back out, got in the camper, and I was sitting there waiting for Reba to come out of the truck stop. We were parked a good way out in the parking lot, so I waited until I saw her come out, and I started easing toward the highway. I kept sight of her from the corner of my eye but kept on focusing toward the highway. She was looking down until she saw me taking off; then she started running, hollerin', waving her hands, and the faster she ran, the faster I'd go! I let her catch up with me, and she ran up to the truck and started beating on the window, so I stopped and rolled the window down.

She said, "Pake, you son of a bitch, was you gonna run off and leave me?"

I said, "Why, Reba, I thought you were in the camper!" (She knew that was bullshit!)

Tuffy Thompson lives near Happy, Texas ("the town without a frown"), and is a two-time world champion steer roper: 1973 and again in 1975. He had a good low-made gray horse called "Dudd" that would buck your ass off! His wife, Judy, would lead him behind the trailer up to thirteen miles to a roping before he would work and not buck. Definitely a true-to-life, real-time rancher, Tuffy runs stocker steer yearlings like we do here. I really like Tuffy, and a more generous guy you'll never meet.

Jim Davis and I both had our family's rodeoing in two rigs, and in between rodeos, we stopped in to visit Tuffy. Tuffy said, "I have a load of bull yearlings from Mississippi and haven't castrated them yet." We loaded up our horses and headed for this wheat field. We bunched them up in a corner, when he said, "Y'all cut one out and head him back toward where we came from, rope him around the neck, stop him, then get started again and tie him down and cut him."

We tied down about twenty-five apiece and had a blast of fun.

Roy "Tuffy" Thompson, 1973 and 1975 world champion steer roper —PRCA file Photo

When we were on the road in '85, we had a music show after the rodeo there at Tulia, and Tuffy was at the dance we played. When it was over, I went over to Tuffy and began visiting with him while the band boys were tearing down the band equipment.

Tuffy said, "You get your ass over there and help them boys load that equipment!"

I said, "Tuffy, it's their job, and I pay those boys to do that."

He said, "I don't care. What would Clark think if he saw you sittin' around while somebody was working like that?"

No matter what I said, I was not gonna convince him it was their job and not mine.

He finally said, "Judy is fixin' something to eat at the house, so y'all come on when they get loaded up."

I said, "You better ride with us 'cause I may not remember where you live."

When we left the fairgrounds, he said, "Take this dirt road here to the right; it's a shortcut to the house." Tuffy was a little bit tipsy, and the farther we went, the higher the weeds got in the middle of the road! Keep in mind this was old Snowball, the truck that we were going all over the United States and parts of Canada in, and now we were running over weeds in the road over five foot tall! It was real foggy, when all of a sudden, we pulled up to a T intersection. Tuffy was in the middle of this long story, when I stopped and said, "Which way here, Tuffy?" He looked right, and then he looked left and said, "Where in the hell are we?"

I said, "Hell, I don't know; this is your country—not mine!"

He kinda giggled and said, "Turn left—that may be the right way."

One year we roped at Del Rio, Texas, and Guymon, Oklahoma, the same weekend. We were all headed to Guymon, when Tuffy got out of a rig with someone and rode with H. L. Todd, who was by himself, just to keep him company for a while. Tuffy opened the glove compartment and found H. L.'s handgun, picked it up, and pointed to the windshield and said, "Is this loaded?" He pulled the trigger, blowing a hole through the windshield! (Guess it was.) H. L. said his ears rang for two days!

I had some cattle on winter wheat near Hereford one winter, when Wade Lewis and Tuffy came over and helped me ship them. Tuffy told me this story: "There was this older man that was shipping his steers one morning, and he had his grandson with him, along with some hired cowboys. The old man made the mistake of penning his steers that morning before the trucks were in sight to haul them to the scales to weigh them. After penning the cattle, the cowboys got off their horses and began telling stories, while the young grandson was there hanging on every word. The older man who owned the cattle was pacing up and down the road, pissed off, looking for the late trucks, while his cattle were standing in the lots, shrinking, costing him money. The grandson came out to where his granddad was and asked. 'Granddad, can whore's have babies?'

"The granddad looked down at him and said, 'Hell yes, son, where do you think them goddamned truck drivers came from?'"

Hold her head up, Newt. She smells alfalfa!
— CHARLEY LYNN

Charley Lynn, 1972 NFSR Pawhuska, Oklahoma. 1972—Ferrell Photo

If you eat dinner with Tuffy at a restaurant, he will not let you pay for the meal. Wade Lewis is the same way. One time Wade and Tuffy were at this café, and they got to arguing over the check, grabbing for the ticket, and by the time they got to the counter, they were scuffling for the ticket, and by the time they got out the front door, they were on the ground wrestling for the ticket! An older lady was driving by and was staring at the scuffle and ran into the back of a parked car!

Wade Lewis at Cheyenne Wyoming. 1988—Jan Spencer Photo

Fast pay makes fast friends.

—WADE LEWIS

Ike Good tells, "One time my brother, Charles, bought a Triangle Ranch horse from Bobby Thompson, Tuffy Thompson's brother, that he named Bob. This horse had a different personality. Tailor-made, meaning that if you had an artist draw a picture of the perfect made steer horse, it would be of ole Bob. Charles tied him to a flatbed trailer back of chute 9 at Cheyenne, and he rared back and lunged forward and got under the trailer fifth wheel, getting grease on him from head to toe. Then one time he and his wife Doris were on their way to Pawhuska to the Ben Johnson and stopped at a roadside park and let him graze on some fresh-cut grass, when he ran off and like to have never got him caught. When Charles got tired of him, he sold him to me. I took him to S. E. Mayo's roping at Panhandle, Texas, and was third in line to rope when I got off to cinch up, and when I did, ole Bob wheeled and spun away from me. There was a baseball field close by, so ole Bob ran to it and began grazing in the outfield. I would get right up to him, when ole Bob wheeled away from me and ran toward the town of Panhandle. I told a friend who had a pickup there to go back to the roping and have them put me at the bottom of the list. We took after ole Bob, who, by this time, was running through residential sections of town. And on this Sunday afternoon, a bunch of colored kids on bicycles with reflectors on their wheels got in on the chase, when ole Bob ran under some lady's clothes line and tore it all down, dragging line and clothes behind him. Finally, these kids and I hemmed ole Bob up in an alley and caught him. I rode him back to the roping to find all the other ropers giving me nine kinds of hell, kiddin' me about my horse. Not long after that, I had enough of ole Bob, so I sold him to Mike "Mule" Thompson from Hobbs."

Ike Good, Pake, and Jim Davis at the Ben Johnson Memorial. 1990—KW Photo

Remember Jason "Rook" Cooper I mentioned earlier? Quite the character Rook. Never fake or false pretenses; some could say a little rough around the edges; always himself—like him or not! Even though we didn't always agree, I always liked him.

One day we were roping steers at Sheridan, Wyoming, when Rook was riding his famous horse Show Time. He roped this steer just across the score line, laid this good steer down nice and easy, ran down the rope, just ready to go through the motions of tying the steer; easily winning first, Show Time decided he hadn't taken the steer far enough, dragging the steer past Rook, taking him out of the money. Rook patiently got back on Show Time, the untie men took the rope off the steer, and Rook quietly rode out of the arena totally disgusted. Shortly after, steer roper Kenyon Burns was riding out back of the barns when he saw Rook in front of Show Time with the horse's bits in both hands, standing face-to-face. He heard Rook say, "I feed ya, water ya, brush ya, put ya in a nice stall, buy the best horse trailer money can buy, and you fuck me, fuck me, fuck me!

Rook painted on the front side of his horse trailer, "I may not be what you want, but I'll be all you want!"

CHAPTER 68

POCKET KNIFE BLUES

When I sat down one evening to read Reba's first book, I noticed at the very front, she handwrote: "I hope you still love me after reading this!" When I got to page eighty-something, she began telling this story, and I thought, "Oh shit! Surely she ain't gonna tell that!" Sure enough she did, and that was what she was talking about at the front. I was not gonna tell this because she put it in hers, but I've had three people request it when they heard I was writing a book.

In the midseventies, I went to Memphis, Tennessee, to the rodeo, and someone there told me of a great calf horse about fifty miles south of Memphis that needed to be bought and put on the rodeo trail. I called this guy, met him at his house, made a deal, and bought the horse. This guy told me the horse was a good barrel horse also. I took the horse home and showed him to Clark, and he said he was too "silky." That's exactly what I named him.

That fall or the next, Reba tried him around the barrels, and he was a great barrel horse as well as a great calf horse. She entered San Angelo, Texas, and placed in the barrel racing against the top girls in the GRA (Girls Rodeo Association). That night we went out to celebrate her winnings, and she told me that Pax Irvine had embarrassed her by hollering at her from a distance when we first pulled in to the rodeo grounds that afternoon something to the effect of, "Hey, Reba, did you get our motel room?" Well, the more we partied and drank, the more this got under my skin, so when we got back to the rodeo grounds, we went to check on our horses, and we walked by Pax's calf horse tied to the fence.

I said, "Reba, do you know whose horse this is?"

She said, "No."

I said, "It's Pax Irvine's calf horse; let's cut his tail off!"

She said, "Fine with me!"

So I pulled out my pocket knife (I told you at the front of this book my pocket knife had gotten me into a bunch of trouble) and cut it just below the bone, straight across.

That morning at the slack, I heard some cowboys kidding Pax, saying, "Hey, Pax, nice trim!" He was madder than an old wet hen!

Seventeen years passed by, and I'm reading Reba's book, and she put this story public. I went to the phone to eat her ass out, but the housekeeper said she was doing an award show that night. Sure enough I turned on the TV, and there she was.

The fats in the fire now!

—JAC MCENTIRE

About three months later, we were at Guymon, Oklahoma, at the rodeo, and Pax was there. I spoke to him, but he didn't speak back. Other steer ropers began to come up to me, laughing about the incident in her book, so I knew then why Pax wasn't speaking. His silence went on until we were at the West of the Pecos Rodeo in Pecos, Texas, on the Fourth of July. Pax and I were both up during the same performance. We both missed with illegal catches and had to go to the backend of the arena to get our ropes off our steers. After retrieving our ropes, I saw him riding up to me horseback. I suspected trouble that was finally going to come to a head after all these years. I could see he was going to be on my right side. I had my left fist cocked and ready down at my left hip if he took the first swing at me. Now, don't get me wrong, I will avoid a fight right up to the end, but hemmed up, I just gotta do it.

He rode up to me and said, "Pake, you know that deal about you and Reba cuttin' my horses tail off twenty years ago?"

I said, "Yeah."

He said, "I just want you to know there ain't no hard feelins'!"

At that moment he stuck his hand out, so did I, saying with a sigh, "Me neither!"

A great hand with a horse, Pax is one of only a few cowboys who won the Pendleton Round-Up in the calf roping and steer roping both.

Chapter 69

AROUND THE KITCHEN TABLE

When Susie was little, she was getting hurt a lot. With us four kids in the back of the pickup truck, twice she jumped out the back before it got stopped and rooted up the drive way, both times ending up with concussions. She also got hit in the nose by the teeter-totter, and then there was the dreaded clothes line.

One day Alice, Susie, and I were all horseback down at the roping pen that was across the tracks. On our way back home, we came through the lots, and I got off to shut the gate, and Susie went on riding old Brownie. Alice went by her, loping to the house, and old Brownie ran away with her. They came around the back of the house on the way to the barn, when old Brownie cut across shorty and ran under the clothes line and drug her off!

When I came around the corner of the house and saw the clothes line, I knew a shit storm had just happened. I went into the house and found Alice and Susie in the bathroom at the sink, trying to get the blood from Susie's nose stopped. Susie was bawlin' and screaming bloody murder when Reba came in and said, "Susie, it duddin' look very bad—look!" Just then Reba put a mirror up to her face, and she began screaming louder!

Like other families, on special occasions, those of us that can make it sit around the kitchen table, reminiscing stories from the past. Susie had her fifty-first birthday on November 6, 2008, and on the night of

November 11, we had a birthday get-together at Jac and Clark's house, and here is the taped conversation of one of our family get-togethers.

Reba, Mama, Daddy, Pake, Susie, and Alice. 2011—Family Photo

I asked Susie about her most memorable birthday.

She said, "One year at a very early age, I asked Mama for an electric blanket because the house was usually cold in the wintertime. After I opened the present, I would show people the box it came in, even the man that delivered the propane. To this day I still sleep with an electric blanket on my bed."

I said, "Pap used to sleep with an electric blanket, and when it quit working, he'd go buy another one and put it under the one that quit, unplug it, and plug the new one in. At one time I counted four or five electric blankets on his bed."

Clark said, "Keeno wouldn't sleep under one."

I said, "Pap told me, one night Keeno couldn't get across the creek, so he came into Pap's house to stay all night. When Keeno went outside to piss off the front porch, Pap reached down and turned Keeno's blanket on.

"When Keeno came back in and got in bed, he said, 'Have you got one of them electric blankets on this bed?'

Pap said, "Yeah, ain't it wonderful?"

"Keeno got up, turned on the light, took all the covers off, took the electric blanket off, folded it up, put it at the foot of the bed, turned off the light, and went back to bed.

Pap said, "Keeno, that didn't surprise me a bit!"

Keeno wuddin' gonna get electrocuted by one of them thar electric blankets!

Clark said, "I've seen Keeno walk to the house already late on his way to town and remember he forgot to turn the propane off at the tank and fret about it, just a-pacing back and forth, so he'd walk over a mile back home to turn off the propane at the tank."

Clark said, "One time, Cordis Martin thought Pap's house needed a fan, so he brought over a huge fan with a big motor on it, big enough to run a two-seater airplane! It roared like an airplane and would nearly blow the covers off the bed!"

Knowing Martin, I just know he thought it was funny.

Jac said, "Isabelle Bowen was a thick, heavy woman. She wasn't very tall, and she had a little ole husband that was as little as Stephanie, real thin. One night she rolled over on Bennett, and the kids heard her say, 'Which one of you kids spilled the matches in this bed?'"

Jac said, "We thought that was the funniest thing we'd ever heard."

Alice said, "I'll never forget the time Pake and I had a horserace. He was riding old Muscles, and I was on Joe Dan. We would do things like this when Clark would get out of sight. Anyway, there was a mud hole at the end of our racetrack, and old Muscles ran right up to the mud hole and stopped, sending Pake flying over his head. Our cousin Eldon Ware, who was marked just like us, red-headed and freckle-faced, was raised in town, at Sun Ray, Texas, and he loved to come and stay with us when his mom and dad, Reda and F. A., would stay down with Aunt Jeannie and Uncle Slim. Now, Eldon was a town boy, and evidently there wasn't much excitement in Sun Ray, so he was game for just about anything we entered him up in, just for the excitement. So we put him on old Muscles and put them in our horserace against Joe Dan, and sure enough, old Muscles did the same thing and sent Eldon flying over his head, taking bridle and all right into the mud hole just like he did Pake!"

Jac said, "Eldon couldn't wait to get down here. He thought y'all had more fun than anybody. He'd say, 'Y'all just have fun all the time!' Rita told me that after several days at our house, on the way home, Eldon would get in the back seat homeward bound, four hundred miles back to Sun Ray, pull his britches down, and get on his belly and let his butt air out that was red as a beet from being gaulded!"

Eldon Ware

Alice's daughter, Garett, said, "What was Judy Goodspeed's daddy's name?"

Clark said, "Buck."

Garett said, "Judy Goodspeed told me that one time, Ike Rude drove to their house to pick up Buck, and instead of pulling in and backing up and loading up, he drove all the way around the barn and then pulled up to the house and stopped.

"Buck said, 'Ike, how come you took the long way around the barn? Why didn't you just pull in here and back up?'

"Ike said, 'I don't have a reverse on this truck.'

"Buck said, 'You mean, we're going all the way to Cheyenne, and we don't have a reverse?'

"Ike said, 'Why hell, Buck, we ain't drivin' backward!'"

If a cowboy can rope, he can rope with a clothesline!
—IKE RUDE

Clark said, "Ike got drunk after the rodeo at Cheyenne, and he had borrowed a horse called "Rock Bar," Jim Snively's bay horse, and he wanted to head for Pendleton by himself. I think Posey unloaded his horse and took his keys.

"Back in the forties, he had a big old roan horse he got from Buck Goodspeed that Ike thought needed some logging. They had killed a bucking horse in the rodeo at Cheyenne, so after the rodeo, Ike tied on to him and began logging his horse, dragging this dead horse up and down the race track.

"Posey had broken the tree in his saddle and had put another one on the dunn horse called 'Dunny.' He thought he needed to tie onto a telephone pole and make him stand out on the end of it, back of the grandstand at Cheyenne.

"I was sitting on the log and said to Posey, 'Stay on 'em; don't get off; don't get off,' but Posey did anyway, and Dunny ran away with the log and ran around the shit house and hung the wing that stuck out in front and tore it all down. Since he had the rope around the log, when Dunny took off running down a gravel road, the gravel cut the rope, and the log came loose. It coulda killed somebody if that rope hadn't come off."

Clark said, "We were at Rock Springs, Wyoming, at a steer roping on our way to Pendleton, and at this arena, many years before, they had a coal mine there and a railroad. These miners wasn't wanting the Chinamen to take their jobs, so they would tie them together and put a stick of dynamite on them and blow them all up together. They buried them up this holler where the roping pen was, and they scratched it up to have this roping, and there were bones, like knuckle bones, all over that arena. This was in about 1952 or 1953."

I said, "What year did they kill the Chinamen?"

He said, "Oh, I don't know, but I do know it was in the years they built the Union Pacific Railroad. They said that even though it has been over a hundred years, the railroad is still paying for damages for wrongful death on those Chinamen."

Clark said, "We kept a postcard a long time from Pap, telling us that he and Buck Goodspeed tied for first and second in the steer roping at Sheridan, Wyoming, in the thirties."

I said, "Clark, how was Joe bred?"

He said, "Well, he was out of a puddin'-footed Morgan mare and old Joe Hancock. I don't know what 'puddin'-footed' meant, but a paint mare."

I said, "Morgan's are short, right?"

He said, "Well, they're half-breed kinda horses—tough, ride 'em every day and work 'em to plow the garden, plow the corn, punch cows on 'em, use 'em every day good horses, that had conformation and easy temperament and easy keepers. We bought him in June of 1945 from Ted Yoakum, and one year I won the calf roping and steer roping at Vinita on ole Joe."

Joe was the best horse by far Clark ever owned because of his speed and stopping ability. All-around champion Todd Whatley rode him one time and didn't hold on to the saddle horn because he noticed Clark didn't either, and Joe broke so hard out of the box it put Todd behind the cantle.

Joe Bill White from Lane, Oklahoma, was gonna ride him at a rodeo, and Clark was helping hold Joe in the box when Joe Bill said, "Will he go?"

Clark said, "You damned right; he'll go when I turn him loose!"
Joe Bill also got behind the cantle and nearly fell off.

Dick Truitt was Everett Shaw's brother-in-law, Nell's brother, and I said, "Clark, where did Dick bulldog the buffalo?"

Clark said, "Sun City, Kansas, between Wichita and Garden City, exhibition only, at a ranch by a feller named Red something." This picture was famous and is in several magazines and halls of fame.

Clark said, "Everett Bowman and Bob Crosby was one of the first ones from the south to go to Pendleton. I guess Ike went after World War I, probably 1922 or '23. Crosby usually wanted someone to split with him, so if he didn't win something and the roper he was splitting with did, then it would cover his expenses. One year Fred Lowry went up there on the train, and Crosby was gonna ride his horse and split with him. Lowry said the racetrack rail was higher than it is now, and the horse's knees were both swelled up bigger than a water bucket, so Lowry didn't try to rope either steer, so he left the horse with Crosby and went home. When Lowry got to Pueblo on the train, the conductor came through the passenger car, calling for Fred Lowry, and handed Lowry a wired thousand dollars for his part of the split. Crosby had won the Pendleton Round-Up."

Clark lowed, "Pap said the only thing he ever learned from Crosby was to travel light. He even took the hubcaps off."

Clark said, "Crosby broke his leg bulldogging in the pasture in New Mexico and didn't have it set or casted, pretending to everyone how tough he was. He just kept limping on it, and when he pulled his boot off, it smelled like a dehorned steer with maggots in it. One hot day at Cheyenne, we were in a car with him, and he pulled his boot off and laid it up behind the seat, and we had to get out it stunk so bad. He finally went to Mayo Clinic in Minnesota but did not like the way things were going, so one day he decided to check himself out early and paid a porter ten dollars to get his britches. He went downstairs to check out, but when he asked the receptionist how much Bob Crosby owes you, she said, 'I can't tell you; they are upstairs taking his leg off!' Bob said, 'When you find out how much it is, send it to Roswell, New Mexico.'

"Later a quack doctor put maggots in it to eat the proud flesh. He'd been better off to let 'em cut it off. He died a thousand deaths over that leg. He broke it in 1929, and we saw him at New York in 1947, so he suffered that long."

Bob Crosby

Susie said, "Daddy would feed cake in the mornings and hay in the afternoon. When we would come home from school, Daddy would want me to drive for him while he put the hay out. I didn't like doing this because I didn't know my right from my left. When he would holler, 'Right,' I'd turn it one way, and if he didn't holler back, I knew it was the correct way. One time he told me that I had to pump the brakes for it to stop. I came to this barbed-wire fence and pumped the brakes once, and it didn't stop, so I drove through the fence, busting out the windshield. He forgot to tell me I had to pump 'em five or six times.

"I had won the spelling bee at school and beat out Kelly Rhyne. I was really proud of myself. Most of the time after I came home from school, I would hear Daddy coming up the hill, so I would pretend to get real busy, so Reba would have to go, and I wouldn't have to drive. I was in the laundry room when Reba came in there and said, 'Daddy wants you.' I thought,

'Oh no, I'm gonna have to go drive again.' So I went into the living room, and he handed me a couple of dollars and said, 'Here—you did good.'"

I asked Jac, "Mama, have you been shootin' any wild hogs lately?"

She giggled and said, "Clark was watching me; ya see, those hogs were rootin' out there in the front yard. If they heard anything, down the hill they'd go. So I had to go out to the garage and be real careful not to make any noise whatsoever. I couldn't turn the light on, but I could see them, but I couldn't see the sights on my gun. So I'd shoot. I wish I'd had a machine gun. Clark would be in here at the window, watchin', and he'd say that those bullets went that much higher than the hogs. One time this sow had three little pigs, and she'd be rootin' in the yard, and here'd come these three little pigs. One day one would run to the right, but two of 'em ran into the brush just east of the house, so I went out there, and I just started shootin', and I killed both of em', just a-blind shootin'. If that sow would have come back, I'd a shot her too!" (This was all taking place at their house four miles northeast of Stringtown, formerly called the Dick Andrews or the Ed George place, of about 2,800 acres.)

Clark said, "Pap had a 410 pistol, and before daylight, he'd go out and shoot a rabbit, and we'd have it for breakfast. Frank Elmore had seven or eight kids, and they didn't have nothin' to eat, but they wouldn't eat rabbits. Me and Lloyd Elmore would catch 'em with ole Fido and a little red she dog. We'd hold 'em and turn 'em loose with about a fifteen-foot start and have us a race. We had a lot of fun doing that."

Susie hollered out from the other room, "Tell 'em about y'all watching the passenger train."

Clark said, "Well, we'd run up the track and get on the bank, and wait on the number 5 train that would come through southbound just before dark. We'd watch through the windows of those fancy dining cars and saw those big black men with those white linen coats on and a towel on their arm. Yeah, it was first class. We'd make a trip over there just to see that train."

Clark said, "Morris Jamison had thirty head of buckin' horses at the Ada rodeo, and after that he brought them to Limestone Gap and gave them to Pap to ride. Pap would ride a fresh one every day. That way he didn't have to shoe 'em. On some of them, when he got off to open a gate, they wouldn't lead through, so he'd have to get back on, ride them through the gate, and then get off and shut it."

I said, "Pap told me one time he was fixin' to get on a bad one early one morning, and Clark was pretty young and was a little jumpy around this bronc, when Pap said, 'Clark, you act like you ain't much of a bronc buster!' Clark said, 'We'll see how much bronc buster you are when you get on that thang!'"

Clark said, "Pap would get on anything, even after he had his back operated on. I've seen him bucked off four or five times."

OUR BIRTH STORY

Written by Stephanie Ann McEntire

December 27, 2013, marked eight days past our projected due date. In the late hour of midnight, I was awakened from a deep sleep to find that my water had broken in bed. Rushes started coming regularly about twenty minutes after. I woke Pake with an excited soul that we were going to meet our new baby very soon! I contacted our midwife, Gail Brown; she said to lie back down and rest as much as possible and keep her posted. My rushes were regular but mild until about four thirty, when they came to an end. There was several moments of rushes starting and stopping once more only sporadic and unproductive. Our midwife and doula, Nikki Imes, showed up at the house about twelve hours after my water had broken. It didn't take them long to assess our current state of progress, which was only two centimeters dilated. Gail called us to a meeting of the minds in our living room, and with a heavy heart, she told Pake and me that the home birth that we had planned and hoped for throughout our pregnancy was just not possible.

In the final weeks leading up to our birth, my blood pressure was elevated beyond normal parameters for a home birth. Many holistic naturopathic remedies were used to try and lower it, but to no avail. Given that I was not yet in active labor, it was safe to assume that my blood pressure was going to increase to dangerous levels during labor, posing a threat to mine and possibly our baby's health. So together we made the decision to drive to Saint Anthony's Hospital in Oklahoma City.

We chose St. Anthony's to be with the well-respected Dr. Ryan because he viewed a woman's right to natural birth as important as we did, and he had one of the lowest Cesarean rates in the state of Oklahoma. Even though a home birth was no longer an option, Pake and I still wanted as little intervention in our birthing process as possible. Gail and Nikki met us at the hospital and got us checked into our room. The hospital staff had me fill out and sign all the necessary forms, got an IV started, and hooked me up to all the usual monitors. Dr. Ryan came in to greet us and introduce himself and give us his recommendation. He recommended Pitocin to get my labor restarted and an epidural to lower my climbing blood pressure. I pleaded with him to let me labor without the epidural because I wanted an unmedicated birth. He respected my wishes, and by four thirty in the afternoon, we were well on our way, and my labor was going strong!

From this point on, my body took over from my mind, and time seemed to lose its presence. I could think about very little other than to focus on my current rush. Each rush grew with intensity and duration as my labor progressed. Gail and Nikki were at my side like faithful friends. As time passed, they took turns rubbing my lower back through my rushes and wiping my neck and forehead with cool cloths. It was amazing how they worked right along with me as I moaned out my rushes and swayed my hips in a figure eight to get deep into "Labor Land." Somewhere in the middle of my labor, Dr. Ryan appeared at my bedside; I was on my knees leaning over the back of the bed, with my head resting on my forearms; he leaned in close to my face and said, "Sweetheart, I'm so proud of you; you're doing a great job; keep doing what you're doing." Then he kissed my cheek and left. If ever there was a doctor who knew just what I needed to hear, Dr. Ryan did. I will remember that forever. Gail and Nikki encouraged me to change positions periodically to increase my progress and facilitate good positioning for our baby. After about six hours of active rushes, I had reached near completion, with just a lip of cervix, which a female resident doctor working with Dr. Ryan was able to stretch to completion, and finally we had reached ten centimeters without medication and were ready to push! I was so proud of myself, and I was exhausted.

Two rounds of IV blood pressure medication were used in an attempt to lower my pressure without success. My blood pressure reached an all-time high of 185/103! Our midwives and Dr. Ryan were all extremely concerned and asked that I take the epidural to bring it down quickly. I still had to push our baby into the world, and as rushes continued to come, his oxygen levels were decelerating, so I said yes! They ran to catch the anesthesiologist before he left the hospital. I received my epidural while enduring several more intense rushes that felt as though my uterus was going to explode.

I looked over at my husband, Pake, who was sitting in a chair not far from my bedside, and I remember seeing the concerned look on his face. I asked him later how he felt at that point, and he said he felt helpless to ease the intense pain he knew I was in. Without knowing at the time, he did all I needed him to do—just love me through it, and he did. Feeling that kind of power coming from my own body was exhilarating and terrifying all at the same time. I could think of nothing except, "Steph, you can do this!" I remember saying that out loud at some point, and Gail telling me, "You *are* doing it."

Right before I completed my labor, when it was at its most intense peak, I looked deep into Gail's eyes and held her gaze; she never looked away, and she said, "I've been right where you're at, and you're doing great, Steph." In that moment, I fell in love with her, and a lifelong friendship was formed. With the epidural in place, the hospital staff called Dr. Ryan in and prepared the room and bed for our delivery. The pain of the rushes was gone, but all the pressure from the rushes remained very prevalent, so I was able to push without being told to. Nikki brought out a Rebozo scarf that she wrapped around her waist and handed me the ends of to hold tight to as I pushed with each rush to bring our baby down. This was a wonderful tool and made it a lot easier to gather myself for each push and gave me something solid to hold onto.

Our baby had his head turned to one side as he entered the birth canal, and the doctor tried to turn it with his hand and was unsuccessful, so they decided to use a vacuum extractor to help aid me in the delivery.

I pushed for about twenty minutes, and even with the epidural, I felt an intense burning sensation as the baby's head was crowning. Once his head and shoulders were delivered, Dr. Ryan told me to reach down and grab our baby under the arms and pull him to my chest. I remember feeling his little body slither out as I brought him to my chest, and a feeling of complete peace washed over me—it was as if everything stopped. I don't remember where anyone was in the room, what time it was, or what was going on around me. All I could see and feel was our beautiful, warm, wet baby on my chest, and I finally got to see his face. The face I had tried to envision countless times during our pregnancy was now in my arms.

A nurse had covered him so quickly with a warm blanket that no one in the room had a chance to catch a glimpse of the sex of our baby. We wanted to be surprised at birth, so even Pake and I didn't know if we had a son or daughter. I peered under that little blanket, and to my delight, we had a baby boy! Throughout my pregnancy I had felt the whole time that I was carrying a boy but didn't have any proof, so I was happy to know my mother's intuition was in good working order. I looked up and saw Pake and said, "Honey, we have a boy!" He was shocked! He furrowed his brow and said, "Really? Are you sure?" He even looked down at the doctor, who was still at the foot of my bed, and said, "Doc, is it really a boy?" Dr. Ryan laughed and said, "Hell, I don't know!" He grabbed the baby by one foot, lifted it a little, and said, "Yep, it's a boy!" I think everyone in the room was highly amused.

We named our son Pecos Pete McEntire. Born at 11:28 p.m., he weighed in at 8 pounds 10 ounces and measured 20.5 inches long. Healthy and strong, he was the most beautiful person I had ever seen. Pake said later he didn't think he could make a boy, since he had three beautiful daughters from his previous marriage.

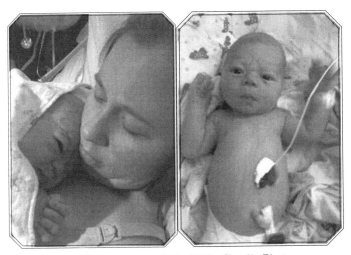

(L) First moments of life. 2012—Family Photo
(R) Pecos Pete McEntire. 2012—Family Photo

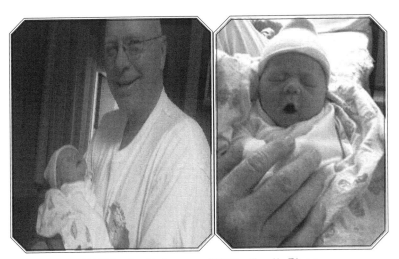

(L) Pake finally has a son! 2012—Family Photo
(R) Daddy's hands—Family Photo

I remember Pecos looking up at me with a serious look on his face as if he was trying to figure out what just happened. He whimpered a few times but never did really cry. I talked to him and took every inch of him into my memory. I was in such a trance I don't even remember birthing my placenta or Pake cutting the umbilical cord—I missed all that. All I could see was our son. I was able to cuddle him and nurse him for what seemed like an eternity before a nurse took him to my bedside to bathe, weigh, and measure him. What I remember most about the aftermath was thanking everyone in the room for their support and efforts; they all got a big kick out of that because I guess they're not used to laboring women being so nice. One nurse said, "We'll labor with you anytime!"

Midwife and dear friend, Gail Brown, with Pecos Pete, four months old. 2013—Family Photo

Doula Nikki Imes and Pecos Pete, five months old. 2013—Family Photo

I was on a natural high like I had never been before—a state of total euphoria. The level of self-respect I have for my body since that day is hard to describe. In several conversations with Gail, I have thanked her for being with me and told her what a wonderful job she did and what a great midwife she is. Every time, in her humble way, she tells me that the birthing mothers do the hard work, and she is just there with them. There may be truth in that, but what Gail and Nikki did while they were with me left a lasting impression on my heart and soul. It's an extremely vulnerable time for a woman, and the people around her can make or break her experience. I was truly blessed to have such a dedicated and strong pair of women at my side, the strong loving presence of my husband, and a wonderful doctor I will never forget.

The next morning, Pake and I looked out the window of our hospital room, and the sky was bright, and a light fluffy snow was forming a blanket on everything below. We felt whole; we had become a family.

Our new family. 2012—Family Photo

Many women asked me to share my birth story, and when I did, many of them said with exasperation, "Why would you choose to go through that kind of pain when you don't have to?" All I can say to that is, for me I needed to feel my body do what it was designed and created to do. I needed to know for myself, and no one else, that I could. Having this knowledge and experience has given me such a sense of pride and has tremendously influenced how I feel as a woman, wife, and mother. I realize I have been given one of the most precious gifts there is on this earth—the ability to bring forth new life.

(L) Pappy and Pecos Pete, two and a half months old 2013
—Family Photo
(R) Pecos Pete, three months old. 2013—Family Photo

Our beautiful baby boy! Four months old. 2013—Family Photo

Heroes & High Bobbin' Good Times

Pecos Pete, five months old, and Steph celebrating their first Mother's Day. May 12, 2013—Family Photo

"Country Music Legend" Roy Clark, Pecos Pete, and Pappy Pake at Shoat Webster's funeral, May 24, 2013, at Lenapah, Oklahoma. 2013—Family Photo

Folks that think havin' kids at sixty ain't fun haven't had kids at sixty!
—PAKE MCENTIRE

Pake, Pecos Pete, and Steph at mailbox at Limestone Gap where I got Steph's letter. 2013—Family Photo

Chapter 70

THE END GATE

Well, that's it folks. I have a lot more, but the publisher suggested I cut it down. It ain't over till the fat lady sings, but she's tunin' up! Did your eyes bleed? Do you now need therapy? I certainly hope not. Maybe I should, but for some reason, I don't feel the need to apologize for anything I've written here, so I'll just say I hope it was entertaining for you. I know it was for me. I mentioned that I was gonna let some folks proofread it before it went to print, and I did. I have mixed emotions about that idea because I had a really juicy book before they asked me to take a lot of things out. I got pleas like, "I'd rather you didn't say anything about the girls in my life: I'm tryin' to forget all that myself."

And from a cowboy friend that said, "Oh hell no, shiiiit! You cain't put that in there! Now, I ain't sayin' that didn't happen, 'cause it did, but I have a nine-year-old grandson, and all he wants to do is pray!"

Sometimes, it's better to ask for forgiveness than for permission!
— GREG SEXTON

I learned a lot from writing—like asking folks questions and them telling me the answer that would remind them of something else. Writing a book is more difficult than I expected.

Thanks to my wife, Steph, for teaching me how to edit the pictures and encouraging me to finish this effort. Also a big thanks to Tom Carter, John Wooley, Gail Werner, Donna McSpadden, Gail Brown, and, most of all, Joan Rhine for politely answering all my dumb questions, keeping this from coming out ass backward.

Mrs. Self, my typing teacher in high school, would be pleased to know that my typing has improved. I enjoyed it tremendously, obviously, or I wouldn't have written it! Remember, I don't do anything unless I enjoy it. I'd like to leave you with one last thing to remember that I didn't invent, but since I like it so much, I'm gonna put my name on it anyway.

Never underestimate the power of print!
—Pake McEntire, June 11, 2013

Made in the USA
San Bernardino, CA
23 October 2014